Forgotten Conquests

Rereading New World History from the Margins

Y. fedonda
C. de bon albrigo
Plaia
TROPICO DI CAPRICORNO
Ningatas
La cananca
Rio di s. Francesco
Y. dis. Catarina
Y. del riparo
PRO: DELLA PLATA
P. del pata
R. negro
Rio poblado
S. Spirito
P. faraiol
Rio tibiquiri
Plaia
R. coriente
R. guarandis
Rio della plata
C. de s. Maria
C. batel
Y. peraliares
C. biancho
Y di loui marini
Y. de aque
Arenagorda
C. de s. ellena
Basianegadi
C. de tre ponte
P. sifondo
MARE OCEANO
Terra di marzo
C. dis. dominico

Forgotten Conquests

Rereading New World History from the Margins

Gustavo Verdesio

TEMPLE UNIVERSITY PRESS

PHILADELPHIA

Temple University Press, Philadelphia 19122

Published 2001
Printed in the United States of America

∞ The paper used in this publication meets the requirements of the American National Standard for Information Sciences—Permanence of Paper for Printed Library Materials, ANSI Z39.48-1984.

Library of Congress Cataloging-in-Publication Data

Verdesio, Gustavo.
[La invención del Uruguay. English]
Forgotten conquests : rereading New World history from the margins / Gustavo Verdesio.
p. cm.
Includes bibliographical references and index.
ISBN 1-56639-833-9 (cloth : alk. paper) — ISBN 1-56639-834-7 (pbk. : alk. paper)
1. Uruguay—Discovery and exploration—Historiography. 2. Uruguay—Description and travel—Historiography. 3. Uruguay—History—To 1810—Historiography. 4. Indians of South America—Uruguay—First contact with Europeans. 5. Uruguay—In literature. 6. Indians in literature. I. Title.

F2723.V4713 2001
985.5'007'2–dc21 00-041193

Based on a Spanish language edition published in 1996 by the former Graffiti Publishers, Uruguay.

FRONTISPIECE. This Jesuit map shows the territory on the northern shore of the River Plate as a land surrounded by two enormous rivers: the Paraná and the Uruguay. This kind of visual misrepresentation finds its correlate in the chronicles of the colonial period that describe the region and its inhabitants. From Paulo di Forlani, *La descrittioni di tutto il Peru* (Rome: 156[?]). Reproduced with permission of William L. Clements Library, University of Michigan.

In Memoriam:

Emilio Verdesio, Sr.

Ernesto Verdesio, Sr.

Juan Carlos Casco

Contents

Preface ix

INTRODUCTION 1

1. THE ENTRANCE TO HISTORICAL TIME 14

2. YEARS OF DISAPPOINTMENT, OR THE LONG EUROPEAN SIESTA 39

3. THE PACIFIC PENETRATION 59

4. EMPIRES IN CONFLICT 72

5. THE ENCYCLOPEDIAS 93

6. THE TENTATIVE GAZE OF THE TRAVELER 110

CONCLUSION: THE TERRITORY AS THE STAGE FOR THE DRAMA OF DIFFERENCE 145

Notes 163

Bibliography 185

Index 201

Preface

This volume studies texts that for the most part have not received the attention of scholars in the field of Latin American colonial studies.[1] It also studies canonical texts by Antonio de Herrera, Pedro Mártir de Anglería (Peter Martyr), Father Bartolomé de Las Casas, and others that have been read and analyzed countless times, but attends to passages that have been neglected or forgotten by most scholars in that field of studies—those dealing with the territory on the northern shore of the River Plate. As a response to this state of affairs, I am proposing not only a reading of non-canonical texts, but a new reading of those canonical texts that focuses on the forgotten fragments in order to attempt a recovery of the history of the discourses and actions produced on and about that lump of land.

As I have stated, many of the texts that deal with the lands on the northern shore of the River Plate are not part of the corpus (and even less of the canon) of Latin American colonial studies. The reason for this omission can be found in a tendency in our discipline to fall victim to what could be called the predominance of the three cultures (Inca, Maya, and Aztec), which prevents scholars from focusing their research agendas on Amerindian peoples who did not organize their social lives around a state or an empire—two structures that resemble those developed by Western culture and, for that reason, seem to be easier to understand than other indigenous forms of social organization. These other forms (tribal, nomadic, and a long etcetera) are precisely the ones practiced by the majority of indigenous groups that populated the Americas at the time of the colonial encounter. If we limit our research to studying what took place in the lands dominated by Aztecs, Incas, and Mayas, and if we do not make sense of the territories occupied by other native groups, our understanding of the colonial encounter will be incomplete. Even worse, it will become a distortion of history.

This is precisely the state of affairs in the discipline: By making the three imperial indigenous cultures and their territories the only objects of our attention, we offer a limited and distorted picture of the colonial encounter. This, in turn, precludes the possibility of a broader, more comprehensive understanding of our field. It is as an alternative to this trend that I propose to study the territory and aborigines of a neglected geographic area (a part of the Southern Cone) outside the three imperial cultures' area of influence.

One of the goals of this book is to study the process of formation of the referents "territory/lands" and "peoples/inhabitants" of what is today the territory occupied by the nation-state Uruguay. In other words, I am interested in the slow discursive invention of that territory and those peoples who populated it before and during the colonial period. Colonial texts in general performed a mapping of the territory; it can be said, following Margarita Zamora (1993: 97), that these texts worked as verbal maps.[2] The study of this mapping is one objective of this investigation.

I am less interested in interpreting the process of the referents' construction (or mapping) from the framework provided by the official national narrative of a modern nation-state (in this case, Uruguay) than in reconstructing the process through which those artifacts or referents entered "world history"—or European time, as Julia Kristeva would have it. In this book, then, there is no room for a perspective proposing that the territory of modern-day Uruguay has had a meaning (or a "being") since time immemorial—an inalterable essence that made (and makes) it what it is today. In other words, I cannot accept that somebody "discovered" and populated Uruguay, because Uruguay, the modern nation-state, had no existence whatsoever in the sixteenth century.

What I propose is simply an "archaeology" of certain referents, a study of the different versions of those referents throughout the colonial period—that is, a study of the slow process (lasting roughly three centuries) through which the referents "territory" and "peoples" entered the cultural framework of Western civilization. My purpose is to emphasize the constructed nature of the "being" of that territory and its peoples by studying the texts that represented and gave meaning to them throughout the sixteenth, seventeenth, and eighteenth centuries. In this respect, this project is indebted to the works of Edmundo O'Gorman. In most other respects, however, it distances itself from his ideas.

For example, the study of European discursive activities that O'Gorman proposed is of limited utility if our goal is to account for the complexity of the colonial encounter. I believe that it is important to make room in this study for indigenous resistance to the Europeans' activities of appropriation. In the absence of texts penned by Amerindians, I have had to study the traces they left in the texts of the conquistadors. Those traces can operate as a reminder that the territory's invention was not a unilateral project; all the human beings who populated the territory (Amerindians and Europeans) contributed to the imaginary construction of that lump of land. In other words, the Europeans' appropriation of the territory did not develop peacefully; the Amerindians also fought for its possession. For this reason, I view this investigation not only as a register of the Western discourses that invented the territory, but also as a record of the struggles among several ethnic groups.

A study of this kind—that is, a study of the past—finds its justification in the attempt to understand the present. The present to whose understanding I am trying to contribute is that taking place within the framework of the modern nation-state Uruguay. That is why I have chosen to focus on the fragments that talk about the lands occupied by this modern nation-state, even though many of the texts analyzed in this work also describe other parts of the River Plate region. The idea behind this research project is to contrast the alternative histories that I have attempted to reconstruct with the representations offered in the official history produced by the Uruguayan state. The narrative of the nation propagated by ideological state apparatuses has silenced those alternative histories—that is, the histories that show the agency of Amerindians, Africans, women, and other marginalized subjects. In their stead, those state apparatuses have proposed a unidirectional and monolithic history—namely, one in which the only possible agent is the male *Criollo.*

However, this book should not be seen as an isolated case study that has nothing to do with the colonization of other areas of the continent. Although the case under study certainly has its peculiarities, it also has many characteristics in common with other regions of the Americas. With this in mind, I envision this investigation as part of a future family of scholarly works that will study areas populated by hunter–gatherers and early agriculturalists throughout the Americas. In this respect, this research project can be associated with other studies, including the one by Alvaro F. Bolaños showing the conflict between European invaders and groups such as the Pijaos (from the area occupied by modern-day Colombia), who, unlike the Inca, Mexica, and Maya, did not organize themselves around a state. I also conceive of this book as belonging to another family of scholarly endeavors: that of studies of the River Plate region—a region that did not host indigenous cultures organized around states—in its entirety. Finally, a study on the colonial period of the territory occupied by the state of Uruguay would benefit from dialogue with similar studies of the territory of Argentina—another modern-day state in the River Plate region where ideological state apparatuses have silenced alternative histories.[3]

This book was originally published in Spanish as *La invención del Uruguay.* Over time, and after many modifications and additions, I have completed the definitive version of the project. I would like to thank some of the people who collaborated with me—academically and otherwise—in this project. I am grateful to my former dissertation adviser, Hugo Achugar, for his shrewd observations, his critical spirit, and his respect for his advisee's ideas. Susana Jakfalvi Leiva helped me discover the wonders hidden in colonial texts; thanks to her classes, I chose to dedicate my academic life to the study of colonial situations. Without Walter Mignolo's invaluable contributions, the theoretical framework of colonial studies would be many years behind. José López Mazz and his collaborators Camila Gianotti and Carola Castiñeira of the Instituto de Arqueología de la Universidad de la República (Uruguay) took an interest in my work and made me rethink long passages of this book. The celerity, efficiency, and cheerful spirit of Janet Francendese, my editor at Temple University Press, made completing this manuscript a pleasant task. And finally, without the support and patience of Pamela K. Gilbert—who read the book twice!—this English version never would have seen the light.

Introduction

In this book, I will study some of the sixteenth-, seventeenth-, and eighteenth-century texts that discursively constructed the referents "lands" and "peoples" of the geographic zone north of the River Plate. This will allow us to see the different forms given to those referents by the European observer, as well as the Amerindian resistance to the Europeans' attempts to appropriate the land.

Unlike in many parts of Mesoamerica and the Andes, the conquest of the lands on the northern shore of the River Plate, as in the majority of the lands populated by nomadic or high-mobility groups, did not take place overnight.[1] In fact, appropriation was a long, slow process, for several reasons. First, the Amerindians who populated the territory did not show any signs of using precious metals, the obtainment of which was the main objective of the first Spanish explorers. Thus, the land was considered "unprofitable" and did not immediately arouse the explorers' interest. Second, the Amerindians' low population density in that area (their number has been calculated at only a few thousand), together with their lack of submissiveness (they were very difficult to subject to Spanish rule, and they did not mix much with the invaders), made exploitation of the land based on indigenous free labor very difficult. The *encomienda* and other forms of forced or free labor, which often served as the foundation of the colonial economy in Mesoamerica and the Andes, were impossible in the lands north of the River Plate. This also means that the contact between Europeans and Amerindians in the region under study was not so close as to promote a process of miscegenation similar to the one that developed in the continent's more densely populated regions. In this respect, this book should be considered an example of the kind of investigation that can be done on territories of late colonization.

As a consequence of this lack of interest in those lands, very few Spaniards came. This was a permanent problem faced by colonizers of the northern shore of the River Plate (as well as of other lands in that vast region) that continued until the first decades of the eighteenth century, as we will see in some of the chronicles produced at that time. This, together with the high mobility of the Amerindians, made the Spaniards' control of the land very difficult. As a result of all these factors, the conquest (or occupation of the territory) on the northern shore of the River Plate was a process that differed substantially from those that took place in Mesoamerica and the Andes. This is why, if we are to map what happened in the lands north of the River Plate, we must take into account the dynamics of the interaction among the ethnic groups in conflict—dynamics that differed substantially from those in Mesoamerica between the armies of Hernando Cortés and Moctezuma and in the Andes between Atahaualpa's and Francisco Pizarro's forces. In both of these cases, the indigenous populations were organized around urban centers, which facilitated control of the land by the European invaders.

The conquest was made easier not only by the fact that the indigenous populations were densely concentrated, but also by the fact that their economic structures and strategies for exploiting the land helped the conquerors survive in an unknown land. This point is made effectively in the studies by James Lockhart (on Mexico) and Karen Spalding and Steve Stern (on the Andes), which demonstrate that the possession and successful exploitation of the land conducted by the Spaniards was made easier by the preexisting structures and strategies of land exploitation of indigenous origin. All three authors emphasize the importance of the *altepetl* and the *ayllu*—the small units of social and economic organization in Mesoamerica and the Andes, respectively—to the Spaniards' effective occupation and control of the land. That is, the invaders adapted these indigenous structures of subsistence in a way that allowed them to settle and prosper in the conquered regions. Lockhart suggests that the similarities between Nahua (or Mexican) and European social organizations made possible not only less conflictive control of the territory by the Spaniards, but also a smoother adaptation by the Amerindians to the new rules (Lockhart 1992: 4). Paradoxically, then, the economic and social structures that allowed indigenous cultural traits to persist over time also facilitated the Spaniards' appropriation of the land.[2]

As mentioned earlier, the Amerindians who lived on the northern shore of the River Plate were highly mobile, not sedentary. Thus, they did not construct buildings or houses similar to the Europeans'; nor did they create villages or keep domestic animals. For these reasons, the territory was colonized very late compared with Mesoamerica and the Andes. In the few places of the region where early settlement was attempted—Buenos Aires, for example—the results were catastrophic: The settlers had to abandon the city precisely because they lacked the resources to feed themselves. Having not found maize, potatoes, or any other staple food cultivated by the Amerindians on the River Plate's northern shore—the Charrúa, Guenoa, and most others of this region were fundamentally hunter–gatherers—the Spaniards could not easily survive. Only later, in the seventeenth century, would a change take place on those lands that would enable European occupation (that is, sedentary and permanent settlement): the introduction of bovine and equine livestock, which I will discuss in Chapter Three.[3]

The situation I have described allows one to see America not as a territory in which European domination spread immediately, but as a continent on which many "pockets" of indigenous resistance existed. That resistance was stronger—and the difficulties for the invaders were greater—in those lands where permanent, well-established strategies for exploiting the land were absent. Where those Amerindian-originated strategies did not exist—as on the River Plate's northern shore—the European settlers were in trouble, and colonization took place at a very late date.

The texts I will discuss are organized in a series of chapters that follow a chronological order.[4] The first chapter includes documents produced by and about the expeditions led by Juan Díaz de Solís, Diego García, and Sebastian Cabot, among others. Solís was not able to leave any testimony of his enterprise, because the aborigines welcomed him with a well-aimed arrow. However, we know about his fate thanks to other texts: The first chroniclers of the Indies (Francisco López de Gómara, Peter Martyr, Antonio de Herrera, and many others) each dedicated a few pages to that ill-fated expedition. Other documents, such as *cédulas reales,* will also be taken into account, although they are not the main focus of this investigation; they are included because they contribute to understanding both the objectives of the expeditions and the conditions under which they took place.

Before Solís's 1516 voyage, the territory of the modern nation-state Uruguay did not exist for Western civilization.[5] At the moment of "discovery," the territory entered what I will call "historical time," which, according to Kristeva (who borrows the term from Nietszche), is the Western version of time. Historical time is understood, then, as a continuum that leads to a certain end and is based on a notion of causality; it is fundamentally verbal and, most important, is generated by writing. Moreover, this temporality is understood as "departure, progression, and arrival"; it has a modeling effect that is promoted by a notion of "world history" based on criteria proposed by the hegemonic civilization—in this case, Europe (Kristeva 1986: 189).[6] The most notable consequence of Solís's voyage, and of the texts that narrated it, was to bring the region's lands and peoples into the cognitive patterns of the Christian and Western world. This shaped the views not only of the expeditionaries but also of the chroniclers and their possible addressees.

The expeditions of Ferdinand Magellan and Loaisa are documented in the writings of some of their crew members. Although no firsthand diaries exist of Cabot's voyage, some official documents (*asientos, cédulas reales*) remain, as do records of legal suits brought against Cabot. Several documents about García's expedition have also survived, among them a 1530 *memoria* and a *memorial* in which García volunteers to undertake a voyage to the Strait of Magellan. Contacts between the aborigines and the invaders became more frequent at the time of these voyages. The sporadic nature of the contacts, however, make them look less like an epic battle than like tentative moves, brief exchanges of hostilities that seem to prepare the stage for a great battle. Today, we know that the story ended without much fanfare—behind the veil of a culpable secrecy in the first half of the nineteenth century, when the *Criollo* leaders decided to exterminate the last of the territory's indigenous inhabitants. Therefore, the texts under study do not narrate—or even allow us to imagine—an epic of the conquest. They are better described, instead, as a realistic and unheroic account of the first failed European attempts to dominate the lands and peoples of the region.

In Chapter Two, I study texts from the historical period—that is, the period that followed the one characterized by the failed Solís, Cabot, and García expeditions. After those unsuccessful enterprises, the Spanish were not interested in the lands north of the River Plate, which is why journeys of exploration and conquest were not very frequent there after 1530. First I will analyze the testimony of a Portuguese sailor, Pero Lopes de Souza, who had some contact with a couple of aboriginal groups. Then I will focus on the expeditions led by Pedro de Mendoza and Juan Ortiz de Zárate, some of whose members had different degrees of contact with the lands north of the River Plate. In 1602, one of the members of Ortiz de Zárate's expedition, the Archdeacon Martín del Barco Centenera, wrote the epic poem *La Argentina*. This text is very important because it offers an extensive description of the Charrúa's actions in response to the Spaniards' hostilities. Another account, by the German (Bavarian) soldier Ulrich Schmidel, a member of the expedition led by the Adelantado Don Pedro de Mendoza (*Adelantado* was a title given by the Spanish crown to some of its captains overseas), is written in German—a fact highlighting that linguistic plurality was present in the region even at such an early moment of the colonial encounter. One goal of this investigation is to call attention to this fact and to analyze texts that have been left outside the Latin American colonial canon because they were written in languages other than Spanish.[7]

All of the texts discussed in the first two chapters could be categorized as having referents common: the "discovery" and (attempted) "conquest" of the lands and peoples of the region under study. They also share some cohesion in terms of the genres to which they belong: *cartas relatorias;* diaries, which can serve as *cartas relatorias,* as Mignolo points out in a passage in which he studies Christopher Columbus's diary in these terms (1982: 60–61,); and *cédulas reales* and other official documents. This group of texts is therefore related to those texts which, in a broader Latin American framework, inform the period that Mignolo, following the most accepted periodization in the field, calls "discovery and conquest" (ibid.: 60).

Chapter Three starts at the beginning of the seventeenth century, when Hernando Arias de Saavedra (also known as Hernandarias), then the governor of Asunción (which is tantamount to saying the governor of the River Plate region), decided to explore the lands he called "*las tierras del Vruay*" to determine their potential for human settlement. Between 1607 and 1619, Hernandarias visited the territory several times. What he saw prompted him to write several letters to the crown citing the wealth and fertility of the land and recommending that a settlement plan be developed.

It should be noted that the term I use for this period, "the pacific penetration" (borrowed from Luis Enrique Azarola Gil [1933: 35]), should not be read as conveying the idea that the explorations in the region were free of bellicose encounters. On the contrary, on more than one occasion Hernandarias himself had to confront resistance from the aborigines. What the term attempts to account for instead is the attitude that inspired those expeditions and the settlements that the Franciscan priests founded in Santo Domingo Soriano—an attitude that is far from the one we see in other parts of Latin America, for which conquistadors such as Cortés and Pizarro are the models. Unlike in other regions of the continent, on the northern shore of the River Plate warfare was not the privileged means of domination. In 1624, a few years after Hernandarias's third and final term as governor, another governor (Francisco de Céspedes) decided to establish a "*reducción de indios*" (a mission) in Santo Domingo Soriano, with the help of Franciscan friars. The same preference for "pacific" colonization over bellicose conquest can be read in the official documents produced during his administration. This attitude was the consequence of two factors: the resistance and mobility of the region's indigenous groups and the Spaniards' lack of human and economic resources to undertake a "conquest" of the territory that would leave it under their absolute control.

Chapter Four discusses the struggles between the Spanish and the Portuguese over the lands of the River Plate region. From 1680 to 1762, the Portuguese intermittently occupied the territory located today in Uruguay's Department of Colonia, where they founded a fortress and village known as Colonia do Sacramento. From 1680 on, numerous documents were produced on both the Spanish and Portuguese sides. Orders, *actas,* and other kinds of legal texts abounded during this historical moment; diaries, histories, and poems have also survived. In comparing the Spanish and Portuguese texts, we see different versions of the same events offered by the subjects of rival European nations. This period also includes the foundation of Montevideo in 1724, a Spanish response to the Portuguese settlement in Colonia do Sacramento, although Portugal's influence in the region would not cease until that country's final defeat in 1762.

The main texts analyzed in Chapter Four include a relation *(relación)* in Portuguese of the siege of Colonia do Sacramento by Silvestre Ferreira da Sylva, a Portuguese soldier who claimed to have written the account in 1748, in his spare time, while defending the fortress. Although this text looks like an official report, everything about it suggests that it was self-published by the author. Another text of this corpus is *Historia topográphica e bellica da Nova Colonia do Sacramento,* by Simão Pereira de Sá, written in Portuguese between 1737 and 1750. This is a typical history in a broad sense, because it includes geographic information and an interpretation of the bellicose events that it covers. Because of their contemporaneity, these two texts offer the chance to compare the soldier's and the historian's views.

Also examined is a rhymed *relación* of the expedition to Buenos Aires in 1778, in which a sergeant of the victorious army narrates the surrendering of the Portuguese island of Santa Catarina to the Spanish forces under the command of Viceroy Cevallos. And I will take into account some of the official documents that help one understand conflicts and events depicted in the main texts under analysis. Among these less central texts are those related to the foundation of Montevideo, because the city's raison d'être was strongly tied to and ultimately a product of the Portuguese presence in Colonia do Sacramento. In this historical period, the land holds a status that is different from that in the sixteenth century. Thanks to the changes introduced by Hernandarias—mainly the introduction of livestock—the land has become a desirable territory and an object of dispute between the two European nations.

Chapter Five is a brief study of what could be called the eighteenth-century encyclopedias on the territory and its inhabitants. The authors of these works are the first to attempt a comprehensive description of the lands and peoples of the region—that is, they intend to create knowledge on the subject from the framework provided by the Enlightenment notions of archive and encyclopedia. The texts by Félix de Azara and the Jesuits (especially Father Pedro Lozano) will not only give the reader an idea of how Europe was giving shape to that territory and its peoples; it will also, occasionally, register the Amerindians' resistance to the European presence.

Chapter Six examines the travel diaries of a selection of diplomats, scientists, and priests from diverse European nations. This group covers a long time span, but most of the texts were written in the eighteenth century. The list of authors analyzed includes Father Gaetano Cattaneo, who wrote his account in Italian; Abbot Antoine Joseph Pernety, who wrote in French on his way to the Malvinas/Falkland Islands; the naturalist William Toller, who wrote in English; and Alonso Carrió de la Vandera (Concolorcorvo), who wrote in Spanish. These authors provide a sampling of the different Western views on the Amerindian "Other" and the American territory that were produced during that period.

Travel accounts are not the only eighteenth-century texts that can be found, as the encyclopedias studied in Chapter Five show. In Chapter Six, I also examine administrative documents written by Spaniards who did not live in the region, because they offer a perspective that differs from the administrative officials'. The rest of the texts from this period can (I hope) be studied in future investigations. This book cannot provide an exhaustive catalogue of the colonial texts that refer to the River Plate region; it can provide only an initial kick toward that goal—it is less a classification à la Linneus than an interpretive and panoramic introduction to a future sub-area of colonial studies. Other texts considered in Chapter Six are those produced by the surveyors who came with Félix de Azara—among them, José María Cabrer, Fernando Borrero, Juan Francisco Aguirre, and Andrés de Oyárvide—at the end of the eighteenth century to measure the territory. The scientific inquisitiveness and rigor of these texts allow them to serve as a more "objective" counterpart to the travelers' accounts.

Having established the corpus to be studied, it is time to say something about the way in which I will read those texts. As I noted in the Preface, this book intends to be a study on the production of the referents "territory" and "peoples" of the northern shore of the River Plate in the sixteenth to the eighteenth century. This study can also be seen as an analysis of the forms in which those texts represent Otherness, as well as a recapturing of the Amerindian resistance through the traces they left in the texts.

To begin the explication of my reading strategies, I must say that I understand "explanation" as an act that implies the existence of a cognoscent subject and a knowable object; further, explanation is achieved in terms that are familiar to the knowing subject.[8] In Western culture, the consequence of this operation is the automatic exclusion of the radically heterogeneous, the absolutely Other.[9] For this reason, the only possible subject of knowledge in the texts about the "discovery and conquest" is the European one, and the European is producing a very concrete knowledge: "America" for the colonial encounter in general, and "northern shore of the River Plate" in the case of the texts studied in this book. I attribute knowledge production to a cultural subject, not to an individual subject, because the notion of "subject" is not a given (that is, it is not something natural) but the product of a construction. The subject, then, is a notion that is constructed in opposition to something else through the exclusion of that something (or somebody). In this book, therefore, that "something that is not the subject of knowledge" will be called Otherness.[10]

The representation of that Other (that irreducible alterity) is what I will look for in the texts to be analyzed. This will not be an easy task, because Western civilization has represented the Other by assimilating it to the known, to the familiar.[11] This modus operandi is evident in the colonial writings that refer to the Americas, which attempt to hide radical alterity. In this investigation, I will try to rescue that alterity from the oblivion to which the European knowing subject—by assimilating it to the familiar and denying difference—relegated it.

I will consider texts not as simple products of a conscious and sovereign will, but as complex artifacts that dramatize a conflict of meaning or a struggle among various meanings (Macherey 1978: 81–82). This conflict, which is present both at the genesis of the text and at the moment it reaches its final form (that is, the moment the text becomes a product or an artifact), is not resolved by the text; it is only shown, exhibited. In other words, the text *manifests* the conflict but does not *state* it (ibid.: 85).[12] That silence (what is not said) informs the text; it is an important part of it and is one of the aspects of the text that needs to be deciphered (ibid.: 86–91).[13] In actuality, the silence that the work keeps in relation to the conflicts that are at the core of its inception (of its genesis) is precisely what critics should interrogate, because what ties the text to the world of ideology is not what it says but *what it does not say.* For the text, as Terry Eagleton (1976b: 34–35) explains, cannot say certain things. Like a skillful dentist extracting a tooth, the interpreter (the critic) must extract meaning from the silences that conceal the ideological conflicts that lie under the production of any textual artifact.

The coexistence of different interests and rival voices in a text creates another task for the critic: to detect the traces of those voices. Jacques Derrida, who coined the concept of "trace," conceives the signification process as a play of differences and traces that does not have room for a presence or an absence in absolute terms—that is, presence and absence constitute the meaningful message (very much like the said and the not said analyzed by Macherey). This is how Derrida explains it:

> Whether in the order of written or spoken discourse, no element can function as a sign without referring to another element which itself is not simply present. This interweaving results in each "element" . . . being constituted on the basis of the trace within it of the other elements of the chain or system. This interweaving, this textile, is the text produced only in the transformation of another text. Nothing, neither among the elements nor within the system, is anywhere ever simply present or absent. There are only, everywhere, differences and traces of traces. (Derrida 1981: 26)

In this investigation, I follow Derrida's and Macherey's suggestions for reading texts. Macherey's idea of unmasking a text's ideological substrate by assigning meaning to its silences goes hand in hand with a process that most people call "deconstruction," apparently against Derrida's will. Although Derrida has always been rather mysterious and imprecise when it comes to defining his own reading practices, he has said very clearly that "deconstruction" is not the word that best conveys his philosophical and discursive practices. However, his method (whatever we call it) does not consist of destroying or disassembling a construct, as some of its practitioners and enemies seem to believe. It involves something very different. It is possible to extract from Derrida's most significant texts (especially *Of Grammatology* [1976]) a certain synthesis of his modus operandi. This method assumes that something that can be called "logocentrism" exists in Western civilization; that this logocentrism has a tendency to divide reality into dichotomous pairs (present–absent, written–oral, etc.); and that this tendency privileges, at the moment of division, one of the elements in the pair. His method interrogates that hierarchical division by inverting the poles—that is, by elevating the value of the previously subordinated element—without leaving things in that state. Rather, the goal is to allow the birth (after inverting the previous order) of a new organization based on different meanings or significations (both old and new) of the elements.[14]

An important aspect of this complex operation is an analysis of discourse that looks for the traces of the elements silenced by the text. This allows one to rediscover the text in all its complexity—an impossible task if the reading does not account for the traces of Otherness. Reading the texts by focusing only on the dominant (or Western) discursive aspects that inform them, without paying attention to elements that make them heterogeneous artifacts (which is what they are, although they are usually understood as homogeneous entities), is tantamount to losing the chance to approach the texts as objects of study and considering them only as objects of consumption. For instance, if we as readers are not capable of seeing the presence of the Other in texts such as Hernandarias's *relaciones,* we run the risk of construing a territory in which the Spaniards ruled freely while the Amerindians were only a decorative element. Or if we read the texts produced by Colonia do Sacramento's Portuguese dwellers without seeing the permanent and hostile presence of their indigenous and Spanish neighbors, we will be unable to perceive the complexity of the human activities (among them, the discursive practices) at that historical time in the territory under study. I will also attempt to reread critically some of the most accepted historical narratives—that is, the official ones—that represent the historical events as a dramatization of the eternal struggles between civilization (understood as European) and barbarism (indigenous), culture (understood as the possession and practice of literacy) and ignorance (represented by orality), true faith (Christianity) and paganism, and so on.

What enables us to reconstruct the volume of colonial discursive and practical realities is the fact that no text, regardless of the extent to which it emphasizes the values imposed by its ideological framework, will fail to allude (even in its silences) to other events or realities that challenge that ideological framework. As Frederic Jameson (1981: 80) states, the historical and ideological subtexts are not immediately present; they have to be reconstructed after the fact. The critic must therefore be patient and use a method that enables him or her to look for the interstices through which the subtext can come to the surface. In sum, the task is to unmask the texts as symbolic acts, as cultural artifacts (ibid.: 20).

This methodological foundation tends toward reconstructing a universe of discourse: that of the colonial period on the northern shore of the River Plate. This reconstruction is based on the belief that every social group has the right to express its communitary interests. That is why I seek a reconstruction of the colonial corpus as a polyphonic totality.[15]

The impoverishing monologic nature of what is commonly understood as tradition can be opposed by studying a reality that was discursively plural. I refer here to what Raymond Williams (1980: 39) calls "selective tradition"—a selection of practices and meanings operated by a dominant culture that discards other meanings and practices that do not fit the hegemonic bloc's interests and agenda. The disciplinary changes that are taking place in the field of colonial studies (which entail, among other things, a notion of literature that differs from the practice of belles lettres) are a step in a different direction, a step that allows for academic endeavors such as this investigation. Those changes are so profound that Mignolo has even talked about a paradigm shift that presupposes a new field of studies (1986b: 137–60). Rolena Adorno, for her part, has endorsed Mignolo's ideas (1988b: 11–15). However, applying the notion "paradigm shift," which originated in the basic and natural sciences, to the humanities is inappropriate. In its stead, I have proposed the notion "new mode of knowledge production" to account for the new scholarly practices in the field of colonial Latin American studies (Verdesio 1997b: 123–25). Using this notion allows one to account for the coexistence of these new scholarly practices with those that respond to old models.

This change in the mode of knowledge production has also taken place outside the area of colonial studies. The Latin American *testimonio,* for example, has created similar theoretical and disciplinary challenges (see, for example, John Beverley's *Against Literature* [1993]). These new disciplinary practices face the challenge of justifying their own legitimacy. One provisional response to such challenges is to emphasize the ethical value of the goals pursued, which can be summarized as the retrieval from oblivion of the multiple traditions that have been obliterated by "tradition." The framework for these disciplinary changes can therefore be viewed as an intellectual climate (a "structure of feeling," in Williams's terms [1977: 128–35]) or a context of decolonization (Mignolo 1989a: 79) that allows for the recovery of lost traditions as it attempts to build new identities. These new identities are forged from and by American subjects, not by the European gaze, for the nonhegemonic or displaced communities (Mignolo 1986b: 138–39).

Legitimation of the new disciplinary practices rests on choices that are ultimately ethical. Therefore, the reader of this book should expect that certain ethical beliefs drive an interpretive model entailing, among other things, the rejection of the existence of a single "tradition" along with the affirmation of the coexistence of multiple traditions, and the rejection of master narratives of domination that render irrelevant or nonexistent the "little" narratives of marginal groups and communities. The discipline's practitioners therefore face a situation comparable to a split personality: They are, on the one hand, members of a certain culture (a community with a specific tradition), but on the other, they are the executors of a series of disciplinary norms and practices (ibid.: 156–57). In other words, we participate in two different contexts of description—our culture and the discipline we practice:

> As members of a culture, *our understanding of the past is guided by the social position (class, gender, generation, etc.) to which we belong.* As practitioners of a discipline, *our understanding of the past is guided by our theoretical and epistemological position in the disciplinary field.* Both kinds of contexts of description

> are, of necessity, intermingled and a constant source of dispute, changing positions and self-analysis. (Mignolo 1989: 86)

Because the majority of scholar–practitioners belong to the dominant European or *Criollo* culture, and thus already possess a first-degree understanding, Mignolo proposes that we look for a second-degree understanding, or a theoretical hermeneutics that consists of reconstructing the modus operandi of our own interpretive community and studying the ways in which a universe of meaning takes shape.[16] In this book, I will offer not only a *theoretical explanation* but also a *hermeneutic understanding* when I interpret the texts under study. To build a theoretical model that accounts for the colonial corpus under study, I must begin by reading the texts from a new (hermeneutic) perspective—that is, by deconstructing the previous readings, especially those that talk about the logocentric opposition of civilization and barbarism from the dominant camp.

The texts I will examine are not innocent, and their meaning is not immutable. On the contrary, they have a history and have been read any number of times according to very specific reading patterns. Thus, they are "loaded" with imposed meanings. (All readings are influenced by a previous series of readings, according to Hans Robert Jauss [1982: 20]). The complex mass of readings, their relationship to the texts, and their conditions of production make up what Tony Bennett calls "reading formations" (1985: 7). These reading formations, in turn, consist of a series of discursive and intertextual determinations that organize and give life to reading practices by connecting readers and texts. In other words, Bennett says, the texts exist only as something already organized, as devices that can be activated only in certain ways, while readers exist only as subjects programmed to perform an equally pre-established reading strategy. These reading formations, then, are the product of the historical struggle for the meaning of texts—or, better yet, for the texts themselves. This study should be inscribed in the framework of the negotiation that is the history of readings and the rules for reading; it should be understood as an attempt to reorganize the reading formations that already exist (ibid.: 14).

Only by intervening in these reading formations can one undertake the theoretical understanding that Mignolo proposes: to describe and explicate a domain or an object of study (Mignolo 1989b: 56). The intervention that I propose should be characterized as a hermeneutic understanding because the members of a scientific community are observers with respect to their object of study, but are participants in the activities they practice (Mignolo 1983a: 16). This hermeneutic understanding of the *old* object of study (the contested reading formations) of the discipline is what paves the way for a theoretical understanding of the *new* object of study. I am talking about a new object of study created by theoretical practices, because all theories *construct their own object of study.*[17] In this book, the object of study is the corpus that I have proposed, and its referent is the discursive universe that arose in colonial times in the territory north of the River Plate.

CHAPTER I

The Entrance to Historical Time

Nos descubrieron. Por fin nos descubrieron. *[They've discovered us. At last, they've discovered us.]*

—*Les Luthiers*

At the moment of "discovery," the lands on the northern shore of the River Plate, until then unknown to Christendom, became a potential object of knowledge for the European subject. The process through which this gnoseological appropriation occurred is very difficult to grasp because the record of the encounter and of the years that followed is so fragmented. For scholars interested in reconstructing a polyphonic situation, the absence of texts by non-European groups presents an additional problem. It is partly for this reason that the history of Western culture and the Western episteme have become the framework for the "discovery" period.[1]

Moreover, Latin America in general, and the River Plate region in particular, continue to be represented through narratives that are strongly based on European ideological foundations. Whether we like it or not, the official history was, and still is, written by members of the hegemonic groups of European and *Criollo* origin, whose perspective—which is almost universally accepted, even by members of the most marginal groups—offers just one of the many possible versions of the historical events that took place in the region.[2] *Criollo* and Europeanized narratives predominate not only at the level of discursive representation, but also in the more factual realm of political activities, such as legislation and state social policy. This Latin America, conceived as an extension of Europe, became Europe's bastard child precisely at the moment analyzed in this chapter, a moment that H. A. Murena (1969) calls "Latin America's original sin."[3]

The territory entered into historical time (that is, discursive time) upon the arrival of Solís's expedition in the River Plate region. In other words, at precisely that moment the region entered the line of sight, and the cognitive framework, of the European observer. From an Occidental perspective, this moment represents the "birth" of the region. The construct "River Plate" began to take shape, giving way to a process of imaginary construction that continues today. With Solís's expedition, and through the texts that narrate its fate, the lands and peoples of the region entered historical, verbal, masculine, and European time. In a land that from a Western perspective was a blank page, these texts found the space and time in which new historical developments would take place.[4]

The moment of cultural clash on the northern shore of the River Plate is characterized by the fragmentary nature of the documents that account for it. The expeditions that arrived in the region between 1516 and 1527 left meager documentary evidence. From 1527 on, the only incursions registered were the expeditions by Lopes de Souza, by Mendoza, and by Ortiz de Zárate. Lopes de Souza visited the land very briefly, while Mendoza undertook the settlement of Buenos Aires. Only occasionally did the members of these expeditions have contact with the territory and inhabitants of what today is Uruguay. Therefore, I will limit my research to studying the fragments of the texts that refer to the "discovery" of the northern shore of the River Plate to see how they produced the first versions of that referent. I will also pay attention to how those texts construct the referent "Amerindians" and, by looking at the traces, to how those texts allow us to see the indigenous reaction to the Europeans' colonizing endeavor.

The question of when Solís arrived on the northern shore of the River Plate has been debated, and several dates have been proposed, including 1508, 1512, and 1516. Two chroniclers and historians of the Indies—Antonio de Herrera (1945 [1601–15]: 111, 220) and Dean Gregorio Funes (1816: 2), who wrote about the colonial period five years after Argentine independence—favor the first date. The 1512 date has enjoyed more popularity, counting among its supporters historians such as Gonzalo Fernández de Oviedo (1959 [1535–47]: 352), López de Gómara (1877 [1552]: 211), Ruy Díaz de Guzmán (1882), Félix de Azara (1847), and Francisco Bauzá (1965 [1880, 1895–98]: 22–30). (Bauzá is not a colonial writer—he produced his works after independence—but his influence in both modern Uruguay and Argentina makes him an important supporter.) The most accepted date, however, is 1516, proposed in several studies by José Toribio Medina (1897)[5] and by Eduardo Madero (1892: 1–15), among modern scholars, and by the prestigious colonial chroniclers Peter Martyr, Father Bartolomé de las Casas (1957 [1875–76]: 365), Martín Fernández de Navarrete (1955 [1825–37]: 39–41), Antonio de Ulloa (1990: 2:216), Father Pedro Lozano (1873: 7–10),[6] and Father Pedro Francisco Javier de Charlevoix (1910 [1756]: 53–55). For many authors, the available documents seem to indicate that the "discovery" voyage took place at this last date (see Medina and Madero). Let us provisionally accept, then, that Solís arrived on the northern shore of the River Plate in 1516. The lack of direct documentary evidence (diaries, logbooks, etc.) led me to look for secondary sources, such as those produced by the colonial chroniclers (some of whom were contemporaneous—or almost—to the facts narrated).[7] These are the texts through which I will offer a reconstruction of the long process that gave shape to the official version of the "discovery" of the River Plate.

Peter Martyr, the first to write about the Indies, was a contemporary of the events narrated. (The first edition of his book is dated 1516.) In his version, the voyage of "discovery" took place in 1515. This is what he says about Solís's arrival in the estuary:

> He found the ominous and anthropophagic Caribs, about whom I have already talked extensively in other parts of this book. These Indians, in the manner of sly [female] foxes, feigned peace signs but were, in actuality, planning a sumptuous banquet. When they saw their guests from afar, they drooled like customers at a cheap diner. Poor Solís landed with as many companions as the flagship boat allowed. A multitude of Indians left their hiding lair and attacked [the Spaniards] with sticks and killed them all before their companions' [who have stayed on board the flagship] eyes. Later, the Indians destroyed the boat. Nobody escaped. Once the Spaniards were all dead, the Indians cut them into pieces and prepared for the future banquet at the beach, while the rest of the crew watched the horrendous spectacle. Terrified by the atrocious episode, the others [on the flagship] did not dare to land or to avenge the death of their captain and companions and left those cruel beaches. (Mártir de Anglería 1892: Década III, Liber X, Caput II, 459–60)[8]

The first thing we notice in this text is that, according to Peter Martyr, the aborigines who populated the territory were "Caribs"—an ethnic group that is usually identified with a different Latin American region. The voyages captained by Christopher Columbus were probably fresh in Peter Martyr's memory; thanks to Columbus's accounts, those mythical "ominous and anthropophagic" Caribs became the paradigm of the American peoples in that historical time. It was very difficult for a European observer to imagine the Amerindians differently. Peter Martyr's characterization of the Amerindians as "sly [female] foxes" ("*insidiosae vulpes*"), which both animalizes and feminizes the described object, is an example of one of the discursive practices the Europeans used to construct alterity. In this case, the Other is reduced to a bestial condition and implicitly compared to an animal that, thanks to the foxes in the fables by Aesop, Fedro, and Count Lucanor, had very negative connotations in the European collective imaginary. This rhetorical device guarantees the European subject's superiority in the representation: The European is a "civilized" human being, whereas the Amerindian is presented as a being that is closer to the animals.[9] Another rhetorical device used is feminization.[10] In this representation, the Amerindians' duplicity is a consequence of their double condition: They are both animals and women (which, by the way, also implies the devaluing of women in general, regardless of their cultural origin).

The scene that this passage depicts is suspiciously detailed—that is, the omniscient authorial voice contributes details, such as the drooling of the "customers at a cheap diner," that no human being who had witnessed the events could have perceived. (Remember, the survivors stayed on the flagship, at a safe distance.) It is through devices and details of this kind that the portrayal of the characters (in this case, the savage, barbaric, and drooling aborigines) is completed and the rhetorical goals of the narration are achieved.[11] Another mechanism put into play in Peter Martyr's narration is the application of the adjective "poor" (or "miserable") to Solís. The narration so far has not given the reader any reason to think of Solís as a character who deserves pity; the use of the adjective "poor," therefore, may presuppose the reader's knowledge, via oral means, of the captain's fate. If this is the case, Peter Martyr may have been telling the story to a public that already knew its sad ending.[12] The eloquent way in which he describes the subsequent massacre is marked by a proliferation of adjectives, including "horrendous," "terrified," and "cruel," that intend to impress (and probably scare) the reader. It can also be said that the animization of the geographic site—that is, the characterization of the beach as an ominous and malignant place—will be used frequently and will enjoy popularity in the Western imaginary throughout the colonial period. The region under study will not be represented in a more benign light until the production of Hernandarias's texts about the fertility of the land.

The following text by Fernández de Oviedo is also contemporary to the events depicted. Fernández de Oviedo declares that he met Solís: "Juan Díaz de Solís was a good pilot and I met him" (1959 [1535–47]: 352).[13] His narration is very brief. He says (perhaps following Peter Martyr) that when the Spaniards arrived in the new lands, they were offered a warm welcome by the aborigines. This welcome persuaded them to leave the boat in order to talk with the Amerindians, but

> a multitude of Indians, lurking and armed, left their lair and killed Juan Díaz de Solís and all the Spaniards who had landed, before the eyes of the ones who had stayed in the flagship, which brought considerable damage and shame for them; and they took the boat and destroyed it first and burned it later. The rest of the Christians having seen this (that without further ado the Indians had killed their captain and pilot and guide), with more than fifty of the best men of the Armada, they lifted the sails and did not dare to stay there, thinking they were too few to confront such a multitude of Indians. (Ibid.)

This version does not differ substantially from Peter Martyr's, except that it does not mention the banquet, and the Amerindians are not called "Caribs." However, treachery is still presented as a trait that defines the Amerindians.

Like Fernández de Oviedo, López de Gómara assumes that the 1516 voyage is Solís's second to the River Plate. He even gives information about events that allegedly happened during the first voyage: "He [Solís] drew crosses on some trees, which are very big in that region; he encountered an enormous river that the Natives call Paranaguazu, which means river as [big as a] sea or big water. *He saw signs of silver in the land and named the river after it.* He liked the land and its peoples, and loaded his ships with brazil wood and returned to Spain" (1877 [1552]: 211; emphasis added). López de Gómara does not contribute anything new or significant to the story, except for one detail: the vernacular name of the river and a version of the origin of the European name that, as will be shown later, is apocryphal. Regarding what happened in 1516, he says:

> [Solís] landed in a boat with fifty Spaniards, thinking the indians would receive him in peace like the other time, because that was the attitude they seemed to show this time too; but when they left the boat, many indians that were hidden *attacked him and killed him and ate all the Spaniards who landed with him,* and they even destroyed the boat. The other Spaniards, who were looking from the ships, lifted sails and anchors without daring to avenge the death of their captain. (Ibid.; emphasis added)

López de Gómara cites exactly the same number of victims as did Fernández de Oviedo (differing from the lower number—all the men who could fit in the landing boat—given by Peter Martyr), but his description of the Amerindians' treatment of the Spaniards differs from Fernández de Oviedo's. Again, as in the text by Peter Martyr, the Spaniards are devoured. This element will reappear not only in colonial sources, but also in nineteenth- and twentieth-century texts.

Las Casas' account of 1559 establishes 1516 as the date of the voyage and continues as follows:

> And he discovered in that voyage *the river that is now called "of Silver," I do not know why,* which name was given by Juan de Solís to the Santa María cape and river. The aforementioned Juan de Solís left the ship with a number of sailors—the ones that fit in the boat they had on the flagship—and landed in a certain part of that coast; the indians killed him and it has been said that they [the indians] ate them all. *I do not know how they [the Spaniards who remained on the flagship] were able to see how they [the indians] ate the Spaniards,* because they [the Spaniards at the flagship] did not dare to stop by the land; unless the indians ate the Spaniards on the very coast, where they could be seen by the Spaniards on board the flagship. (1957 [1875–76]: 365)

Las Casas, a defender of the Amerindians, poses a couple of interesting questions in this passage. One has to do with the origin of the name Río de la Plata (River Plate), and the other with the alleged cannibalism of the Amerindians who populated the river's northern shore. I will deal with the first question later. Las Casas' strategy regarding the second question is cautious, to say the least. First, he makes it very clear that he is not the one who asserts the aborigines' cannibalism: "It has been said" is the form he uses. Second, he questions the plausibility of those accounts without rejecting them in a conclusive way. The most relevant point for this investigation is that he does not join the choir of Europeans who accuse the Amerindians of practicing anthropophagic rituals.

Of all the chroniclers of the Indies, the one who gives the most detailed version of the expedition's itinerary (perhaps because he had access to the diary or logbook of one of the members of the crew) is Herrera. After describing Solís's route before arriving in the River Plate region, Herrera says:

> Later they entered the water that they called Sweet Sea (because it was not salty and because it was so wide), which ended up being the river known today as "de la Plata" [of Silver] which was then called Solís's. From there the captain left with a ship, that was a latin caravel, in order to explore one of the mouths of the river: he ended up close to a middle-size island, located at 34 and two-thirds degrees.
>
> They navigated, sighting land all the time, until they reached this point. They discovered some mountains and other rivers, and they occasionally saw people on the shores; especially on the shores of the River Plate, they discovered many houses of indians. And they saw indians who were looking at the ship and offering the Spaniards all they [the Indians] had, by displaying it on the ground. Juan Díaz de Solís wanted to know what kind of people they were. He also wanted to take some of them with him, to Castile. He landed with as many men as fit in the boat. When the indians (many of whom were hiding with their arrows prepared) saw that the Spaniards were close enough, they surrounded them and killed them all, in spite of the artillery fire that was coming from the flagship. Later, taking the bodies from the shore (but still at a distance where the people

> in the flagship could see them), they started to cut off their heads, arms, and feet and to roast the entire bodies. After that, they ate them. After this horrible spectacle, the caravel [the flagship] left for help and sailed to look for the other ship of the expedition. Later, both ships returned to Cape St. Augustine, where they loaded brazil wood. From there, they departed for Castile. This was the end of Juan Díaz de Solís, more famous as a pilot than as a captain. (1945 [1601–15]: 308)

The only peculiarity in this account is the addition of another name for the river: Sweet Sea. Other than that, Herrera's narrative follows the other ones very closely.

Martín del Barco Centenera, an archdeacon with Ortiz de Zárate's expedition, describes the "discovery" this way:

> In the year 1513, counted from the birthdate of he who suffered for our sins, Juan Díaz de Solís sailed toward the Paraná river and landed on a shore where the Timbus' deceit caused his death. [This] little river of great fame is known nowadays, because of this deceit, as the river of treason.
>
> Solís had come to the same shores as a pilot in Magellan's voyage to the strait. Notwithstanding the travails, he asked King Charles to be sent to conquer the region. He entered the river with misfortune, until he suffered the last one of them [misfortunes]: his soul and body separated, giving the Paraná a silver name [*nombre de Plata*]. (1602: 7–7v)

A couple of details can be singled out in Barco Centenera's account. The first is the date he gives for the expedition—1513—which has not been suggested in any of the texts we have examined so far.[14] The second is that he not only proposes that the expedition to the strait led by Magellan preceded Solís's, but also that Solís was a pilot in the convoy that circumnavigated the world. One of the elements for constructing the referent "Indians" is still present: their tendency to deceive the Spaniards. In this case, the *insidiosae vulpes* (sly vixens) are the Timbú, an ethnic group that makes its first entrance onto the stage of the "discovery" narration. The Timbús' actions give the infamous river yet another name: river of treason.

Despite the minor variations, these texts show a structure that is repeated by the majority of the chroniclers, which allows us to perceive a main version of the story that might as well be called "official": Solís and his companions (regardless of their number) were received with deceit by the Amerindians of the region (whether they were the Caribs, the Timbú, or a generic group without a name), who killed them in an ambush. According to some of the sources, there is more to the story: After the massacre, the aborigines ate the Spaniards. (In Herrera's version, they were barbecued—a detail that would make Lévi-Strauss drool.)

Independent of the texts' truth value, what the chroniclers do not seem to perceive is that the Amerindians (regardless of their ethnic origin and of whether they killed or ate the Spaniards) were acting in defense of their territory. An investigation such as this one must pay attention to this fact, because it represents one of the most conspicuous silences in the corpus. By proposing an interpretation that differs from the chroniclers', I will attempt to restore meaning to aboriginal agency—a meaning that is completely different from the one European subjects have given to the same events.

The only chroniclers who offer information about the story's specific setting are Barco Centenera, who, by attributing the ambush to the Timbú, forces us to locate the action in the area of the rivers that connect to the estuary known as the River Plate, and, indirectly, Herrera, because he measures—in leagues and degrees—the distances that the expedition sailed. Using Herrera's testimony and fragments from other documents about the River Plate,[15] some late–nineteenth-century scholars reached very different conclusions. Madero (1892: 16) believed that Solís landed where Montevideo is now located, whereas Medina (1888: cclix–cclxi) proposed modern-day Maldonado, Puerto de la Candelaria, as the stage. But Medina warns:

> When the profound inaccuracy that dominates the ancient maps as regards the location of diverse sites (whether they are bays, capes, rivers, or lakes) is admitted; when we see that with regard to the events we have been studying two prestigious cosmographers like Santa Cruz and Chaves disagree (to which should be added that we cannot resort to any accurate date) . . . , when we confront this situation, we must acknowledge that any attempt to establish with any precision the itinerary of the voyage of discovery of the River Plate will run the risk of being erroneous. (Ibid.: cclxi)

The conditions for reconstructing the events are very discouraging, because the other sources available—the chroniclers' texts—are as imprecise as the maps to which Medina refers. Even some of the most noticeable sites, such as the Paraná and Uruguay rivers, are confused with other geographic features—most often with the estuary known today as the River Plate. However, despite the disagreements between authors and maps, some scholars do not even hesitate: They think they can deduce accurately the place where Solís found his end. Herrera says that Solís, after taking possession of the "discovered" lands, continued his navigation until he reached an island located at "34 and two-thirds degrees" of latitude. According to Medina (1888: cclxxvi–cclxxvii), this is the island known today as Martín García, and the landing must have taken place on a shore of the mainland located in front of the island.[16] This hypothesis finds its most important argument in a pair of texts that were almost contemporary to the "discovery": the *Historia* by Fernández de Oviedo (who repeats what the cosmographer Santa Cruz allegedly told him) and the caption that accompanies the 1544 map depicting the findings of Sebastian Cabot's expedition to the region. Fernández de Oviedo says: "And they reached a land and river called San Lazaro, in front of which *there is an island called Martín García, because a steward from the expedition led by Juan Díaz de Solís died there* at the time of the discovery of the River Plate" (1959 [1535–47]: 356; emphasis added). In the map of the region attributed to Cabot, the caption states:

> The indians call this great river hurnai. In Spanish, the River Plate takes that name from the River hurnai (which has a great volume of water) that enters the great River Paraná. It was discovered by Juan Díaz, *piloto mayor* of the Catholic kings of glorious memory. He discovered an island and *he named it Martín García, because he buried a sailor named Martín García there.* This island is located thirty leagues from the mouth of this River. The discovery exacted a very high price, because the indians of the land killed him and ate him. (Harrisse 1882: 356; emphasis added)

Medina accepts the data in these documents (which are almost contemporaneous to the events narrated), and he concludes that the death of the steward (or sailor) Martín García took place on the homonymous island. Regardless of whether we accept his conclusions, one thing is clear: The sixteenth-century documents do not give the modern reader a lot of information about the place and events of the "discovery." Yet despite the fragmentary nature and lack of accuracy of their accounts, the early chroniclers left an indelible imprint in the social imaginary of the region. Their testimony about what I have called the official version of the arrival of the Spanish in the River Plate, and the topographic and toponymic (that is, the first names given to the geography of the region) references they provided as hints for deducing where the action took place, inspired the chroniclers and historians of the eighteenth century. Most of them repeated what Peter Martyr, Herrera, and the others narrated in their texts. For instance, the Jesuit Father Charlevoix accepted the story of the deceitful hospitality of the Amerindians and tells the rest of the story thus:

> He landed with very few men, without taking any precautions, determined to take some of those indians in order to send them to Spain. He did not even notice that as he advanced the barbarians were retreating, leading him to a wood which they entered. He followed them almost alone and when got there the indians (whom he could not see) shot a shower of arrows that killed him and the men who followed him. The indians undressed them immediately, made a fire outside the woods, barbecued them and ate them in front of the Spaniards who had stayed at the boat (or the ones who had escaped to it), who had no choice but to come back to their ship as soon as possible and sail back to Spain. (1910 [1756]: 54–55)

Once again, we are confronted with the macabre barbecue. The only element Father Charlevoix adds to the story is the significative moment in which the Amerindians take the Spaniards' clothes off—symbolically depriving them of their "civilization." A few years after Charlevoix wrote this version, another Jesuit told the same story. Father Lozano followed Herrera almost verbatim, changing only the style and adding adjectives—for example, using the expression "very high mountains" ("*altísimas montañas*" [1873: 9]) and describing the Amerindians as "perfidious and inhuman" ("*alevosos e inhumanos*" [ibid.: 7–10]). Another author who repeats the story is Fernández de Navarrete:

> Solís wanted to explore the land and to take some men [indians] in order to send them to Castile. For this reason, he landed in the company of some sailors. When the indians, many of whom were hidden and armed with arrows, saw them far from the sea, attacked them and *killed Solís, the Factor Marquina, and the Accountant Alarcón plus six other men.* After that, they cut the heads, hands, and feet off their victims and barbecued their entire bodies and ate them, showing their horrendous inhuman nature. *All this happened next to the island called Martín García, located on the southern coast.* (1955 [1825–37]: 41; emphasis added)[17]

Fernández de Navarrete, then, presents as a certainty that the action took place near the island of Martín García. He also contributes the identities of some of the victims, although he does not say where that information came from.

The last of the historians to be discussed in this section is Félix de Azara, who not only believed that the voyage of 1512 took place, but also that it had been the occasion for some contact between Solís and the Guaraní (Azara 1847: 2). His opinions are very interesting because, among other issues, he discusses the name of the river. In that passage, he criticizes Father Lozano for having stated that Solís christened the river with his own name, and he scolds López de Gómara for saying that the captain of the expedition was responsible for the denomination "Río de la Plata." By criticizing his predecessors (ibid.,: 2–3), Azara introduces a metadiscursive attitude that is absent from the texts cited so far:

> He saw that some Charrúa indians were observing him and erroneously thought that they belonged to the same nation as the Guarani indians he saw on the opposite shore in his previous voyage. For this reason, he wanted to confer with them and he carelessly [without taking any precautions] took a boat and some men and sailed toward the shore. Immediately after their landing at the mouth of an arroyo, the indians he saw and many others that were hiding jumped them and killed them all, except for one [Spaniard] who saved his life. This arroyo, located between Montevideo and Maldonado, is today known as *Arroyo of Solís.* The writers López, Lozano, and León Pinelo (1623) say, in addition, that the Charrúa barbecued and ate the dead Spaniards. But I do not believe them, because

> customs among barbarians are very persistent: if they had that custom in the past, they would still have it now, and that is not the case; besides, they do not have any memory of such a banquet. This story was put into circulation, no doubt, by a brother of Solís and by his brother-in-law Francisco Torres, who were pilots of the expedition and witnessed the fateful event that [probably] scared them so much that it made them return to Spain, where they offered such a sad and ugly picture of the region that it discouraged other men from undertaking the exploration of that river—which with good reason they called *River of Solís.* (Ibid.: 7–8)

This passage is filled with new information, some of which presents substantial discrepancies when compared with the official version. For example, the Charrúa Indians are associated with the events for the first time.[18] Another new element is the reference to a survivor of the massacre and subsequent cannibalistic banquet. The location of the events also seems to differ considerably from the sites proposed by Fernández de Navarrete, Madero, Medina, and Fernández de Oviedo: The area in which Azara places the Arroyo of Solís is far from the island of Martín García (Department of Colonia, in the westernmost part of the territory). For this investigation, Azara's speculation on the origin of "River of Solís" is interesting because it offers a psychological interpretation of the event that inspired the name of the river. According to this interpretation, the name of the ill-fated navigator would remind future visitors to the region of the sad end that the pilot met there.

One element in this passage has even greater relevance for this investigation: the discussion of the Charrúas' alleged anthropophagic habits. One must remember that, before Azara, no one thought of making the Charrúa responsible for the carnage and subsequent banquet; it had only been said that the "natives" or "Indians" of the region had eaten Solís and his company. It is understandable that Azara would be interested in answering an implicit accusation: By the time he wrote his text, it was believed that the aborigines who inhabited that region were the Charrúa. Although Azara does not state it in this passage, his observations are based on his own contact with members of this ethnic group.[19] I see no good reason to doubt the truthfulness of his testimony regarding the Charrúas' cannibalistic practices, or lack thereof. However, we should not forget an important detail: Azara's observations in situ were made at the end of the eighteenth century, almost three centuries after the events he discusses took place.

This is a fact that we cannot ignore, as the anthropologists Leonel Cabrera Pérez and Jorge Femenías (1990: 16) point out. According to Cabrera Pérez and Femenías, diverse processes of acculturation, displacement, and extermination of the area's aboriginal populations occurred in the area in a relatively short period of time (ibid.: 17). Thus, making generalizations about the period under study here based on data obtained in the eighteenth century—a historical moment that abounds with documentation—implies a static view of a complex, dynamic process (ibid.: 17). We must be even more careful with respect to the validity assigned to the first chroniclers' assertions about anthropophagic practices—especially if we take into account that cannibalism was one of the traits that the European observers' imaginary predicted would be found in the "unknown lands." This does not mean that we should rule out the possibility of a coincidence between the European imaginary's pre-existing representation of unknown lands and what really occurred on the shore of the River Plate in 1516. It only means that we, as twentieth-century observers, should question the reliability of texts produced by very imaginative and misinformed (when not simply ill-intentioned) European chroniclers.

Thus, scholars should avoid making such careless assertions as: "Modern critics do not doubt that the discoverer of the River Plate—who was killed and eaten, as documents contemporary to the events do assert—had his unfortunate encounter with the *Guarani of the islands,* because they were the only Indians of the River Plate region that practiced anthropophagy" (González and Rodríguez Varese 1990: 10). This opinion is, in actuality, supported by some of the primitive chroniclers—who do not say anything about cannibalistic practices among the Charrúa but do discuss the Guaranis' anthropophagic rituals. Among them are Fernández de Oviedo ("There is another group called Guarani, on the southern shore, who are caribs and eat human flesh" [1959 (1535–47): 372] and Diego García ("The first indigenous group at the entrance of the river, on the northern shore, is called charruases: they eat fish and game and nothing else; other groups inhabit the islands and are called guarenies: these ones eat human flesh" ["Memorial de Diego García," in Medina 1908b: 172]. Luis Rodolfo González and Susana Rodríguez Varese accept as an irrefutable truth that Solís "was killed and eaten, as documents contemporary to the events do assert." However, as I noted earlier, it is not wise to accept the word of the Spanish chroniclers at face value if what we are looking for is to figure out what happened.

In any case, what is relevant to my investigation is that posterity accepted—if not as "true," at least as hegemonic—the narrative that presents Solís as a victim of the cannibalism of the region's aborigines, be they the Charrúa or the Guaraní.[20] In this fashion, the activities of the area's indigenous groups became the object of a discursive re-elaboration that makes the members of those nations look more like fictional characters than like actual human beings. However, there is no doubt that the aborigines actually did something: They attacked the intruders who arrived on their lands. From this perspective, we can see indigenous subjects (whatever their ethnic affiliation) who defended themselves and, in doing so, slowed the occupation of their lands. The rules of the game, then, are clear from the first moment of contact between the European and Amerindian cultures: Their members are the historical agents who will fight, throughout the colonial period, for possession of the land.

These historians' discursive attitude is strongly influenced by the European episteme. Their strategies for perceiving alterity (lands and peoples) come directly from Columbus, the first European to arrive in the Americas. Columbus's worldview—the ways in which he processed information—continues to be the paradigm that is reiterated (with some changes) by the authors cited here. It can be argued, however, that some of the historians we will read later (Lozano and Azara, for example) repeat Columbus's paradigm only partially, perhaps because they participated in different historical moments of the Occidental and Christian episteme.[21] Further, Lozano and Azara wrote from a disciplinary framework. Despite these differences, however, Lozano and Azara still construct the Other based on cognitive mechanisms that depend more on previous knowledge than on empirical observation.

It is in this sense that Columbus's discourse is paradigmatic: It was the one produced by a European explorer who had to confront a new reality, the so-called New World. His discourse, especially from the second voyage on, is paradigmatic in yet another sense: It is the discourse generated by those who have not succeeded in their endeavors but try to justify them using discursive means. The justifications can take different forms: Sometimes they are natural catastrophes (such as storms or hurricanes); sometimes, the vastness of the lands explored (impossible to survey with the means at their disposal). Yet the most recurrent justification is the assertion that the wealth the expeditioners were looking for actually existed, despite the meager samples that they took home. The only problem, they claim, was that the wealth (gold, pearls, silver) lay a little farther away than the last site they reached. The explorers promise, despite any perils or pain they might have to confront, to prove the existence of the yearned-for treasures if they are given the chance to return to the explored lands. In the unsuccessful explorer's discourse, failure cannot be uttered.[22]

Yet another narrative paradigm dominates colonial discursive production: that of Cortés, the victor who subjected the savages to the law of civilization. In his letters, Cortés mythologizes America, the conquest, and the conquistadors, who are represented as heroes who confront difficult tasks that they will perform successfully—not only to Cortés's own glory but also to his nation's. Beatriz Pastor calls this kind of narrative the epic project of the mystifying discourse of the conquest (1988 [1983]: 308).[23] Its ideological foundation originates in the same episteme that made Columbus's discourse possible, but their respective narratives differ. It is preferable, then, to reserve the term "epic" for narratives such as Cortés's.[24] For in Columbus's case, we are dealing with texts motivated by the personal interest of an individual who has failed to carry out an assignment; texts that resort, as a desperate move, to improve the speaker's or writer's situation, to verbal actions (or discourse) that may change his or her fate.[25] The instrument that these failed explorers used to improve their situation is, then, a discursive activity—or, more concretely, a narrative.[26]

The textual bits and pieces we have seen so far belong to the family of texts that conform the other side of the victorious-conquest coin: They narrate not a triumphal enterprise but a failure. The difference between the texts by, say, Columbus or Cabeza de Vaca and the historians we have read (Peter Martyr, Fernández de Oviedo, and the others) is that in the latter's texts, the subjects of discourse do not try to justify or legitimize the explorers' actions. Despite this basic difference, the historians try very hard—by means of a cultural solidarity of sorts—to propose all kind of extenuating circumstances that explain the debacle suffered by Solís's voyage of exploration. For instance, the treacherous, sly nature of the Amerindians and their alleged cannibalism are presented as unfortunate hindrances that help portray the enteprise in a tragic light. In the following paragraphs, I will study texts produced mainly by explorers who narrated their own failures—which are far more numerous than those following the relatively unusual model of the Cortesian epic of the victorious conquistador.

The next European incursion into the River Plate took place in 1520, when the convoy led by the Portuguese pilot Ferdinand Magellan arrived in the region. Records of what happened during the short time the expedition spent in the area, like those accounting for Solís, are very scarce, although in this case more than one navigation diary has survived. When we peruse the texts produced by members of the crew, we face a European gaze that differs somewhat from the one we have seen so far. That is, these are not historians who intend to organize, or give a totalizing view of, reality. Unlike Columbus and Cortés, they are neither discoverers nor conquistadors attempting to produce an image of the referents (the explored "land" and its "peoples") that will help them attain their professional goals or fulfill their personal agendas. The gaze of the crew members on the circumnavigation voyage is closer to the gaze of the voyager who watches the landscape from a moving point. As a consequence, the crew members' observations are both more superficial and less committed than those of the historians and the conquistadors.[27]

The best-known navigation diary from this expedition was written by the Italian chronicler Antonio Pigafetta, who says very little about what he saw in the estuary:

> We kept our route very close to the coast until we reached the 34° 40° of southern latitude, where we found a great sweet-water river. *Here is the place where the cannibals dwell; that is, the ones who eat human flesh.* One of them, *of gigantic stature, whose voice resembled a bull's,* approached our ship in order to reassure his companions who, fearing we could do them some harm, were drawing away from the coast in order to retreat inland with their belongings. We landed in the number of one hundred men—in order not to miss the oportunity to see them from a close range and to talk to them—and followed them with the intention of capturing some of them, but they walked so fast that, even though we ran, we were not able to catch up to them. (1888: 426; emphasis added)

It is obvious in this passage that the official history of the "discovery" was already well known—to the point, in fact, that the territory was known as the land where the cannibals live. In addition, this brief passage is testimony both to the ease with which the European imagination tended to see prodigies in unknown lands and to the way in which that interpretive community projected the models and representations available in its own cultural repertoire. Barco Centenera (as will be shown later in this chapter) and Alonso de Santa Cruz, who told Fernández de Oviedo (1959 [1535–47]: 361) about the existence of "fish men" ("*hombres marinos*"), are good examples of European subjects' propensity to fantasize about remote and unknown lands. It is possible that the European observer looked at the New World with awe and excessively open eyes, as Alfonso Reyes suggests (1942: 41). Jean-Paul Duviols, for his part, proposes that the New World was a very little known and mysterious place and, for that matter, one that was appropriate for the materialization of European dreams (1985: 69). However we choose to explain this behavior vis-à-vis the unknown, the fact is that the minds of Renaissance Europeans were programmed in a way that made it easier to confirm the pre-existing models that had become part of the Occidental collective imaginary than to undertake inquisitive investigations of the lands that they "discovered" (Pastor 1988 [1983]: *passim*). This tendency provides us with a framework for understanding Pigafetta's assertion about the existence of giants with taurine voices on the shore of the River Plate—giants that might be related to the Patagonian giants who allegedly lived near the Strait of Magellan.[28] To supplement that framework, it helps to remember how Azara described the region's Indians: In general, he said, they were as tall as the Spaniards, and in some exceptional cases (for example, the Charrúa), they were an inch taller (1847: 248). This does not mean that the Europeans could not have seen an Amerindian who was considerably taller than most members of his ethnic group. A more likely explanation, however, is that this is a European construct—inspired by the literature about *terrae incognitae*—not a description of what the Europeans actually saw. Later in the text, confirming the popularity of the official history, Pigafetta synopsizes the sad story of Solís and his sixty fellow Spaniards who were killed and eaten by the Amerindians on the shores of the nefarious river (1888: 426). He does not say anything about the name of the aborigines, though.

Another chronicler, Maximiliano Transilvano, says even less about the visit to the river, "a place where captain Juan Díaz de Solís was killed and eaten—together with certain Spaniards of his crew—by the anthropophagi that are called Cannibals" (1888: 265). His is the most synthetic version so far of the official history, but it is the same story nevertheless. The diary written by Francisco Albo is of great relevance to the history of the toponymy of the territory's coasts. The expression "Monte Vidi," referring to the place known today as the *cerro de Montevideo* (Montevideo hill), makes its first appearance in his text: "We reached 35 degrees when we encountered the cape of Santa María; from that point on the coast runs from East to West; and the land is sandy. *Straight from the cape there is a mountain shaped like a hat, to which we gave the name Monte Vidi,* that is erroneously called today Santo Vidio; there is a river of the Ducks between this mountain and the cape of Santa María." (1888: 216; emphasis added).[29]

It is interesting to note that none of the members of Magellan's expedition quoted here identifies the place as "Río de Solís" or "Río de la Plata." Instead, they use a more generic name: cape of Santa María. Albo does so, as does Pigafetta, who writes: "This river forms seven little islands, the smallest of which is called cape of Santa María, where precious stones can be found" (1888: 426). And Transilvano writes: "This voyage, with fair weather, arrived in the cape of Santa María" (1888: 265). Other crew members identify the region using the river's name, but the name that they use differs from those we have seen: "At twenty degrees of antarctic latitude, we were in high seas and we sailed one thousand five hundred miles toward the occident where we found ourselves close to a river that is one hundred and eight miles wide at its mouth, which is located at thirty five degrees of anctartic latitude *and to which we gave the name of river of San Cristobal*" (anonymous, "Relación de un portugués," in Medina 1888: 396; emphasis added). This name, although not favored by posterity, appears in yet another anonymous *relación* from the same voyage: "Sailing along the length of the coast in search of the Cape of Santa María, located at 34 degrees and 3/4; as soon as he [the captain] was able to see it [the cape of Santa María], they continued sailing to the west–northwest, always trying to find a strait, and they found themselves in a big freshwater river, *to which they gave the name San Cristobal,* and it is located at 34 degrees" (anonymous, "Navegación y viaje," in ibid.: 399; emphasis added).

The rest of the process of consolidating the current name of the estuary (usually called "river," even to this day) will be shown when we study the expeditions conducted by Loaisa, Sebastian Cabot, and Diego García. Before entering the study of those expeditions, however, here is what Herrera says about Magellan's voyage. After referring to the arrival in the cape of Santa María, Herrera continues:

> That same day in the afternoon, they entered the River of Solís, also called of Silver, and they sailed through it for two days; because it is low and because of some confabulation between the pilots, the captain did not want to sail the river anymore, because at its deepest, the river was not even three fathoms deep. They stayed there for six days in the water because they found it as good as the one of the River of Seville; *they also fished extensively and many people from the land approached them in their canoes; because they did not dare to get closer, Hernando de Magallanes [Magellan] ordered his people to prepare three boats, and the people of the land escaped without allowing the captain to take any of them.* (1945: 3:290; emphasis added)

The aborigines appear in this text, as they do in Pigafetta's *relación.* The picture is vague in terms of description, but it is also considerably more verisimilar: It seems reasonable that the Amerindians (whatever their ethnic origin) retreated inland at the sight of those strange-looking men. According to the same historian, another encounter took place:

> During the night an Indian arrived in a canoe and entered the flagship without any fear; he was dressed in goat's skin and Magellan ordered his crew to give the Indian a linen shirt and a red cloth undershirt; once he was dressed, they showed the Indian a silver cup in order to see if he would be able to recognize it [the metal]: he put it against his chest and said that there were great quantities of it in the land. The next morning he returned to the shores and he never came back. (Ibid.)

There are no other records of this episode. Regardless of whether it is a true account, the passage can be useful if it is considered as data about the first encounters between the region's aborigines and the European explorers. It shows that the first friendly gesture to cross Magellan's mind involves putting European clothes on the Amerindian, an operation that intends to make the Indian look more like a European subject—at least in terms of clothing, an important part of physical appearance. The goatskin of indigenous origin is a sign of savagery, whereas the linen shirt is a sign of "civilization."[30] This substitution ultimately fails to achieve its goal—that is, to assimilate the aborigine to European civilizational patterns—because the clothes do not change the Amerindian, who escapes from the ship as soon as he is able to do so.

In the exchange about the existence of silver in the region, Herrera also records the only lines of intercultural (and interethnic) dialogue preserved in the texts that refer to Magellan's expedition. From these lines, one can conclude either that the Amerindian was a liar (or he was sly—*taimado*—in the chroniclers' terminology, like the aborigines who killed Solís) or that he did not distinguish very well between silver and other metals. There is no ethnographic or archaeological evidence of the use of silver by the region's Amerindians. In any case, the dialogue reminds us of the European explorers' avidity for precious metals, which will justify their arduous navigations. The Others they encountered were no more than an instrument for finding the treasures that their employers on the other side of the Atlantic expected.

Despite its brevity, this text clearly depicts attitudes on both sides of the colonial encounter. The Spanish were looking for precious metals; the Amerindians sought to escape from the intruders. Regardless of our ignorance about the exchanges that took place and the actual words that were uttered at the encounter, it is obvious in the text that the Amerindians had some agency—consisting, on this occasion, of resisting the conquistadors' presence by refusing to continue to have contact with them.

From 1525 to 1527, three expeditions—led by the knight commander Loaisa, by Sebastian Cabot, and by Diego García—departed from Spain and ended, for diverse reasons, at the River Plate. Only García's expedition had the River Plate as its original destination. Loaisa's destination was the *especería* (the Asian lands where spices could be bought), and Cabot's was the Maluco (the Moluccas). The members of Loaisa's crew who left written records say very little about the River Plate region, where they had an accident. The gaze that I perceive in their testimony (in the sense I gave the term while analyzing the texts about Magellan's voyage) resembles the observational practices in the accounts of voyagers who were not involved in colonizing that particular area, whereas Cabot's and García's texts show a gaze that is closer to that of the paradigmatic colonial texts. The captains met (actually, they almost bumped into each other) in the River Plate region because Cabot decided to change the destination of his expedition. The unexpected encounter produced a conflict of interests,[31] and they signed their accounts in order to defend their interests in court, as well as to elaborate their own kind of epic narrative.

The texts about Loaisa's expedition are important only insofar as they discuss the evolution of the river's name. In some of the *relaciones* of this expedition, it is called River of Solís (Juan de Areizaga, "Relación que dio Juan de Areizaga," in Medina 1888: 36; Rodrigo de Acuña, "Carta de D. Rodrigo de Acuña," in ibid.: 64); in one dated 1527, however, the name "River Plate" makes its first appearance: "In the river of Solís, also *called of Silver,* the Day of the Holy Innocents, the armada endured a severe storm that split it in three parts" (Francisco Dávila, "Relación de Francisco Dávila," in ibid.: 49–50); emphasis added).[32] This *relación,* according to Medina, is the first document to record the name by which the river is now known. Medina recounts the process through which that name became popular as follows: "It is evident that the news about the wealth to be found up the river had, ultimately, the same sources: the sayings of Juan Diaz de Solís's companions who were living on the island of Santa Catarina. These sayings were propagated in Spain by Diego García and the crew of the *San Gabriel* vessel, who were the first ones to replace the name River of Solís with River of Silver (River Plate)" (1897: cclxxiv–cclxxv).[33]

The companions of Solís to whom this text refers—Enrique Montes and Melchor Ramírez[34]—were stranded on Santa Catarina when one of the expedition's ships developed problems. The ship *San Gabriel* mentioned in the text belonged to Loaisa's expedition, and Francisco Dávila was a member of its crew. García, who traveled with Solís in 1516, became the captain of the expedition that returned to the River Plate in 1527. It is in the following text that Medina proposes García as the agent for propagating the river's new name:

> And these people [the Indians of the region] say that there is plenty of gold and silver and great wealth of precious stones; this is all we know about these discovered lands and this is the sample of *silver that I have brought.* One of my men that got lost with one of our ships fifteen years ago was forced to stay in the region and he traveled throughout this land of Paraguay and brought two or fifty or seventy five pounds of silver and gave them to the Indians and Christians that lived in that land. I obtained this sample from the latter. (1908b: 359; emphasis added)

The following text, by García, is included in a *memoria* that he presented to the Spanish king when asking for permission to undertake another expedition:

> Your Highness knows that I brought silver and samples of gold and copper to this Court, plus a piece of metal with the figures of two bishops and the holy father sculpted in it; and that I was very well informed by the indian who gave me the aforementioned piece of metal about where to get that kind of object. He told me that he had gotten it in the southern region and I know very well where that part is; and I commit myself to discover that place. ("Memorial de Diego García," in ibid.: 172)

The reason for the Solís River's name change can thus be found in the silver that the two castaways from Solís's expedition showed not only to García but also to other sailors (among them Cabot) between 1525 and 1527. Despite the name change, Silver River (or River Plate) was not universally accepted at the time. Proof of this can be found in the cosmographer Alonso de Santa Cruz's declaration in a deposition for the suit that García filed against Cabot: "He says that he saw captain Diego García heading toward the river called of Solís, which was never called of Silver before the aforementioned captain Diego García led your Highness's armada to that region" ("Información hecha en Sevilla," in Medina 1908a: 2:167).[35] This document supports Medina's hypothesis about the river's name change.[36]

García's suit against Cabot originated in the armadas's unexpected meeting in the rivers that form the River Plate basin. As we have seen, Cabot's orders did not allow him to explore the estuary's basin; he was headed toward the *especería*—or, more specifically, to the Maluco. His destination is clearly stated in the passage: "You offer to go with your ships through the Strait of Magellan, also known as Strait of All Saints, in search of the lands of Maluco" ("El asiento que se tomó con Sebastián Caboto," in ibid.: 1:421). Cabot decided to change his route and abandon his voyage to the *especería* for several reasons (among them, greed). Hence, García was surprised when Cabot arrived in the River Plate region: García did not expect to find any Christians in those lands.

Two events involving members of the García and Cabot expeditions are relevant to this investigation. One of them relates to the accountant Montoya; the other is the encounter between Cabot and the cabin boy Francisco del Puerto, the only survivor of the massacre of Solís and his crew. The first episode interests me because it involves direct contact between the Spanish and the area's Amerindians. According to the testimony of several eyewitnesses ("Información hecha en Sevilla," in ibid.: 2:151–64), Cabot, who had decided to return to Spain and was anchored in the harbor of San Salvador, sent Montoya to one of the islands near the cape of Santa María to kill seawolves and prepare their meat for the journey home. While Montoya was fulfilling his mission, Cabot's remaining crew was attacked by Amerindians (the documents do not specify their ethnic group[37]), causing Cabot to abandon the harbor and head quickly toward the cape of Santa María. When Cabot and his crew arrived in an area close to the islands that Montoya had visited, they saw several crosses and smoke signals. The entire crew, except Cabot, thought that the signals might be coming from Montoya's people.[38] Cabot refused to look for his men and decided to leave the River Plate. He later excused his behavior before Spanish officials:

> When asked about whether he knew, when he arrived in the cape of Santa María, that the location was approximately one league from the island [where the seawolves lived], he responded that coming down the river he ran into some Indians in their canoes and asked them if they had seen two Spanish brigantines. The Indians responded that they came from the cape of Santa María, but they had not seen any brigantine or any Spanish people. This happened around fourteen leagues before Cabot arrived in the island of the Wolves [seawolves]. He declares that nobody gave him any information about the whereabouts of Montoya's men. (Ibid.: 2:162)

This alleged encounter is the second dialogue between the aborigines and the European visitors for which we have any record. Like the dialogue cited earlier, this one is characterized by laconism and pragmatism on the Spanish side: The Spaniards ask for information; when they get it, they leave the scene, without further ado. The Amerindians' role is incidental: They exist solely to fulfill a narrative function—in this case, to state that they have not seen any Christians, and thus to justify the conduct of the declaring witness. This is reminiscent of the passages in Columbus's diary in which the aborigines tell the admiral only what he wants to hear. Amerindians are given voice (that is, they are allowed to speak) only when what they say supports or advances the interests of the European subject of discourse. For this reason, what we find in most colonial texts that include indigenous speech is "a monologue in which the real interlocutor had been reinterpreted and transformed to the point of becoming a simple sign of confirmation of the narrative subject's perceptions" (Pastor 1988 [1983]: 41).[39]

In the same document, Cabot refers to his encounter with Francisco del Puerto, but he does not specify where he found the cabin boy. His tone again is laconic, a characteristic that the narrative shares with the dialogues between Spaniards and the Other:

> They went to the Solís River, where this declaring witness found a certain Francisco del Puerto, who had been taken prisoner by the Indians who killed Solís. He gave the witness great news about the wealth of the land; and . . . he [Cabot] decided to enter the Paraná River and sail up to another river called Carcarañá, that is the one that, according to Francisco del Puerto, descends from the hills where the gold and silver mines were located. ("Información hecha en Sevilla," in Medina 1908a: 2:158)

Once again, the witness, whose voice is filtered through Cabot's discourse, is quoted to confirm the existence of precious metals; the same device can be found in Columbus's diary. The difference between most of the texts that appropriate the voice of the Other and the one cited here is that the speaker in this case—Francisco del Puerto—is not an Amerindian. However, it should be noted that, after betraying his former compatriots and allowing the aborigines to ambush the Spaniards (killing seventeen of the men of Cabot's armada), del Puerto decided to stay with the Amerindians (see ibid.: 1:169, 2:160; Harrisse 1882: 422–23). It could thus be said that del Puerto holds a status similar to that of the Amerindians.

In another passage in the same declaration, Cabot narrates how he sent del Puerto as an interpreter to obtain information from the Chandul Indians about another European armada that had allegedly arrived in the river; he did not know at the time that the armada was García's. Del Puerto told Enrique Montes, one of the interpreters Cabot brought to the region, that "it was Cristobal Jaques, a captain at the orders of the King of Portugal" ("Información hecha en Sevilla," in Medina 1908a: 2:159).[40] This passage once again shows the informative function that del Puerto had for the Cabot expedition.

The interesting thing about these textual fragments is the attitude toward the unknown their subjects of discourse show. In Herrera's passage about the encounter between Magellan and an Amerindian, the dialogue is presented as a non-conflicting, quotidian fact. The text does not suggest any communication problems or difficulties; it does not even mention the mediation of a translator. The same can be said about Cabot's account, in which communication is represented as something natural, as if the parties involved did not speak different languages. It should also be noted that the European subject showed a complete ignorance of the ethnic and linguistic diversity among the aborigines. This ignorance is best illustrated by the Europeans' apparent belief that capturing an Amerindian of any ethnic origin would provide an interpreter who could communicate fluently with all of the aborigines. Rodolfo Schuller's remarks about this topic are very reasonable:

> Who were, then, those who called the Indians from the cape of Santa María the "Charrúa"? They were the interpreters the Conquistadors had brought from Santa [Catarina].
>
> In what language did those interpreters speak to the Indians of the River Plate? They spoke to them in the lingua franca of Brazil: Guaraní.
>
> For this reason, we see that in the first texts [about the region] almost all the ethnic groups are named by words of Guaraní origin. Just because the name Charrúa is a Guaraní word we should not deduce that the tribe to which it was applied was of Guaraní origin. (1904: lxxxiii)

The fact that the interpreters the Spaniards brought were fluent in only one of the languages spoken in the region should give us an idea about the communication problems in the colonial encounter. That is also why certain ethnic groups (and most geographical locations) were given Guaraní names, as Schuller argues (ibid.).[41] Texts of Latin America's colonial period abound with examples of "noise" in the communication channel, the most dramatic of which is perhaps the famous legendary encounter in Cajamarca in which Atahualpa threw away the Bible because it did not speak to his ear.[42]

The brevity with which events are recounted in the colonial testimonies about the River Plate does not contribute in the least to a better understanding of the cultural exchanges of the colonial encounter. In actuality, it was less an encounter than a clash. How these texts refer to facts is important in itself, because it tells us something about the European subjects' attitude toward communication with the Other. In other words, the carelessness with which they narrate such contacts reveals the value that those contacts had in the framework of the dominant axiology in Renaissance Europe: The Other was not as important (or as interesting) as the precious metals hidden in the lands to be possessed and conquered. That lack of interest is also evident in the text narrating the encounter between Cabot and del Puerto. Cabot's declaration seems to indicate that he is not interested in finding out how del Puerto survived the massacre that ended the lives of all his companions; how the former cabin boy adapted to the indigenous society; or why he chose not to rejoin the expedition and to stay with the Amerindians. Although it may seem reasonable that such information would not appear in a declaration for a lawsuit that had nothing (or very little) to do with del Puerto, the text is nevertheless symptomatic of the general rule dominating the accounts of European captives in the River Plate and neighboring areas. Take, as another example, Cabot's finding Enrique Montes and Melchor Ramírez on Santa Catarina. In his account of that occasion, Cabot says nothing about Montes's and Ramírez's life among the Indians.[43] The tendency not to recount stories of Europeans' adaptation to indigenous societies also helps to reveal the European subjects' attitude vis-à-vis the Other. Despite the many theoretical, historical, and ideological problems in his book *The Conquest of America* (1992 [1982]),[44] Tzvetan Todorov provides a useful model for measuring this attitude:

> First of all, there is a value judgment (an axiological level): the other is good or bad, I love or do not love him, or, as was more likely to be said at the time, he is my equal or my inferior (for there is usually no question that I am good and that I esteem myself). Second, there is the action of rapprochement or distancing in relation to the other (a praxeological level): I embrace the other's values, I identify myself with him; or else I identify the other with myself, I impose my own image upon him; between submission to the other and the other's submission, there is also a third term, which is neutrality, or indifference. Thirdly, I know or am ignorant of the other's identity (this would be the epistemic level); of course, there is no absolute here, but an endless gradation between the lower or higher states of knowledge. (Ibid.: 185)

At the gnoseological level, then, the lack of information about the captives' lives among the Amerindians reveals how little the European subjects knew (or wished to know) about their Other. At the axiological level, that lack of information reflects the attitude of those who do not think it worthwhile to obtain knowledge about beings considered inferior to the knowing subject.[45] At the praxeological level, it is obvious that the explorers of the River Plate wanted to adapt the Amerindian Other to their own cultural structure, not vice versa. A good example of this is the scene in which Magellan puts European clothes on an indigenous subject. Unfortunately, those who chose (or were forced) to adapt to the social and cultural rules of the Amerindian Other have been silenced—exactly like the Others themselves.[46]

The extant colonial-period texts allude in an incomplete way to the "lands" and "peoples" on the northern shore of the River Plate. One might expect discursive polyphony, given the variety of sources available, yet the opposite is true: The discourses are all written (and they all construct the referents "lands" and "peoples") from the same perspective: the European gaze. The object that those texts construct, and the referent they produce, is Otherness—understood as the totality formed by the lands and peoples "discovered." This Otherness only partly interests the European subject of discourse, because the subject's goal is to appropriate the land's wealth. As a consequence, the Amerindian as Other is less important than the lands where the precious metals await the arrival of the conquistadors and their miners. To appropriate the lands, the conquistador (Solís, for instance) plants crosses at every site he visits. These Christian signs are accompanied by other acts of possession, some of which may have been unconscious—that is, naming and referring.

The act of naming is crucial for colonial discourse in general, especially in Columbus's diary, the paradigmatic text. In his text, the naming of unknown lands functions as a demarcation of the territory, as a sign of its possession: "Through writing—of the names imposed [on the land]—, the land that was nobody's possession becomes somebody's" (Jitrik 1983: 98).[47] By using the language, conceptual repertoire, and discursive strategies available in their culture and episteme, the European subjects of discourse appropriated and conceptually modified a geographic and human reality that they had not previously known. And at the same time that these subjects produced an image of the Other, they created a space for their own enunciation, a space from which to emit their discourse ("Montaigne's 'Of Cannibals,'" in de Certeau 1989 [1986]: 67, 73).[48] We see these devices at work in the texts about the northern shore of the River Plate, texts that signal the beginning of a process in which a once unknown alterity (the region and its people) begins to take shape as a referent ("northern shore of the River Plate") in the European cognitive world.

At the same time, this referent or construct served as a tool for appropriating the New World. This mechanism presupposed that the cultural rules governing both worlds—that of the Amerindian and that of the European—were ultimately the same. Magellan's and Cabot's encounters with the aborigines reveal a complete lack of awareness or acknowledgment of difference. At the same time, Pigafetta's report about giants reminds us of how easily the European subjects found in the Americas exactly what they expected to find, dismissing all possible discrepancies between their expectations and what actually existed.

The European version of the colonial encounter in the River Plate is the only one we have access to; it is the only one that has been heard so far. In addition, the events and circumstances surrounding Solís's expedition were repeated almost verbatim by most of the chroniclers studied in this chapter. The documents record more than one version of individual facts only when the Christians come into conflict—as in García's suit against Cabot. For conflicts that arose during exchanges with the Other, what remains for the modern reader is only the so-called official history.

This monologic situation notwithstanding, it is possible to discern the presence of the Other in these texts. The texts show the Amerindians fighting against the Spanish, escaping from them, and working with them—as in the case of the aborigines who warned the Spaniards about Jaques' arrival in the River Plate. Despite their mystifying representation, the Amerindians appear in the text in traces that remind us that the Spanish conquest of the territory was not an easy task—and, more important, that the conquest was not achieved without tenacious resistance by the original inhabitants of the territory.

CHAPTER 2

Years of Disappointment, or the Long European Siesta

After the expeditions cited in Chapter One, voyages to the northern shore of the River Plate became less frequent, and Europeans were deterred from settling there for two main reasons: First, the famous silver was never found, causing the region to be classified as *tierras de ningún provecho* (lands of no profit, or unprofitable lands); and second, the region was considered dangerous. The Amerindians had already killed dozens of Spaniards. Settlement did take place in other parts of the River Plate region (Buenos Aires, Santa Fe, and Entre Ríos, all located within modern Argentina), but those populated centers had very little or no contact with the area under study.

The account by the Portuguese sailor Pero Lopes de Souza (1531) contains very valuable information about the region's Amerindians. The following passage narrates an encounter with a group of Amerindians at what is today the harbor of Arazatí (Department of San José, Uruguay):

> Two leagues after our departure, 4 canoes carrying a large number of people came to meet us. When I saw them, I prepared to wait for them. They rowed so hard that it seemed they were flying. When they met me they were carrying bows and arrows and javelins made of wood. They were wearing multicolored [of one thousand colors] tufts of feathers. They came to us without showing any fear: they embraced all of us. But we were not able to understand their language; it was not like the one spoken in Brazil [Guaraní]. They spoke [made sound] from the crop, like Moors. Their canoes were half a fathom wide and 10 to 12 fathoms long; they were very well made of cedar. They had tufts of feathers at the end of the oars. Each canoe had 40 men, and they rowed standing up. Before the night fell, they

> returned to their tents, which seemed to be close to the place where we encountered them. (Lopes de Souza 1926: 47–48)

According to Aníbal Barrios Pintos, there is no doubt about the ethnic affiliation of the Amerindians Lopes de Souza sighted and greeted: They are the Charrúa (1991: 43). Despite Barrios Pintos's certainty, I think we should be more prudent in assigning a specific ethnic identity to these Amerindians because of the lack of ethnographic knowledge about them. In his passage, for instance, Lopes de Souza says clearly that the Amerindians he saw were navigators, but not all scholars believe that the Charrúa had canoes and navigated the region's rivers. Lopes de Souza also says that the Amerindians were friendly. The embrace he recounts is, in fact, the first between the Amerindians and the Europeans in the texts that talk about the colonial encounter in the region. That moment of communion suggests a much less violent encounter than the one recounted in the texts about the Solís expedition. The highest value of that moment of friendship lies in the fact that both groups—the Amerindians and, in this case, the Portuguese—were heavily armed. The feathered Amerindians appear in Lopes de Souza's text, then, as friendly but fearless navigators. They also appear as speakers of a language that sounds very different from those spoken by the Amerindians known to the members of the crew—that is, the Guaraní.

Lopes de Souza writes about another encounter with the same Amerindians, this time in the area of the Cufré brook (today's Department of Colonia, Uruguay):

> Two leagues from the Saint John River, I saw again the same people I had seen earlier at their tents. They came in 6 canoes, without weapons. They came to greet us with pleasure. The wind was hard, and the sea was high. They tried to convince me to follow them to a river that was close to their tents. I sent a sailor swimming in order to find out how good the mouth of the river was. He reported that the mouth was too narrow and that it was not safe to trust the Indians, who were many—it seemed to me that there were about 600 men. He also described the tents made of 4 rugs that formed a square house without a roof—they were covered only by nets similar to ours. After I heard this, I said farewell to them and gave them a lot of goods, and they gave us a lot of fish. And they followed us: some swimming and some in their canoes. They swim like dolphins, and although the winds favored our navigation, they swam at the same speed reached by the ship. These men are all very big and robust and it seems to me they are very strong. All their women are good-looking. [The Amerindians] cut their fingers off like the ones at the cape of Santa Maria, but they are not as sad as the latter. (Ibid.: 57)

In this fragment, the Portuguese sailors' distrust is evident when they refuse the invitation to follow the Amerindians upriver. The large number of Indians (600 according to the fragment, but 240 if we take into account that Lopes previously established as 40 the number of Indians per canoe) could understandably have discouraged the Portuguese. The tents that Lopes de Souza reports seeing are typically Charrúa, according to Schuller (1906: 11). However, as I noted earlier, it is advisable to be prudent when ascribing ethnic traits to the aborigines who appear in these texts. For one thing, some of these traits were common to more than one ethnic group. A good example of this is Lopes de Souza's declaration that the Amerindians he saw practiced the same mourning ritual—cutting off their fingers' phalanxes—as the Indians he had sighted at the cape of Santa María (Department of Maldonado, east coast of today's Uruguay).

This passage addresses two other important issues: First, the aborigines—regardless of their ethnic identity—are described as big, strong, and, no less important, great swimmers; second, food is exchanged during the encounter. This allows us to add another kind of indigenous action to those we have seen: Not only did the Amerindians fight against, flee from, and negotiate with the Europeans; they also traded with them. Indigenous agency thus can be surmised, little by little, by reading the traces the Amerindians left in European texts that paid little attention to them.

The next passage will provide a better understanding of Lopes de Souza's remarks about the cheerful attitude of the Amerindians from the tents compared with those he saw at the cape of Santa María:

> The people from this land [the cape of Santa María] are very big and robust men; their countenances are very ugly; they have long hair; some of them pierce their noses and introduce pieces of shiny copper in the holes; all of them are covered by furs; they sleep in the countryside where night surprises them; they do not carry anything but furs and nets they use for hunting; they also carry a stone *pilouro* [ball] the size of a falcon with a one-and-a-half-fathom-long thread, at the end of which are feathers; they throw the *pilouros* using an object that resembles a sling. They also carry javelins made of wood and maces that are also made of wood, the size of a covado. They eat only meat and fish; they are very sad, and they cry most of the time. When a relative dies, they cut off their fingers—one finger's phalanx per relative. I saw many an old man with only the thumb left. Nothing made them happy, and they were always sighing. They were always sad: I think that is the only thing that made them happy. (1926: 62)

In addition to the mourning ritual, perpetual sadness is a notable trait among these Amerindians, according to Lopes de Souza. But his account should not be taken literally, because cases similar to this one—that is, the "welcome with tears"—have been recorded elsewhere in the Americas. The Amerindians' tears, therefore, might have been less the consequence of a way of life than a ritual played in front of foreigners (Schuller 1906: 10–13).

Scholars who have studied this document disagree in assigning these Indians to a specific ethnic group. Barrios Pintos says that they are Chaná-Begua

(1991: 40); Schuller says that they are Chaná-Timbú (1906: 12). Whatever their ethnic identity, these Indians, like the others Lopes de Souza saw, seem to be very strong—perhaps because of their diet of fish and meat, which are notorious for their high protein value. This piece of information somewhat contradicts assumptions that the region's environment was hostile enough to make its hunter–gatherers' livelihoods difficult. As we will see in Chapter Six, this may be an inaccurate assessment of the situation in pre-Columbian times. Lopes de Souza also informs us about the Amerindians' appearence—notably, that they pierced their noses, a practice he did not find among the aborigines in the western part of the territory. In sum, Lopes de Souza's account provides a glimpse at some of the aspects of indigenous social and cultural life that apparently did not interest the chroniclers we have read thus far. Thanks to the Portuguese pilot, we have at least a vague idea about the Amerindians' diet, appearance, behavior, skills (swimming, rowing, hunting), and emotional traits.

Because the expedition led by the Adelantado Don Pedro de Mendoza had only occasional and very superficial contact with the territory under study, I will not dedicate much discussion to it. One text, however, does contain information about the lands on the northern shore of the River Plate: the account by the German soldier Utz (or Ulrich) Schmidel, a member of Mendoza's crew who wrote of his adventures in this already famously hostile territory. After writing about his arrival in the River Plate and, later, the harbor of San Gabriel (in the westernmost part of today's Uruguay), Schmidel continues:

> We landed in the River Plate the day of the Epiphany of 1535. There we found a place inhabited by indians called Charrúa. There were around two thousand adult men. They eat only fish and meat. They abandoned the place and took their women and children with them; that is why we have not been able to find them. The harbor where our ships are is called San Gabriel. The [male] indians go naked but the women wear a little rag made of cotton covering their parts from the navel to the knees. (1947: 37)[1]

In this fragment, Schmidel's tone is almost neutral, and he describes only what he has been able to see: that the Indians hunt and fish. He also presents the Charrúa as a nongregarious group and describes their appearance in a way that suggests an intention to be accurate, an attitude illustrated by the spelling he chooses to represent the name of the Charrúa: "zcharruas" or "Zzcharruas." This is what the translator of a Spanish edition says about that choice: "The German spelling offers a simultaneous pronunciation of -j- or of -k- to the -ch- —for example, *Dach* is pronounced *daj,* but *Chor* and *Wachs* are pronounced *Cor* and *Wacs.* . . . But: how could he reproduce the Spanish modern -ch-, whose sound does not exist in German? How to describe the Charrúa in a way that could prevent his compatriots from pronouncing 'jarruas' or 'karruas'? The German Jesuits in the Indies have appealed, in this case, to a compound of letters -tsch-, but their predecessor [Schmidel] used the strong sounding German -z- and writes 'zcharruas' or 'Zzcharruas'" (Wernicke in Schmidel 1984: 27). This attempt to use a spelling that could achieve a sound as close to the original as possible gives us an idea about Schmidel's attitude vis-à-vis representing the new realities, entities, and peoples he encountered in his voyage. Despite his good intentions, however, Schmidel was not able to produce a discourse on the Amerindians that differed substantially from his predecessors'—although his text does reveal a less imaginative, or fantastic, gaze.

More information is available about the expedition led by the Adelantado Ortiz de Zárate, thanks to the Archdeacon Martín del Barco Centenera. In addition, a document has survived that can operate as a counterpoint to Barco Centenera: a letter by the expedition's treasurer Hernando de Montalvo, who as an administrator seems to have been more cautious and tidy than the archdeacon. Barco Centenera's *La Argentina*[2] (1602) is a poetic attempt to narrate (mainly, though not exclusively) the events that occurred in the lands of the River Plate region from their origin to the moment in which he wrote his account. The peculiarity of this history is that it takes the form of an epic poem in royal octaves (*octavas reales*). This form is not unknown, however, in Latin American colonial letters: An antecedent that was very close to *La Argentina* both geographically and chronologically is Alonso de Ercilla's *La Araucana,* an epic poem that narrates the Spanish campaign in the lands of Arauco (today's Chile). Ercilla's poem is generally considered to have served as a source of inspiration for Barco Centenera,[3] and both authors, in turn, were inspired by classical models, such as Virgil, Lucan, and Homer, and by Italian models, including Tasso and Ariosto. Both Ercilla and Barco Centenera, however, have been criticized for transgressing the formal rules that these models set down for epic poetry. Ercilla, for instance, has been taken to task for the lack of unity in his poem and for its lack of an epic hero.[4] Barco Centenera has been criticized even more harshly by literary scholars.[5]

Barco Centenera's history differs from the others in that it tries to avoid boredom and fastidiousness. But this is not its only distinguishing trait: Another peculiarity is that, according to the poem's dedication, *La Argentina* was written "so that the world may have all the information and a true relation about the River Plate."[6] This definition leads us directly to one of the fundamental problems faced by historiography in general, and by colonial Latin American historiography in particular: the truth value of the texts.

Put simply: What does it mean to write a true narration of true facts? In other words, what requirements must a historiographical text fulfill in order to be considered true? This question has been answered in many ways throughout history; for the historiography of the Indies from the sixteenth century on, however, one thing is certain: One must have had personal experience, or direct contact, with the events narrated (Mignolo 1981: 386–90). An explanation of this criterion can be found in one of the paradigmatic colonial texts: "We will tell what we saw and considered as true, as eyewitnesses, and we will not talk about the false relations written by those who only heard about the events, because we know that truth is a sacred thing" (Díaz del Castillo 1984: 110). Before this historical period, the general principles organizing the discipline had already been established regarding the truth value of historiographic accounts. According to Mignolo, truth value was

> founded more on pragmatic criteria than on logico-semantic ones and, therefore—at least in the chronological period under study—, direct relations between logical and historiographic criteria are not established. For this reason, historiography will make the truth values strongly depend on the "efficient cause"—the historian—and the "final cause"—the goal of history: *magistra vitae.* (1981: 369)[7]

Thus, the truth value of historiographic knowledge depended on the combination of determinate skills that the historian possessed (to be literate, a wise man, etc.) and on the goals of the text (to teach how to live a good life, etc.). According to Mignolo, historiography gets its epistemological support not at a logical but at a pragmatic level:

> If the word of the gods carries in itself the guarantee of its own truth, the word of men needs the guarantee of the wise man. Truth is legitimized, ultimately, by the end of history, because we could not consider as truths those that contradicted the dominant ideas about what constitutes good living. The epistemological support, in this case, lies in ethics, and its guarantee lies neither in the divine word nor in the human word but in the word that emanates from power. (Ibid.: 69–70)

When we reach the core of the legitimation mechanisms for historical truth, we find an extremely ethnocentric notion of truth. This notion can be paraphrased as: "The only true statements are those that repeat what my culture (or episteme) considers true." This poses a series of contradictions to, and conflicts with, the historiography of the Indies, because, at the same time that this region was being "discovered" and colonized, the European episteme was processing a change that impinged on the form in which it conceived the accumulation and production of knowledge. That is, the European episteme evolved from a conception that understood knowledge as an established entity (which the wise man would transmit to future generations) whose means of transmission was the word (which would be received by the ear) toward a conception in which the eyes and hands became the means through which a *new knowledge* was discovered. In this new conception of knowledge, the repetition of established, fixed knowledge lost its importance (ibid.: 388).

Thus, the legitimation of historiographical knowledge about the Indies based on the values sanctioned by the powers that be collided with the new epistemological need to say or discover new things. The conquistadors who wrote about the Indies faced precisely this challenge: to find a compromise between the requirements for the legitimation of their discourse and the new realities that did not fit the imaginary models forged by the European episteme of the sixteenth and seventeenth centuries.

The question about how signs relate to what they signify underlies all of the texts about the Indies, especially those that attempt to decipher systematically an alien and unknown reality—that is, the histories. The conflict between sign and referent, between expression and *denotatum,* arises on every page of the texts under study. The encounter with the unknown forced the European subjects to provide names, or signs, for beings and objects that did not exist in their own cultures. Barco Centenera, like most of the earliest historians of the Indies, had to face the conflict between his worldview and all that he saw as a witness to a new reality, the New World. Julio Ortega describes the characteristics of the discursive family to which Barco Centenera's text belongs:

> These texts, understood as discourses that classify and register [objects], presuppose a model of perception and representation and, for that matter, develop a series of cognitive and formal processes that represent the systematic and central character of a culture capable of making the New World a completely readable object. . . . Thus, legibility, *the conversion of the diverse into the similar,* is a model with a powerful descriptive and categorizing capacity; but *because the objects exceed the possibilities of both the act of naming and of comparison, the activity of the subject,* organized by binary oppositions, becomes *a decisive mediation that is superimposed upon the observed object.* (Ortega 1988: 101; emphasis added)

The mediation conducted by the interpreter or by the text consists of harmonizing the new and the already existing, the known and the unknown, the American reality and the ideological context upon which European society's perceptive and cognitive mechanisms were founded (Pastor 1988: 4).[8] In this regard, I follow Pastor in saying that America, for the European observer, was equal to the sum of all the knowledge and legends circulating about *terrae incognitae* at that time (ibid.: 5). In her analysis of Columbus's discourse,

Pastor says that the European subjects who wrote about the Indies in the early stages of the colonial encounter did not discover anything; rather, they identified and verified (ibid.: 6). In other words, Columbus was looking for the old reality, not the new reality that surrounded him. Through the data that they drew from their experience in American lands, these early Western observers performed an interpretive activity within coordinates set by their culture and society—in this case, the conceptual framework created in the classical and medieval corpus of writings about unknown lands (Pliny and Marco Polo, among others[9]). In performing such an interpretation, these Western observers simply verified what was already known about both *terrae incognitae* and their savage peoples—an activity that, Jitrik surmises, may have comforted European readers who, like the writers, saw their knowledge confirmed (1983: 87). To some degree, this informational load was part of the luggage that the chroniclers of the Indies took to America, and Barco Centenera is no exception: In his writings, we can see the coexistence of the reduction of Otherness to the similar and the need to say new things—the need to contribute new data that enriched the cognitive lore of his culture. Judging from the dedication cited earlier and from the first stanza of his poem/chronicle, Barco Centenera deemed the veracity and inherent interest of the knowledge he was offering to be self-evident. In that first stanza, Barco Centenera invokes Apollo in the classical manner to ask his help: "Help me so that I am able, *without deceit,* to make public the memory, in the form of *a new history,* of *admirable things* (1602: 1; emphasis added). Note that this stanza gives us a first hint about those to whom he is addressing his message: He is telling his story to the world. It is likely, however, that his conception of the world did not include many nations. Further, the veracity ("without deceit") of this new knowledge ("new history") about "admirable things" is grounded in the sources of information that Barco Centenera cites in the following stanza: "I am also going to deal with strange events that I was encountering. *Many of them I personally saw;* I heard other people's testimonies about other events because I asked some people; and they responded to me. I talked with them about admirable things I was greedy for—and was anxious to write about them" (ibid.: IV; emphasis added).

Thus, Barco Centenera gets his information from two basic sources: personal experience as an eyewitness and firsthand accounts related by witnesses of events that he could not see himself. In Mignolo's study of the classification of historiographical sources according to their value, the two invoked by Barco Centenera are the most reliable (Mignolo 1981: 377).[10] For this reason, Barco Centenera (like Ercilla before him) is very proud to state that nobody has better information than he: He was either present when the events occurred or he took pains to obtain the best firsthand testimony available.

When Barco Centenera tells of the "discovery" of the River Plate and other early expeditions, however, he does not bother to cite his sources. He simply offers his version. He does the same when he proposes a story about the origins of the region's Amerindians. In a tirade that starts on page 2 and ends on page 7, he offers a very creative narrative that employs an already familiar cognitive strategy—the assimilation of the Other to the Same. First, he postulates a biblical origin, then a Spanish origin, for the Tupí. More specifically, he locates the Tupí's geographical origin in Extremadura, from which the Ricinos from Trujillo had been expelled because of their savage and cannibalistic customs (Barco Centenera 1602: 2v). Barco Centenera offers an equally creative story when he attributes a Carib origin to the Guaraní (ibid.: 5), and he completes this fantastic genealogy with a Latino/Guaraní etymology for that term: "If we want to look carefully at this issue, Carib means good burying of flesh; this we know from Latin, a language in which caro means flesh. And in Guaraní language, we can say Iby, which means ground where humans are confined. Carib is this tyrannical people" (ibid.: 5).[11]

In his text, Barco Centenera provides the region's Amerindians, who are absolute strangers to the European subject, with a history that ties their past to "world history"—that is, the history that presents Europe as the privileged historical agent. And he offers even more: He presents a pseudo-etymological explanation that clarifies the "true" meaning of the names of the local ethnic groups. In cantos II and III (ibid: 8v–23v), he completes his strategy of reorganizing the observed alien reality while describing the geography, the fauna, and the flora of the region. The multitude of unfamiliar plants and animals in the region under study presented European observers with a world that they did not understand very well—a world that, as Ortega suggests, exceeded the classification and organization capabilities of the Western episteme. Thus, Barco Centenera's statement that he saw mermaids in the River Plate should not surprise us; a century earlier, Columbus himself had reported seeing specimens of this mythological being (Colón 1982: 124). Barco Centenera writes:

> The mermaid, beautiful and lovely,
> appeared as a beautiful lady,
> moaning in the middle of this lake
> while she spread her golden mane. (1602: 21)

La Argentina notes other such unusual beings. The most extravagant of these stories may be one in which he tells of the worms that turn into butterflies, only, in the final stages of their quasi-Ovidian metamorphosis, to become mice:

> When the cane matures, a worm is engendered inside it.
> Then the worm perforates the internode
> and gets out of the cane transformed into a butterfly.
> With its wings it begins to fly, but after a while
> it loses them and becomes a perfect mouse. (Ibid.: 22v)

And Barco Centenera sights another mythological being, the carbuncle, in the River Plate:[12]

> Not far from here I saw several times,
> with my own eyes the Carbuncle.
> Nobody judge this as a figment of my imagination,
> because I almost captured one of them.
> I went to a thousand pains and one thousand annoyances
> in my search for this animal. But happy are those who
> are able to capture Anagpitan[13] alive. (Ibid.: 21v)

In sum, all of the beings that Barco Centenera saw in the River Plate region had already appeared in the books that formed the European reservoir of knowledge about unknown lands. The colonial writers' interpretive labor, their mediation between observed reality and the reader of the text, consisted of distorting the facts to adapt them to familiar patterns—that is, to the available cultural parameters.[14] This does not mean that the European observers consciously distorted the reality they perceived; rather, the knowing subjects "read," in the reality they perceived, only what the constraints of their own cognitive framework allowed them to understand. In other words, Barco Centenera belonged to a culture, an episteme, and, most of all, an interpretive community (in the sense given to the term by Stanley Fish) that predisposed its members to interpret the world in a determinate manner—actually, in the only manner possible for that culture. From the vantage point of our contemporary episteme, it may seem odd—or even funny—to read descriptions of mermaids, worms that turn into mice, carbuncles, and other entities that modernity has relegated to the realm of fictional discourse. Yet the educated Renaissance subject accepted those entities, and many more, not only as part of literarature (at least, in epic poetry based on Ariosto's *Orlando*), but also in texts that were considered scientific works (such as Pliny's *Historia naturalis*) or historically reliable accounts (such as Enea Silvio Piccolomini's *Historia rerum ubique gestarum*).[15]

The ideological limitations of that macro-interpretive community (Europe, the West) are laid bare when one studies the strategies its members used when trying to interpret the new lands in a way that differed from the archetype of the unknown lands established by the texts of Marco Polo and other Medieval voyagers (that is, when they tried to account for the new instead of repeating the already "known"). Barco Centenera provides a good example: After one hundred years of exploration and settlement, the archetype of the unknown lands remains almost untouched in his poem. That is to say, none of the contradictions between the known and the new seems to have given the archdeacon sufficient reason to abandon the archetypical representations. The European interpretive community's rigidity—and, above all, its position of power—allowed its members to keep repeating formulas and constructs despite the challenges that contradictory empirical data constantly posed to them.

In *La Argentina,* the act of naming geographic sites and species of animals illustrates this interpretive community's strategies for representing alterity. The European lexical reservoir cannot, of course, account for the wide variety of animals found in the territory under study. Barco Centenera solves this problem by applying European (or Old World) names to these unfamiliar species.[16] This strategy appears for the first time in Columbus's diary (Colón 1982: 43), in which the admiral describes in Andalusian (Spanish) terms the woods he found in the Caribbean. He does the same when he tries to give an idea about the average temperature in the new lands (ibid.: 45). In these two cases, the European subject of discourse confronts a new topographic reality that he cannot describe without help from the realities that are already known.

In some cases, the decision to use this strategy is understandable. For example, when Barco Centenera needs to describe the ñandú (*Rhea Americana*), he logically calls it an "ostrich" because of the two birds' strikingly similar appearance (Barco Centenera 1602: 16v). However, when he uses the same strategy to describe felines (probably pumas) that are very different from species in the Old World (ibid.: 18), he comes closer to distorting reality than explaining what the New World animals look like. Similarly, in some passages he calls American birds of prey "neblí" and "falcons" (ibid.: 16v); the discrepancy between his lexical and conceptual arsenal and observed reality is, in these cases, considerable.

The apocryphal European genealogy that Barco Centenera offers for the region's Amerindians works as a mechanism to confront and domesticate an absolute alterity. The passage on the "Caribs" is not the only segment of the text that attempts to decipher (and neutralize) an absolute alterity (the Amerindian, the radically Other). Other ethnic groups are also represented in the poem. For example, Barco Centenera describes the Charrúa thus:

> The people who live in this region are called
> Charruahas. *They are very strong and Mars has bestowed*
> *upon them the gift of his strength, his valor and his power.*
> Abayuba (a very healthy youngster) is, among these people,
> the one who carries the banner, in front of his uncle, cacique Zapican.
>
> *This is a very brave people* but they have no agriculture.
> They are very bellicose (in war and battle).
> They are very daring. When they get tired of the place
> where they live, they move somewhere else—because their
> houses are made of rugs, they can move fast. (Ibid.: 75; emphasis added)

The first thing one notices in this passage is Barco Centenera's imprecision in attributing a name to this ethnic group. Although he does not reach the degree of distortion to which Fernández de Oviedo subjected the name (he called these people "Jacroas" [1959 [1535–47]: 372]), his "Charruahas" differs considerably from the most accepted spelling. In the rest of the poem, the name suffers slight variations, appearing as "Chauarria" (Barco Centenera 1602: 114v, 115) and, in the plural, as "Charruahaes" (ibid.: 76). This lack of coherence in naming practices and negligence in phonetic reproduction are common among the first chroniclers of the Indies, as is Barco Centenera's hesitation in identifying an adequate phonetic reproduction.[17] One could argue that this hesitation signifies a disrespectful attitude toward the Amerindians—that is, a lack of interest in representing the Other adequately. Others would say, instead, that the hesitation was a consequence of the natural cognitive limitations of the European interpretive community—that is, that the hesitation resulted from the difficulties romance-language speakers faced when they had to reproduce sounds in indigenous languages that were not "normal" for them, especially when their sole tool for transcribing those "new" sounds was the Latin alphabet. These two explanations are not mutually exclusive, however. It is possible to consider these texts as combining the denial of alterity as such and the incapacity to transcend conceptual and ideological limitations.

Barco Centenera was able to perceive the Charrúas' bravery, though one could argue that he had no choice, given the Amerindians' repeated attacks on the Spaniards. The proliferation in *La Argentina* of adjectives that allude to the Charrúas' valor ("brave" and "bellicose") and the references to their strength bear witness to the impression that those Indians made on Barco Centenera. It is also possible that Barco Centenera used such praise of the enemy's talents as a rhetorical device to add value to the Spaniards' ultimate victory—for example, when he exaggeratedly describes the Charrúa as able to run after deer and catch them (ibid.: 75v). This device can be also found in *La Araucana,*

Barco Centenera's model, when Ercilla presents the Araucanians in Homeric fashion. Intending to represent a formidable enemy, Barco Centenera, following Ercilla's example, tells us that Mars himself protects and guides the Charrúa army. *La Araucana*'s influence is also evident in the passage of *La Argentina* that depicts a battle between Zapican's (Çapicano's) men and Ortiz de Zárate's soldiers (ibid.: 78v ff.). In this passage, each instance of man-to-man combat is presented individually—a model that Ercilla himself took from classical epic poetry. One detail militates against the credibility of *La Argentina*'s battle scenes: the author's absolute certainty with regard to the names of the Charrúa combatants. One wonders how he managed to become so familiar with the names of an enemy who did not even speak Guaraní, the lingua franca of the region.

At this point, it is opportune to recall that many documents suggest the Spaniards had a great deal of trouble understanding indigenous languages. When Barco Centenera tries to reproduce the indigenous word we now pronounce as "Uruguay," for instance, he is capable of writing only "Vruay" (ibid.: 86) and "Vruaig" (ibid.: 103v). Thus, the fact that he is able to give a proper name to each indigenous warrior seems less the consequence of the chronicler's access to privileged information than of the need to copy the esthetic model established by Ercilla—wherein every indigenous warrior had his own name. I will not propose a truth value for these texts; I will, however, point out that there are many reasons to suspect that the Charrúa warriors did not bear the names that Barco Centenera attributes to them.

The analysis of the representation of the Other (be it a geographic, an animal, or a human entity) in Barco Centenera's text suggest that the narrative it produces is less a description than an interpretation. According to Hayden White (1978: 51), historians interpret material to fill gaps in the documents they study. This suggests a manipulation of the historical text, which, in turn, causes some critics to view the historical object of study as a construct (Gossman 1978: 27). Interpretation as mediation is something that producers of historiographic texts add to the documents or events that they study—it is not present in the events that the texts describe.

The object of historical discourse, then, is a construct; it is created by the discipline itself. The cognitive operation that historians perform includes their own lucubrations and data that can be confirmed empirically (for example, the nomadic habits of the Charrúa). This is how, in Barco Centenera's text, data obtained from reality become those mysterious worms that turn into mice. This is also how the Charrúas' speed (a piece of data obtained from observation) becomes hyperbole: "*They are so fast that they run after the deer and they actually catch them.* They also chase the ostriches until they catch them" (Barco Centenera 1602: 75v; emphasis added). In another passage, Barco Centenera charges the Charrúa with certain bloody practices: "When these mean people capture prisoners, they take their eyes out and cut their feet and hands with fierce cruelty. They say all this gives them greatness" (ibid.: 115v). (As we will see later, these charges are not confirmed by other sources.) Notice Barco Centenera's macabre detail about the Charrúas' satisfaction after performing the alleged mutilations. Add to this his use of the words "fierce cruelty," and the picture of a bloody and malignant people is completed. However, as I noted earlier, the construction of the Charrúa as Others is a complex process involving a dialectic between descriptions based on empirical observation (for example, the Charrúas' benevolence toward their captives [ibid.: 76] and their self-mutilation after the death of a relative [ibid.]) on the one hand, and the author's creations or interpretations (of other data) stemming from his interpretive community's epistemic foundations on the Other. This dialectic once again dramatizes the relationship between representation and ideology: The representation of the colonial subject (the Amerindian, the Other) is achieved via one or more of the so-called borrowed languages (science, historiography, and ethnography, among others).[18] It is through the use of these borrowed languages (especially historiography and ethnography) that the European subject gives shape to the referent "Charrúa," the element that occupies the lower position in the binary or logocentric hierarchy,[19] in the colonial period.

How does a discourse create (or, according to some authors, denote) its Others as referents? There are many ways to present the problem of reference. Peter Strawson's is useful because it studies utterance in a pragmatic context. This distinguishes Strawson from his predecessors in the field of analytic philosophy, who studied reference by trying to establish truth values depending on the extensional existence of the object to which a determinate proposition was referring. The classic studies in this field are by Gottlob Frege and Bertrand Russell. Both establish (from different perspectives) a similar criterion: There is no true proposition if the proposition does not refer to an object that exists in the world (outside discourse). Thus, both Frege and Russell put less emphasis on the pragmatic dimension of the act of referring than on the object that is being referred to. Strawson, for his part, believes that it is not useful to ask about the existence of the object to which discourse is referring if we are not capable of taking into account the possible uses of that discourse (1973: 65). His ideas have inspired literary critics such as Françoise Meltzer (whose other source of inspiration is Frege), who proposes the notion of "cognitive referent."[20] That is, Meltzer postulates a referent that does not require extensional confirmation. Another author of interest is Anna Whiteside, who maintains that reference is the product of the collaboration between a text and its addressee. In this conceptual framework, reference is not immutable; it will depend on the many possible contexts of emission and reception (Whiteside 1987: 201). In other words, everything can be referred to as long as discourse is uttered in an adequate context.[21]

Following Strawson's idea that reference is not produced by expressions but by persons, both Whiteside and Meltzer incorporate the addressee into the referential process—or act, as Thomas E. Lewis prefers.[22] In this investigation, too, the context and the role of the reader who decodes the text are considered fundamental elements of the referential act. These are the elements that help us understand why Barco Centenera's readers believed what he wrote—that is, why his readers assigned truth value to his text. The entities that he describes, the prejudicial representation of the Amerindians he offers, and many other assertions that may sound ridiculous to the twentieth-century readers were not incredible to his Renaissance readership: They were the truth—a truth decreed by the European episteme before it confronted factual evidence. The educated European subject (except perhaps Michel de Montaigne) expected unknown lands to be plagued by monsters and populated by savage Indians.[23] Thus, the referents "northern shore of the River Plate" and "Charrúa"[24] are not objectively true or false (that is, true or false independent of the context of production and reception). Rather, they may be false for one person but true for another. For a Spanish reader in 1602, Barco Centenera's description of the River Plate *was* the River Plate; his version of the Charrúa *was* the Charrúa. In other words, "Charrúa" and "River Plate," for the European reader, were *created by* that referential act entitled *La Argentina.*

Montalvo, the treasurer of Ortiz de Zárate's expedition, provides a different discursive perspective—that of the bureaucrat—and the way in which he narrates the clashes between the Spaniards and the Charrúa differs dramatically from Barco Centenera's account. That notwithstanding, Montalvo shows a similar contempt for the Amerindians of the region:

> Some indians called charrúa, who live on the shores of this river, came to see us. These indians are loafers who neither practice agriculture nor have a fixed residence. They eat fish, deer, and ostrich. They approached our ships in three or four canoes; and they brought their kind of food in order to trade with us, because the Adelantado always treated them well—he always traded with them, regardless of the value of the goods brought by the Indians. And so they [the Indians] came to the San Graviel [*sic*] harbor, where the Adelantado made the captain, treasurer, and interpreter Francisco Ortiz de Vergara ask the Indians whether one of them could carry some letters to Juan de Garay [who was camping somewhere else]. (1915: 297)

Montalvo's portrayal of the Charrúa as the opposite of "civilized man" (because they neither cultivate the land nor have a fixed domicile) is synthesized in the expression "loafers." But apart from reproducing the construct "Charrúa" that we have already seen in other chronicles, Montalvo offers a very "civilized" version of the relations between the two cultures of the colonial encounter in the year 1573. He portrays them not only as trading (performing the *rescates*) with each other, but also as showing mutual respect and good treatment. Trust is also an ingredient in this picture: According to Montalvo, the Spaniards trust the Amerindians enough to ask them to be their messengers. However, also according to his account, the aborigines did not deliver the letter, and this provoked a sour response from the Spaniards: They took a Charrúa *cacique* prisoner. This is Montalvo's version of the facts:

> The cacique did not comply with his promise; instead, he left and called for the help of the indians from the area, so that he could lead an attack against the Spanish military camp. And he did so: one day, when the treasurer Francisco Ortiz de Vergara, the piloto mayor and some soldiers were exploring a river called San Juan at the Adelantado's request, they ran into the cacique of the Indians. He had just called his neighbors and was making great fires—which are the signals they have for their gatherings. (Ibid.: 297–98)

In this version, the Charrúa are again shown as sly people who fail to fulfill promises.[25] One can, however, ask several questions about this situation: How well did Ortiz de Vergara perform as an interpreter? And even if he was very good at his job, was he good enough to communicate specifically and accurately in the Charrúas' language? If the answer is yes, we must conclude that Ortiz de Zárate's expedition was very lucky to have him—the odds that a European expert in the Charrúas' language existed in 1573 were very low. But regardless of whether the interpreter understood what the Amerindians were saying (or was able to communicate precise messages to them), this is a crucial moment in the history of Charrúa–Spanish exchanges, because the moment that the Spaniards decided to punish the Indians' lack of integrity by kidnapping the "sly" *cacique* (Montalvo in Levillier 1915: 298), the hostilities between the groups began. Barco Centenera, for his part, does not say anything about the possible reasons for the *cacique*'s capture. He only narrates the episode after explaining the prisoner's identity: "He [Abayubá] was brought to the military camp by some captains; when he arrived, Juan Ortiz took him prisoner because he knew the cacique was very respected by his people" (Barco Centenera 1602: 78v). This is how Montalvo tells the rest of the story:

> Because the Charrúa found out about the capture of their captain, their main cacique came (accompanied by some of his men) to the military camp to ask the

> Adelantado to free the captive captain—who was a cousin of the main cacique. In exchange, he offered to deliver the letters his people had previously failed to deliver; he also promised to liberate a Christian they had with them (a cabin boy who had been whipped by the Adelantado as punishment for a theft that he had committed) and provide the canoe the Adelantado had previously asked for. The Indians did as promised, and the captain freed the cacique. (1915: 298)

In this text, the Charrúa "captains" are not mentioned by name; Barco Centenera, however, calls them Zapicán and Abayubá: "The cacique of these people is Zapican, who has a very brave nephew called Abayubá—a very handsome lad" (Barco Centenera 1602: 78v). The archdeacon's tendency to give names indiscriminately to the Indians may explain the discrepancy between the two versions. It should be noted that these two authors also disagree on the degree of kinship between the Charrúa *caciques:* Montalvo says that they are cousins, while Barco Centenera asserts they are uncle and nephew. They do agree on one issue, however: Montalvo and Barco Centenera both refer to the Spanish prisoner who was traded by the Charrúa *cacique* (Abayubá). In Barco Centenera's version, the cabin boy is living with the Amerindians because of the punishment inflicted on him by the Adelantado. (Remember that, according to Montalvo, the cabin boy had been whipped.) In other words, he escaped from the Spanish camp and sought refuge among the Amerindians: "There was a mistreated sailor who escaped from the camp and went to live with the Indians. He [Zapican] traded the Spanish sailor and the canoe for his beloved Abayubá" (Barco Centenera 1602: 79). Both chroniclers also attribute malice to Yamandú, the *cacique* of an unidentified ethnic group in the area (Montalvo 1915: 307). Barco Centenera is even harsher than Montalvo on Yamandú: He repeatedly calls him "dog" ("*perro*") and "evil" ("*malvado*") in cantos XI to XV.

Together, these two texts about the same events help create a polyphonic effect that is absent from the other accounts examined thus far. The discrepancies between Montalvo's and Barco Centenera's accounts, however, belong to the same episteme. For that reason, the polyphony that they produce does not offer an indigenous perspective. The region's Amerindians, as always, remain silent. But their actions—and their agency—can be surmised. In these texts, new forms of indigenous agency appear as traces. They include disobedience (that is, if the Amerindians truly understood what the Spanish interpreter requested but refused to comply); deceit (if they pretended to agree to carry the message); and diplomatic negotiation (when they traded prisoners with the Spaniards). In the rest of the fragments from *La Argentina* quoted earlier in this chapter, the agency of the Charrúa is manifested mostly in their bellicose defense of the territory. In those fragments, the Charrúas' actions remind us that occupying the territory was not easy, and the Amerindians' agency was fundamental in determining the course of events on the territory. In fact, Ortiz de Zárate's troops eventually had to abandon the area dominated by the Charrúa in defeat. Thus, European settlement could not develop immediately, partly because of the Amerindians' brave resistance.[26] Ercilla describes a similar situation—that is, a long, difficult struggle between invaders and high-mobility indigenous peoples who did not organize around a state or urban centers—in *La Araucana* when he relates the successful resistance of the Mapuche Indians from the territory known today as Chile.

Both *La Argentina* and *La Araucana,* therefore, refer to situations with similar characteristics that differ substantially from the bellicose encounters that took place in Mesoamerica and the Andes. As I noted earlier, the encounters that led to the spectacular falls of Mexico–Tenochtitlan and Cuzco were not the most typical kind of clash between invaders and Amerindians. On the contrary, in many regions the conflict was long, and the actions developed slowly. Thus, despite the success that the epic narratives of triumph relate, pockets of resistance did exist in many parts of the continent. On the northern shore of the River Plate, one of the consequences of that kind of resistance was that the first permanent European settlement could not be established until 1680.[27]

The *Mestizo* Ruy Díaz de Guzmán, born in the Government of Paraguay (the old capital of the River Plate region), wrote the historical account known as *La Argentina* circa 1610. *La Argentina* was not published, however, until much later. We do know from the testimony of chroniclers such as Lozano, Guevara, and Azara that the work was consulted and cited frequently in manuscript form, and for that reason, it became known by the title *La Argentina manuscrita* (Rojas 1924: 342).

Díaz de Guzmán offers a representation of the region's territory in which the unknown—"*papagayos y monos diferentes de los de Africa*" ("macaws and monkeys different from those in Africa"; ibid.: 18)—is presented via a series of comparisons in which one of the terms is familiar to the addressee—European culture. However, in his comparisons, Díaz de Guzmán never uses a mythological monster or entity as the familiar element. Instead, he uses an animal that is already familiar within European culture (the monkeys and macaws, for example). Yet the author is more interested in referring to historical events than in describing the peculiarities of the local landscape and fauna—perhaps because, as a native of the region, he did not feel the need to describe a landscape or animals with which he was very well acquainted.

According to Enrique de Gandía, "Ruy Díaz is the first author from this region who uses the word patria [fatherland], and the first who refers to these provinces as the fatherland of the people born in their territory. In the history of the notion [feeling] of fatherland among us—Hispanic Americans from the River Plate—, he occupies, chronologically, the first place" (1945: 16). De Gandía (1946) also says: "Neither professors nor students should forget this important fact: *La Argentina,* by Díaz de Guzmán, is our first patriotic historical work—the first one that evokes the past of these lands as the fatherland of the men [*sic*] born in them."

It is difficult to deny the patriotism that de Gandía ascribes to Díaz de Guzmán. However, it is the patriotism of a *Criollo*—or, better yet, of a well-to-do *Mestizo* of colonial times who perceives America as his fatherland. The fact is that Díaz de Guzmán's situation of enunciation is profoundly European. As J. Jorge Klor de Alva has pointed out, a large number of *Mestizos* in Latin America participated fully in, and had access to the benefits of, the Occidental way of life (1995: 255). This caused many *Mestizos* to endorse European culture, the colonial government, and the values that government promoted—take, for example, Díaz de Guzmán's reference to the conquistadors as "*nuestros españoles,*" or "our Spaniards" (1882: 14). To measure Díaz de Guzmán's cultural positioning, we can examine how he deals with his ethnic heritage: Although he talks extensively about his Spanish father's prestigious lineage, he remains silent about his indigenous mother. It would not be fair, however, to overlook the passages in which Díaz de Guzmán praises the *Mestizo* of the Americas (1882: bk. 1, chap. 18), as Rojas points out (1924: 329). These passages add more evidence to the portrait of the ambiguity of the *Mestizos*' social position (in terms not only of social hierarchy but also of their feelings toward the two worlds they come from) before independence.

These ambiguities notwithstanding, Díaz de Guzmán's Europeanized perspective is revealed clearly in the version he offers of the Spanish epic in the River Plate region. The Spaniards came to America and the River Plate with the mission to civilize and evangelize the savage, "*caribes y carniceros*" ("carib and bloodthirsty" [1882: 18]) Indians, who opposed any rational form of social organization. This is a narrative that was shared by the majority of the European chroniclers of the Indies, and it takes a form that resembles an epic tale.[28] In Díaz de Guzmán's history, the Amerindians somewhat resemble those we saw in Barco Centenera's *La Argentina,* at least in terms of the position they are assigned in a logocentric structure. One of the few passages describing indigenous subjects tells of an American region that is "*muy poblada de gente caribe y carnicera*" ("densely populated by carib and bloodthirsty people" [ibid.]). Sometimes, however, he makes positive remarks about the Indians—for instance, he describes the Charrúa as "a very spirited and brave people who eat only game and fish. They are very bold and cruel when they fight, but very humane and compassionate with their captives" (ibid.: 25). This fairness toward the Other (especially compared with Barco Centenera) can also be seen in Díaz de Guzmán's naming of geographic sites. He usually places the autochthonous name next to the Spanish one: "That great River Plate, that the Natives call *Paraná Guazú,* which means river as big as a sea—not to be confused with another river called Paraná" (ibid.; emphasis added).

Cases such as this one give modern readers a glimpse of the silenced Other. These traces of their discourse (the indigenous name of a river, for example) and of their culture allow us to recover at least some of their presence, for the only form in which the Other appears in the texts under study is as a trace.[29] Whether the colonizer likes it or not, his or her discourse is permeated—or better, poisoned—by the traces of the elements that have been displaced in the hierarchical binary pairs she or he produces in order to understand, and account for, the world.

CHAPTER 3

The Pacific Penetration

Pero lo cierto es que yo nunca vi una vaca. *[Yet, the truth is that I never saw a cow.]*

—*Los Tontos*

After Ortiz de Zárate's departure, the lands on the northern shore of the River Plate fell into a deep oblivion. By 1576, hunger and hardships, ongoing hostilities by the Amerindians (presumably the Charrúa, to judge from Barco Centenera's account, whose area of influence was believed to include the San Salvador region, where the Spanish military camp was located), and the absence of precious metals had persuaded the Spaniards to abandon their only settlement on the northern shore of the River Plate.[1]

Despite the difficulties, the Spanish monarch showed interest in the region at least once before Ortiz de Zárate evacuated the military camp: In 1559, King Philip II appointed Jaime Rasquín governor of Paraguay. Rasquín, however, never reached his destination. (For details about this failed expedition, see de Gandía [1942].) After the camp was abandoned, according to a *cédula real,* Philip II planned to establish a settlement on the island of Maldonado "because many ships frequently got lost in that area, and the Natives capture their crews. If we had a settlement there, the ships could seek refuge in it, and the people would be protected" (in Azarola Gil 1927: 10–11). Six years later, Governor Valdés de la Banda proposed a similar project to King Philip III, Philip II's successor (ibid.: 16–19). For various reasons, however, the settlement of Maldonado never took place.

The lands on the northern shore of the River Plate did not receive any further attention from the colonizers until Hernandarias was appointed governor of Paraguay. The first serious exploration of the territory took place during his first administration. (Hernandarias served four terms as governor.) This historical moment also marks the beginning of the exploitation of cattle in the territory, which, according to Emilio Coni, took place in 1611 on the island of Vizcaíno and in 1617 on the shores opposite the island of San Gabriel (1929: 1–2).[2] Hernandarias's introduction of cattle initiated many economic and social transformations, and from that moment on, the way in which European observers perceived those lands changed dramatically.

Hernando Arias de Saavedra was the son of a member of the expedition led by the Adelantado of premonitory name, Alvar Núñez Cabeza de Vaca. This is confirmed by a *relación de servicios* (relation of services) dated 1612 in which Hernandarias addresses the king regarding his services to the crown (reproduced in Azarola Gil 1933).[3] This document also sheds light on the many activities Hernandarias performed as a governor in the service of the Spanish crown, most of which are related to "discovery," conquest, and the settlement of territory inhabited by Amerindians. Expressions such as "we encountered some Natives" and "the Natives rebelled" are common in this document, giving an idea about the indigenous peoples' response to Hernandarias's attempts to colonize their lands. The Amerindians of the northern shore of the River Plate do not appear very often in Hernandarias's texts; when he does mention them, however, he presents them as warriors. For example, while writing about clashes between the Charrúa and members of the expeditions led by the adelantados Ortiz de Zárate and Juan de Garay, he says: "Those charrúa indians had killed and captured many of the Adelantado's soldiers in the San Graviel harbor. For this reason, *he [Juan de Garay] took twelve cavalry soldiers and put them on certain boats. When he was crossing the Paraná river, he encountered the Charrúa, who counted more than two thousand. The Indians, who had killed many Spaniards in the past, fought very bravely*" (in ibid.: 207; emphasis added).

This fragment narrates one of the several battles between the Charrúa and Garay's troops—of which Hernandarias was a member. Although the same Charrúa who inhabited the northern shore of the River Plate are meant, the text says clearly that the clash took place on the shores of the Paraná River—another area that this nomadic indigenous group favored.[4] The text confirms that, because of their previous victories over the Spaniards, the Charrúa were known by the beginning of the seventeenth century for their talent as warriors. Hernandarias's citing of the Charrúas' martial skills and their large number of combatants (perhaps an exaggeration) makes Garay's subsequent victory even more praiseworthy—a rhetorical device that we saw in both *La Argentina* and in its model, *La Araucana.*

Additional references to the Charrúas' territory can be found in a *relación* addressed to the king dated July 2, 1608. In this text, Hernandarias narrates the "*descubrimiento de la Vanda del norte que es la costa de los charrúas*" ("discovery of the northern shore that is the coast of the Charrúa" [ibid.: 207]). As we can see, in the Spanish imagination the name "Charrúa" is closely tied to the territory to the north of the River Plate—a territory that, according to other documents, Hernandarias wants to populate. In a letter dated May 5, 1607, he writes:

> For the security of Buenos Aires, I have determined to explore, next year, with some of my people, *the shore known as Vanda [shore, coast] of the Charrúa.* I also want to establish a settlement at *a harbor located in the area known as Montevidio.* People tell me this harbor is very good and it is located thirty leagues from this city [Buenos Aires]. It communicates with a very good river, and very close to the harbor there is an island that may help us sight enemy ships. (Hernandarias 1937: 143; emphasis added)

Two things are particularly noteworthy in this passage: the name "Charrúa" is again associated with the northern shore of the river, and the harbor area is still being called "Montevidio." Hernandarias saw this place as a potential advance post that could protect Spanish possessions from threats by French, Dutch, and English ships, which by then had become frequent. His understanding of the problems and needs of that part of the region also caused him to see other possible uses for the harbor and settlement. In the May 5, 1607, letter, he makes his plans for Montevideo more explicit:

> If we found a town in the area located between Peru and Asuncion and another one on the province East of the Uruguay River—a very fertile province densely populated by Indians—, located less than forty leagues from the ocean, we would be able to populate the Santa Catarina harbor [in Brazil]—which is very good and capable of admitting ships of great draft without any risk; it could also be closed with a chain, which would make it easier for us to protect it.
>
> If we could send to Spain the silver produced by the Potosí mines that belong to Your Majesty through this [new] route, Your Highness would save great expenditures because this route is shorter and it is appropriate for stagecoaches. Besides, the route by sea between this harbor [Montevideo] and Santa Catarina is also brief, and it is less stormy than the current route. (Ibid: 151)

Hernandarias's idea, then, was to establish Spanish settlements along the northern shore of the River Plate to create a new route for transporting the silver extracted from the Potosí mines. Raúl A. Molina views this project, which goes beyond creating a new route for the silver, as proof of the governor's powerful intelligence and vast knowledge of the region's problems: "The important cities of Concordia, Salto, Paysandú and, close to the Santa Lucía harbor, the capital of modern-day Uruguay are located today in the places [Hernandarias] picked for the establishment of settlements" (1948: 164).

Hernandarias's multiple talents as a statesman are illustrated even more clearly in the text that follows. In his July 2, 1608, *relación* to the king, Hernandarias offers many more details about the exploration campaign ("*descubrimiento,*" in the terminology of that age) than he did in his 1612 *relación de servicios.* For example, he explicitly cites the number of men he took with him, the route he followed, and the different geographic zones he visited. The letter's abundance of information reveals a very observant, detail-oriented author. For example, this is how he describes the Uruguay River:

> These people brought news about a river named Uruay. Down the river, navigation is peaceful and pleasant. The lands around it are good for settlements, although they have found few Natives who, apparently, live far from the shores of the Uruguay river, on the coast of smaller ones [rivers]; we know so because the people I sent saw fires and smoke; the majority of them live north of Santa Fe. (In Azarola Gil 1933: 208)

The explorer's pleasure grows as he travels more deeply into the territory. As he progresses in his exploration, he discovers more and more natural assets: "The coast is good, and it has many harbors; many rivers from the mainland flow out to the sea" (ibid.). Although the mainland seems to be deserted in Hernandarias's account, traces of the Amerindians appear in his citing of fires and smoke. Although Hernandarias does not reach Montevideo proper (the harbor with a hill) during this exploration, he does manage to reconnoiter the river that he names "Santa Lucía" because he sees it on that saint's day:

> This Santa Lucia harbor is located in a river around thirty leagues from this city [Buenos Aires]. There is an island in the middle of its mouth that protects it [the harbor] from all kind of winds. It is capable of hosting many ships because there are no shoals in it and it is nine fathoms deep. All this I know because I was able to investigate the area thoroughly, thanks to some canoes I found there. In sum, *I think this may be one of the best harbors that we have discovered,* because in addition to all the advantages already mentioned, t*here is plenty of wood* in the surrounding areas. *The land is very beautiful* and, in addition to all this, *the great quality and fertility of the land* make the development of densely populated agricultural settlements possible. (Ibid.: 209; emphasis added)

Hernandarias's *relación* is the first document to praise the harbor of Santa Lucía and the surrounding area. It is also the first text to call attention to the abundance of wood, the presence or absence of which was a critical factor in deciding whether to establish settlements. In Hernandarias's opinion, the Santa Lucía area should be taken into account in any decision to populate the northern shore of the river because of the quality and fertility of its land. Yet the explorer's gaze in this historical period notices more than practical advantages: Hernandarias also remarks on the territory's beauty. This representation differs substantially from earlier descriptions, made during the period that I call the "entrance to historical time," in which the most frequent images are macabre cannibalistic banquets and deserted, "unprofitable" lands. Hernandarias's praise for the new lands continues to build: "They are good for labor. Although there are very good lands in this *Gobernación,* none of them compares to this one, because it has an abundance of all kinds of things, and it is fertile and good for all kinds of cattle. In addition, there are many brooks, gorges, and rivulets very close to each other. There is also plenty of wood and firewood for the building of edifices and ranches where cattle could be raised" (ibid.).

Hernandarias's references to fertility and abundance—two elements that are completely absent from the early explorers' texts—marks a dramatic change in the construction of the referent "northern shore of the River Plate." The proliferation of desirable traits that Hernandarias sees also leads him to suggest something that will make him a central character in the region's history: the introduction of cattle. "If Your Majesty decides to populate this land," he writes, "it will become a very prosperous land in a very short time, because of the quality of the soil and the reigning good navigational conditions: it is very easy to navigate to Spain and Brazil from there—and the produce and hides from the region could be thus easily shipped and carried. . . . Besides, *the conversion to the Catholic faith of the many Natives who live inland would be a great service to God,* our lord" (ibid.: 210; emphasis added).

The sequence of Hernandarias's argument is interesting in itself. First, he outlines the economic advantages of populating the land; and second, he cites potential moral and religious profit. Like Columbus's discourse, Hernandarias's allows for the coexistence of a religious mission and an economic enterprise. In both cases, the economic side of the conquest and colonization is given priority over the evangelical mission.

With his ideas and projects, Hernandarias sealed the fate of the northern shore of the River Plate: The region would become a site for Europeans to develop agriculture and raise cattle. His gift for observation and his entrepreneurial spirit led him to form the conclusion that the land, that great prairie, was underexploited. Yet Hernandarias also had geopolitical concerns: "I was looking for sea harbors in order to place spies in them who could announce the arrival of pirates to the people in this city [Buenos Aires]; these pirates always sail along that shore [the northern shore], as they did last year" (ibid.: 208). Hernandarias, in fact, had already mentioned these concerns in his May 5, 1607, letter.

Hernandarias's political wisdom is as evident as his devotion to the crown. The *relación* reveals a few other things about the governor. One is the mercantile spirit with which he studies the new geographic area. In this respect, he does not differ dramatically from most Spanish and *Criollo* colonizers. His gaze imaginarily transforms rivers, brooks, gorges, and prairies into potential wealth—that is, into exploitable natural resources. His is not, then, the gaze of a naturalist or a scientist; it is the gaze of a statesman—or an economist. Like Columbus, the first to view America in this way, Hernandarias sees in every object and landscape the possibility of eventual profit. But Hernandarias is perhaps savvier than Columbus and his successors in early exploration (Cabot, García) in that he is less interested in discovering precious metals than fertile lands. He knows—thanks, perhaps, to the time that has elapsed since the time of "discovery"—that, in the long term, the true wealth of the New World will be found in its land. Having said that, I should point out that the Spaniards' (and the *Criollo*s') change of attitude toward precious metals was very gradual. Some of the myths from the early days of the conquest—such as the seven cities of Cibola, El Dorado, and, finally, the city of the Caesars—still had currency at the beginning of the seventeenth century. This may explain why Hernandarias, whose political realism is indisputable, fell prey to the temptation to organize an expedition to the fantastic city of the Caesars. Not surprisingly, he did not find it.[5]

Yet, except for this expedition (a residue of the old way of conceiving the conquest and colonization of the continent), Hernandarias's attitude seems to be that of the statesman who carefully examines every inch of land that he explores to produce a thorough inventory of his findings.[6] Unlike the descriptions by the early explorers, who imposed their prejudices on the observed territories, the geography Hernandarias describes is not adorned or disguised by his discourse. As someone who has lived all his life in the New World, Hernandarias is not as impressionable as the region's first explorers, and, for that matter, in the lands he explored, he did not see the prodigies and monsters predicted by the texts by Marco Polo and Pliny.

Hernandarias's detailed representations of the land are not matched, however, by his descriptions of the Amerindians. On the contrary, references to the Charrúa and other aborigines of the territory are very scarce in his texts. His portrait of these Amerindians is not only incomplete; it is somehow incidental—making his texts very similar, in this respect, to those produced by conquistadors who ignored or neglected the Other. It is interesting that a man born on American lands would show so little interest in his neighbors, the Amerindians. At a cultural level, his *Criollo* condition does not distinguish him from the conquistadors born in Spain: The *Criollo*s and the Spaniards shared an episteme, a culture, and, most of all, a set of values. Despite the appellations that traditional historians have applied to Hernandarias—including *"hijo de la tierra"* ("son of the land")[7] and *"padre de la patria"* ("father of the fatherland)[8]—the reader should remember that the colonial *Criollo* was mostly a transplanted Spaniard. Hernandarias was no exception. His cultural positioning can be surmised, not surprisingly, from his texts and from his actions throughout his life.[9]

I am interested in the consequences of Hernandarias's ideological, social, and cultural positioning as a *Criollo* mostly in terms of his attitudes toward the Other. It would be interesting to study his positioning in the framework elaborated by Todorov to measure the relationship of the European subject with his or her Others. A close reading of the diverse letters studied in this chapter reveals that Hernandarias positioned himself at one of the extremes of the praxeological axis. He did not show any signs of interest in adapting to the Amerindians' way of life; instead, his plan was to reduce the aborigines to the rules of European culture and society. The abundant existing documentation records his many attempts to confine the Amerindians from different areas of the *Gobernación* to Jesuit and Franciscan missions, or *"reducciones"* (Aranguren 1963: 147–58).

Hernandarias's knowledge of the Amerindian Other (gnoseological axis) is poorly documented in the texts we have read so far. However, the evidence seems to show that he did not have an "anthropological" interest in the aborigines. The only kinds of interaction with the Other suggested in the texts are warfare and attempts to incorporate the Amerindians into religious missions. This kind of contact can provide only very superficial knowledge of the Other. Hernandarias's texts (informed by an ethnocentrism that is common to all the European observers studied in this book) are not the best sources of information about the Amerindian Other.

Finally, it is not difficult to deduce Hernandarias's position at an axiological level. It goes without saying that the values he privileges in his texts are not the indigenous but the European ones. This seems to be at odds with the image of Hernandarias that has been produced by traditional historiography, which presents him as the protector of the Indians. Father Lozano calls Hernandarias *"defensor de los indios"* ("defender of the Indians" [1873: 3:287]; Juan Estevan Guastavino calls him *"protector de los indios"* ("protector of the Indians" [1928: 301–303]). Raúl Molina dedicates a chapter to proving these authors' assertions (1948: 243–300). To judge from the available documents, Hernandarias's benevolence, when compared with that of his contemporaries, is undeniable. The freedom he granted to many of his slaves, the benevolent labor legislation he proposed and approved, and many other actions are proof of his kindness.[10] It is far from my intention to deny the good-heartedness of these actions. I simply intend to read Hernandarias's texts from a perspective that differs from the dominant perspective in traditional historiography—that is, to read these texts as artifacts produced by a member of the European interpretive community; to decode the silences in the text; and to rescue the traces of the Others from the shadows to which the colonizer's text has confined them.

What can a scholar do with a corpus of texts that registers only the voices of the victors (those who wrote the official history) and that does not offer much information about the vanquished? For one thing, the scholar can question the ideological foundations that inform those texts' universe of discourse. And for another, he or she can look for ways in which the presence of the repressed elements—in this case, the Amerindian—is registered in the texts that, albeit unwittingly, narrate their resistance to the conquest.

The texts to which I will now turn my attention are more explicit about the Others' actions—mostly, their interactions with the European subject—than are Hernandarias's. Moreover, some of the things these texts say—and some of the things they remain silent about—will help us reconstruct the exchanges between the cultures in conflict.

The plan proposed (and undertaken) by Hernandarias for exploring and populating the lands on the northern shore of the River Plate was continued by Governor Céspedes, who, a few years after the introduction of cattle into the territory in 1617, initiated the colonization of several geographic sites. According to the available documents, Céspedes sent some of his men to the other shore of the river (he was residing in Buenos Aires) with the purpose of populating the territory. The date of this operation can be established as no later than 1625, thanks to the following passage, taken from a document dated in that year:

> [Father Juan de Vergara] went to the two new *reducciones* [missions] established in the jurisdiction of this city of Trinidad, located on the other shore of this great River Plate. He entered the land populated by *the Garrua [sic], a very bellicose people,* with only one religious companion, *who preached, with much love and effort, the gospel and our Catholic Faith to the caciques and Indians who required it.* These *reducciones* were named San Francisco de Olivares of the Garrua [*sic*] and Saint Antonio of the Chana. The aforementioned religious man baptized many Indians of all ages. *Men and women asked for baptism,* and he baptized them all, putting his health and comfort in danger. ("Información hecha en la ciudad de la Trinidad," in Peña 1916: 73–74; emphasis added)

This passage is interesting not only because it contains the usual representation of the Charrúa (who on this occasion are misnamed "Garrua") as warlike people, but, more important, because it offers a different view of those Amerindians. That is, it presents the Charrúa as a people prone to conversion. This is the first time we see this ethnic group adopting Occidental rules or customs. Thus, by 1625 there was at least one *reducción* of Charrúa Indians on the northern shore of the River Plate, where they were taught the gospel by a couple of abnegated missionaries. In the same report, Captain Salvador Barbosa, a witness to the two priests' endeavors, declares:

> After he took office, Don Francisco de Céspedes (who is still the Governor of this Province) tried to confine the Indians of the Charua [*sic*] and Chana nations, who live on the other shore of this great River Plate, to a *reducción.* Since the discovery of this area [the River Plate], one hundred years ago, *it has been impossible to reduce them or to pacify them. He [Céspedes] tried to do it with soft manners.* He called for the Indians, and assured them both that their visit would be beneficial and that nothing bad would happen to them. (Ibid.: 110–11; emphasis added)

From this document it is possible to deduce that, although the government's intention was to dominate and control the Amerindians (especially the Charrúa and the Chaná), they had not been able to do so until that moment (1625)—hence, the need to change strategies for approaching them. This time, Céspedes tries to pacify them "with soft manners." The Charrúas' resistance is registered in the following document: "Since the city of Asunción was founded, there was news about the provinces of Uruguay [the northern shore of the River Plate], because *the early explorers were never able to conquer them*—knowing about this, one of their successors, Hernando Arias de Saavedra, conducted a raid to them [the provinces of Uruguay]" ("Información hecha en la ciudad de Buenos Aires," Archivo General de Indias, 74-4-13, quoted in Azarola Gil 1933: 38; emphasis added). Another text that mentions the Charrúas' defending their lands is the following:

> We heard that *the indians from the northern shore of this river,* fifty leagues from this city [Buenos Aires], *caused much harm [to us] by capturing and killing people from our ships.* We also heard that *the neighbors of this city could not cross to the other shore or exploit the wealth of that land,* of which they have great need. That is why I sent an Indian who speaks Spanish to some of the caciques. ("Carta del gobernador Céspedes," in Azarola Gil 1933: 214; emphasis added)

The indigenous presence in these texts is considerably more notorious than in Hernandarias's. In this text, the Amerindians appear as an obstacle preventing the neighbors of Buenos Aires from exploiting the wealth of the lands now called "of Uruguay." The testimony of Zayas, one of the declaring witnesses in the "Información hecha en la ciudad de Buenos Aires," confirms the situation: The Spaniards were trying to dominate the Amerindians, and the Amerindians were resisting those attempts. Of course, this struggle was neither a permanent state nor the only way in which the cultures related to each other. Dialogue was an option, as was cooperation, as Coni points out:

> In synthesis, we can say that the situation between the Charrúa—neighbours of the Argentinean capital—and the Spanish authorities at that time, was not of open war, although their relationship was not very cordial. For instance, when the Indians were asked to help the people of Buenos Aires, they refused to do it. Nevertheless, there are documents that state that in 1611—during the government of Marín de Negrón—a Charrúa cacique from the "northern shore" went to work, accompanied by twenty of his men, at Buenos Aires harbor, where he helped to repair a fence. (Coni, as quoted in Menéndez 1953: 54)[11]

This is the situation during Céspedes's term, too. It shows a spirit of cooperation and dialogue amid some hostilities. Remember that even chroniclers as prejudiced as Barco Centenera (who wrote his chronicle fifty years before Céspedes's government) referred to cases of dialogue, commerce, and cooperation between the Amerindians and the Spaniards. Barco Centenera, however, was careful to omit the cause of the Amerindians' hostile reactions: the bad treatment they received from the Spaniards. Remember that in the episode that narrates the imprisonment of Abayubá (studied in the previous chapter), Barco Centenera (unlike Montalvo, who tells the whole story) fails to mention the reason that Zapican decided to attack Ortiz de Zárate's military camp. This treatment started as early as the arrival of Cabot's expedition. (The Amerindians did not, of course, give Solís the chance to mistreat them.)

Céspedes's attitude was more respectful—and more important, more intelligent—than his predecessors'. His efforts to pacify the Amerindians would have been more successful had he gotten help from the colonial authorities in Spain. However, the authorities' lack of political vision militated against the success of the governor's efforts. It is clear from our vantage point that the establishment of towns on the river's other shore would have advanced Spain's interests in the region, because it would have prevented—or, at least, made more difficult—the foundation of Colonia do Sacramento by the Portuguese fifty-five years later. In Azarola Gil's opinion, that Portuguese settlement would not have been established if the Spanish authorities had listened to Hernandarias and Céspedes:

> It is unnecessary to state that those events [the foundation of Colonia do Sacramento] would have never happened had Céspedes' plan been carried out. The Portuguese would never have decided to build a city on a spot located between two inimical towns [Buenos Aires and, probably, Montevideo], one of which dominated the route of the maritime expeditions and isolated San Gabriel [the area where Colonia do Sacramento was founded] from its Brazilian headquarters. (1933: 44)

The importance of these considerations will become more evident in the next chapter, when we study the period covering the foundation of Colonia do Sacramento and Montevideo. What interests me now is the softening of the conflicts between the Spaniards and the Charrúa. To judge from the *relación* by Captain Barbosa, the pacific strategy obtained far better results than did war and disrespect. The document abounds in expressions such as, "They came to tell us that they would subject themselves to confinement in a *reducción* voluntarily; and that they would do it now" ("Información hecha en la ciudad de la Trinidad," in Peña 1916: 210). The Amerindians' reaction is the result of treatment that offered them gifts and praise rather than bullets: "They [the Spaniards] adulated them and gave them plenty of silver from their pockets, plus other things the Indians liked" (ibid.). The missionaries were thus able to bring Amerindians with them to Buenos Aires: "After this, the Indians were happy, and the Spaniards returned to this city [Buenos Aires] to tell the Governor about the exchange; they brought with them some Indians and caciques. After he heard the report, the Governor expressed great joy" (ibid.). Barbosa's account also informs us that the city regaled the indigenous visitors during their stay (ibid.: 211). Before this event, Céspedes had asked for help from the director of the Jesuits, but he excused himself, citing a lack of priests in the region. Father Juan de Vergara had to go alone to pacify the Amerindians and establish the *reducción,* but despite the lack of human resources, his enterprise was a success: "The Indians listened to him and communicated with each other, because what they were hearing was news to them; later, more than two hundred men and women came to ask to be baptized. The aforementioned priest baptized them himself" (ibid.: 212). Although the number of baptized Amerindians may be exaggerated, it is significant that any of them would ask for baptism. The Amerindians' positive response was caused, no doubt, by the friendly treatment they were now getting. In support of this deduction, I offer Céspedes's testimony: "I again sent Indians to the caciques, who later came [to see me] and subjected themselves to the authority of Your Majesty. *All this was done very smoothly,* seeing that smooth was the treatment they received from us, too. *They did for me what other governors could not make them do by force*" ("Carta del gobernador Céspedes," in Azarola Gil 1933: 214; emphasis added).

The respect that the Céspedes administration showed for the Amerindians should not lead us to confusion: The treatment was simply another strategy for subjecting the Amerindians. In other words, the purpose of this treatment was to force them to move toward the European end of the praxeological axis. The apparent acknowledgment of the Other once again took place via the mechanism of assimilation—that is, the desired result was to make the Amerindians adapt to the new culture that was being imposed on them. This is exactly what happens in the situation narrated by the following text by Céspedes:

> On this occasion, I can tell Your Majesty that the Indians from Uruguay have come here [Buenos Aires] in the number of more than twenty. They are great players of the organ, double bass, and other instruments. *They play during mass, and they dance in front of the Holy Sacrament. They are as knowledgeable in these matters as if they had learned about them in Your Majesty's court.* They learned in a very short time. It is important that the number of Indians increase instead of diminish, because I have spent so much effort and money to reach this point. (Ibid.: 215)

The Amerindians' adoption of social mores and codes of European origin—that is, their dancing and behaving like seventeenth-century Spanish courtiers—is the ideal outcome from the colonizers' point of view. Regardless of how absurd this picture may seem, it is the degree of acculturation that Céspedes wanted the Amerindians to reach. The acculturation of the Amerindian and the appropriation of the Other through assimilation are two strategies that reflect the same European attitude: the denial of absolute Otherness.

Although the aborigines appeared to be heading toward total acculturation, the lack of available human resources (especially priests) led to the depopulation of the *reducciones* of San Francisco (Charrúa) and San Antonio (Chaná) ("Información hecha en la ciudad de la Trinidad," in Peña 1916: 212).[12] This happened despite the efforts of Céspedes, who gave the Jesuits full control over the operation: "I give them, on behalf of Your Majesty, full, unlimited and unrestricted power for the foundation of as many *reducciones* as possible" ("Poder del gobernador Céspedes a la Compañía de Jesús," in Azarola Gil 1933: 213). Not only did he give the Jesuits unlimited power; he also repeatedly asked the Spanish crown to send people and resources to populate the land.

The texts studied in this chapter, beginning with Hernandarias and continuing with Céspedes, reflect a change in the European subject's attitude. All over the American continent, the chivalric ideal, whose ultimate reward is victory, is beginning to make way for the seventeenth century's more pragmatic (and realistic) view. The "conquest" is completed; now, colonization begins. The task, then, is to adapt the old strategies to a new goal, which, at least in the lands called "of Uruguay," is to undermine the Amerindians' resistance.

The Other is now interpellated by pacific means such as adulation, gifts, and religious ceremonies. The goal has become the assimilation and acculturation of the Other. The Amerindians' resistance is the only aspect of alterity in which the Spanish authorities are interested. The documents studied in this chapter say very little (or nothing) about other aspects of alterity. At best, they express that the Charrúa and the Chaná are harmful (*"dañosos"* ["Carta del gobernador Céspedes," in Azarola Gil 1933: 214]). Despite the paucity of information about the aborigines in these texts, the conquistadors' discourse is not totally free of the Other's presence, because its mechanisms of exclusion cannot stop the repressed element—that is, the Amerindian—from being registered. The Amerindian lurks not only in the shadows of the woods but also in the silences of the text.

The texts studied in this chapter register other changes in the region, as well. The landscape is now represented as an object of desire, and cattle have been introduced. These developments transformed, completely and forever, the economic and social conditions for the population of the northern shore of the River Plate. This was true not only for the European-based societies that developed later, but also for the Amerindians. After Hernandarias's introduction of cattle, the inhabitants of the region that had become known as "Uruguay" no longer had to chase fawns in order to survive; their nutritional needs were more easily satisfied by the livestock.

Another fundamental transformation in the region was brought about by the appearance of a new human group—that is, people who left the cities because they were attracted by the countryside's abundance of cattle. Those subjects were Amerindians, Europeans, and *Criollos.* Over time, they mixed and became the *Mestizo*s who were the precursors of the gauchos.[13] Thus, the economic structure of the territory, and its social organization, started to undergo radical modifications. *Alea jacta erat.*

CHAPTER 4

Empires in Conflict

Cielito cielo que sí
Baya un cielo para todos,
Mirá que lindos patriotas
Los Portugueses y Godos . . .

[Cielito, cielo, *yes,*
This is a cielo *for everybody,*
Look what great patriots
The Portuguese and the Goths are]

—*Anonymous, circa* 1821–23

Apart from Céspedes's short-lived *reducciones,* no European settlements were founded in the lands of Uruguay until 1680. In that year, the Portuguese established a military camp in San Gabriel—an event that started a series of conflicts in the region that lasted roughly a century (1680–1776). During this period, other towns and military camps were established, of which the most significant is Montevideo. The texts studied in this chapter record the conflict between the peninsular empires—Spain and Portugal—that developed during this historical period.

At the start of the seventeenth century, Hernandarias had increased the potential wealth of the land, but, as we have seen, his attempts to populate it failed because of the crown's lack of interest. Céspedes's "pacific-penetration" projects ended the same way. Only when a new historical agent, the Portuguese crown, entered the region in 1680 did the way in which the European subject viewed the land change dramatically: The colonizers' lack of interest gave way to an exaltation of the landscape, and the lands of Uruguay, no longer "unprofitable," became an object of dispute.

The Spanish and Portuguese were not the only actors in this century-long drama, however. The indigenous peoples who populated the territory, as well as those living elsewhere (especially the Guaraní and Tape from the Paraguayan Jesuit missions), played a fundamental role in the period's most significant events. Their alliances with the European crowns, and with other indigenous groups, were crucial to the resolution of more than one dispute. Their preference for one of the European sides of the conflict was, then, an important factor during the period. And one more actor (besides the Portuguese, Spanish, and Amerindians)—albeit an occasional one—entered the stage: the French, who attempted to establish a colony on the coast of Maldonado (in the easternmost part of today's Uruguay). Stopping that attempt drove the Spanish decision to populate the northern shore of the River Plate. Thus, all of these actors made the territory an object of dispute and negotiation; I propose, therefore, to understand this historical period as a drama in which diverse actors struggled for possession of the territory and in which some were trying to appropriate what they coveted, while others were trying to defend what they already owned.

Spanish possession of San Gabriel was not under dispute, because it was widely known that this area fell within the imaginary line established by the Tordesillas treaty. That was the state of affairs until 1678.[1] From that year forward, the Portuguese crown proposed a different interpretation of the treaty's dividing line. The Portuguese did not bother to take the Spanish to court; they simply occupied the area of San Gabriel. On November 18, 1678, the Portuguese regent prince ordered Don Manuel Lobo, the governor of Rio de Janeiro, to populate the northern shore of the River Plate. His instructions are illustrative of the reasons that motivated such unexpected behavior. The prince's decision was motivated by two factors: a conviction that those lands were legally owned by Portugal, and recognition of the territory's fertility and potential wealth: "[I order you] to populate *the lands under my dominion,* which are now deserted, located in the demarcation of the division of the southern lands that extend throughout the River Plate, Buenos Aires, and Montevideo, *because of their fertility.* The Castilians have already established several colonies in the territory that belongs to this crown" ("Instrucciones del príncipe de Portugal," in Azarola Gil 1931: 164; emphasis added).[2]

This strategy of occupation also aimed to formalize the frequent raids that the São Paulo *Bandeirantes*[3] were making on the territory. Legalizing these raids made exploiting the River Plate's prairies a more comfortable and less risky enterprise. The fertility of the land and the absence of permanent Spanish settlements inspired the prince's daring plan to occupy the territory. Of course, his claim regarding the existence of Spanish colonies in the disputed land is arguable: Although the Jesuits had established a few missions in the northern part of the Uruguay River, the *reducciones* barely qualified as military camps or colonies. But the claim served the prince's political aspirations.

Whatever the legal strength of the Portuguese prince's arguments, in July 1679 Lobo began preparing for the expedition that would result in the establishment of a town and fortress in January of the following year. He gathered three infantry batallions and a cavalry squadron, three priests, sixty black slaves (forty of whom were his own), some Amerindians, and eight women (Azarola Gil 1931: 35–36). These data suggest the military character of the expedition; had the goal been otherwise, Lobo would have included more women. This text also contains the first reference to African slaves in the territory—another historical agent, another Other, that will reappear during the colonial period in the lands of Uruguay.

The Spanish reponded in kind to this Portuguese military enterprise: Governor Garro, in the middle of a profuse epistolary exchange with Lobo about the legitimacy of Portugal's claim to the land, decided to send troops to prepare for an assault on the Portuguese fortress.[4] In an attempt to prevent armed conflict, Lobo wrote to all of the civil and religious authorities in Buenos Aires. The bishop of Buenos Aires responded in a letter dated July 16, 1680; in it, he declared his support for Garro's decision and actions, because the situation created by Lobo's actions "forced us to defend these lands by any means. Our right is based not only on the dominion we acquired to these lands since the conquest, but also on our pacific possession, for more than one hundred years, of its hills, prairies and waters" ("Respuesta del obispo de Buenos Aires," in ibid.: 183). The Buenos Aires *cabildo* responded in similar terms: "You leave us no choice, because you are disturbing our pacific possession of the land, which our King and his predecessors have possessed since the moment of the conquest" ("Respuesta del cabildo de Buenos Aires a don Manuel Lobo," in ibid.: 184).

These texts show the attitude that was most common among the representatives of both empires: They continually tried to legitimize their rights to possess and, most of all, to exploit the land. To do this, they attempted to produce histories of the land that justified their acts of possession. In this case, for lack of a better argument, the bishop and the *cabildo* appeal to the antiquity of the Spanish presence in the region that Lobo is occupying, as well as to the acts of dominion—that is, the use and usufruct made of the waters and hills—by the Spanish crown since its men arrived in the region. As we will see later, both empires' arguments will become more sophisticated over time.

What is interesting at this point is the change that these legitimation narratives register in the way the referent "territory" is constructed. The land is now represented not only as an object of desire, but also as an entity with a past—a past provided by the Portuguese and Spanish narratives that attempt to possess it.

In the name of one of those possible pasts, Garro attacked the Portuguese fortress, which Lobo defended to the end. In 1681, San Gabriel, which had come to be known as Colonia do Sacramento, was recovered by the Spanish army after bloody combat. The Spanish could not have carried out the carnage that ended the dispute without the help of hundreds of Amerindians from the Jesuit missions. This is very important, because it marked the beginning of a practice that would recur whenever the Spanish needed numerical superiority for a military campaign. Yet the Spanish were not the only ones who resorted to the Amerindians' help: The Portuguese, too, knew that their forces alone were not sufficient to protect the fortress. Thus, the Amerindians would also become an object of dispute during this period. The occupation of the land and recruiting of Amerindians as soldiers did not, however, exhaust the list of devices and strategies used to achieve the appropriation of alterity—which the European actors in this conflict (like Céspedes) considered the ultimate goal in assimilating the Other to Western cultural patterns.

The prince regent had other priorities in the first stages of colonizing the San Gabriel area, however, which is why he did not emphasize the acculturation and subjection of the Amerindians to the crown in his instructions to Lobo. What really mattered was maintaining a friendly relationship with the aborigines: "And if they do not want to subject themselves to us but accept our friendship and trade, you have to treat them well and regale them, so that, by these means, you are able to profit from that deserted land" ("Instrucciones del príncipe," in ibid.: 166).

The intelligent policy of the Portuguese toward the Amerindians left very few options open to the Spanish. Garro, faced with the success of the Portuguese strategy, gave the following instructions to Vera Muxica, who was in charge of the assault on the Portuguese fortress: "After inquiring about the whereabouts of the Charrúa, try to attract them to us. Offer them whatever they are interested in, so that you manage to stop them, by good reasons or by force, from talking to, and helping—induced by their deceitful manners—, the Portuguese" ("Instrucciones del gobernador Garro," in ibid.: 174; emphasis added).

As these texts show, the times had changed: The epic figure of the conquistador has disappeared as such.[5] The empires, closer to pragmatism than to a chivalric ideal, no longer want to defeat and subject the Amerindians.

They now intend—using means that are more political than bellicose—to incorporate or assimilate the Amerindians into European cultural patterns. The people who are now in charge of the operations come neither from a lineage of swineherds (like Pizarro) nor from an ancestry of dairy farmers (like Lope de Aguirre). Most of the Spanish and Portuguese captains are professional soldiers or politicians who are experienced in diplomatic and political matters. Their ambitions are also more moderate, and their respect for authority and hierarchies is more reliable: The governors sent by the Portuguese and Spanish are loyal servants who will never disobey orders. For that reason, a rebellion such as the one conducted by Lope de Aguirre and his Marañones could not have happened in this historical period. The River Plate region in general, and the lands of Uruguay in particular, never experienced a cruel and overpowering conquest like those suffered by other regions of the continent, which gives the colonial history of the River Plate region an idiosyncratic character. It is during an era dominated by bureaucrats, politicians, and diplomats that the struggle between the two empires for the lands of Uruguay takes place.

Although the founding of Colonia do Sacramento was not prefaced by great battles against the Amerindians, populating the site was not a peaceful process. The hostilities between the European forces, which also involved hundreds of allied Amerindians, were at times bloody, and at times diplomatic. The military defeat of the Portuguese in 1680 became, in 1681, a diplomatic victory that allowed them to recover their lost colony. To use an expression from soccer, the Portuguese won in the federation what they had lost on the field.

I will now turn my attention to the *Historia* by Pereira de Sá, a text that comprehensively describes the events that occurred from the foundation of Colonia do Sacramento to the siege it endured in 1735. This text was written between 1737 and 1750, according to Capistrano de Abreu (1900: xxxiv), and although it partakes of the Western and Christian traditions, the *Historia* drastically opposes the Spanish point of view. This is evident from the first page, which synthesizes the Portuguese perspective on the conflict: "In the first book, you will see malice winning over valor; in the second, you will see negligence obfuscating bravery; and in the third, you will see the Portuguese standard win over a malicious opposition" (Pereira de Sá 1900: 1). It is probably unnecessary to point out that, according to the text, malice is an attribute of the Spanish, whereas valor is the most salient trait of the Portuguese. This is the point of view from which Pereira de Sá tells the story not only of the foundation, siege, and diplomatic reconquest of Colonia do Sacramento, but also of the events following the reconquest up to 1735.

But before he starts telling this story, Pereira de Sá dedicates several pages to justifying Portugal's rights to the land. As noted earlier, around 1680 both the *cabildo* and the bishop of Buenos Aires defended Spanish rights to the territory by citing its pacific possession for more than a century (or "*desde la conquista*" ["since the conquest"]). Pereira de Sá, for his part, appeals to arguments that bear a heavier juridical weight, invoking the right of property (or dominion) given to Portugal by the Tordesillas treaty (ibid.: 5–6). His argument is not very original, however: Throughout the one hundred years of conflict, that treaty had been used to bolster the arguments of both sides. Everything depended, of course, on how one interpreted the imaginary dividing line. Pereira de Sá argues: "[But] the Spaniards, with shrewd politics, confused the issue, and moved the line in a way that limited the extension of the Lusitanian [Portuguese] possessions" (ibid.: 6). The Spanish, in turn, accused the Portuguese of moving the dividing line. In the final round of negotiations over possession of Colonia do Sacramento in 1776, one Spanish official, the Marquis of Grimaldi, proposed to the Portuguese negotiators "to determine, based on astronomical observation, the true demarcations of each of the superpowers, in accordance with the Tordesillas treaty" (Grimaldi 1982 [1849]: 7:4). This is what the representatives of the adversary crowns did during the century-long conflict: They moved the dividing line back and forth and repeated their claims to seniority in occupying the region. Thus, each empire proposed its own argonauts and discoverers. Pereira de Sá recounts an example of such an alleged voyage of "discovery," although he is not able to establish a precise date for it:

> According to many, Martim Afonso de Souza, then the Senhor Donatario of the Town of San Vicente, was the discoverer of the River Plate. He attempted, together with his brother Pedro Lopes, to explore the farthest end of that extensive jurisdiction. He discovered the San Gabriel island and noticed that the mainland was plagued by Barbarians. So full of Savages that land was, that, afraid of the dangers, he turned around, like the Trojans—and he reached San Vicente with more fortune than the Trojans had when they reached Italy. (Ibid.: 7–8)

Notice that the beginning of the passage is imprecise about sources: It says "According to many" ("*Quizerâo muitos*"), which is tantamount to saying, "It is well known" or "Everybody knows." That is, Pereira de Sá's failure to produce specific sources forces him to resort to vox populi as his only possible argument. In the next sentence, Pereira de Sá narrates the "discovery" of San Gabriel—the territory under dispute. According to his account, the Portuguese argonoauts refrained from landing in San Gabriel for good reason—it was heavily populated ("plagued") by barbaric savages. Prudence in this case proved more powerful than the will to know. Another noteworthy detail in this text is the comparison of the brothers Sousa and Eneas, which is so exaggerated that one suspects an ironic intention on Pereira de Sá's part—that is, the Trojans were escaping from their heavily besieged city, which had already been partly destroyed by the Aqueans, but Sousa fled because he was scared of a group of "savages" who were supposedly "inferior" to the European subject. It is interesting to compare this (Portuguese) version of the story with the one offered by the Spanish a few years later. In the Spanish version, the Marquis of Grimaldi asserts that the first explorer who reached the land was Sebastian Cabot, in 1496, followed by Solís, in 1508 and 1515 (Grimaldi 1982 [1849]: 8).[6]

One of the many texts produced during this period is the diary of the Portuguese soldier Silvestre Ferreira da Sylva, who helped defend the fortress during the 1735 siege. In his diary, Ferreira da Sylva not only records events related to the siege; he also advocates the legitimacy of the Portuguese occupation: "*There is no doubt about Portugal's rights to these land*s, because of its uninterrupted possession since 1501. At that time, this River Plate, which was completely unknown to all European nations, was discovered and demarcated, by the execution of all acts of possession, by the Florentine Amerigo Vespucci" (Ferreira da Sylva 1748: 1–2; emphasis added). The lack of agreement on this topic (and on other topics) between Pereira de Sá and Ferreira da Sylva, even though they were contemporaries, is interesting, as Capistrano de Abreu points out (1900: xxxiv). It seems to indicate that more than one legitimation narrative was operating at that time, at least on the Portuguese side.

Pereira de Sá's representation of the Amerindians resembles that offered by the region's first European explorers—up to Barco Centenera, at least. The traits that attract his attention are the Amerindians' savagery, valor, strength, and, sometimes, impiety. Pereira de Sá inscribes his discourse in this tradition, because he draws the material with which he constructs the image of the Amerindians (regardless of their ethnic affiliation) from the same old model. In one passage, he says that the Amerindians are considered the most impious in America ("*havidos . . . pelos mais impios de toda America*"), and that their presence intimidated even the most intrepid spirits ("*intimidava aos animos mais intrepidos*") (Pereira de Sá 1900: 14). Elsewhere, he says that the aborigines do not have any friend but their own interest *("nâo conhecerem mais por amigo, q. o interesse"*) and that they are thought to be ungrateful by nature ("*ingratos por natureza*") (ibid.: 15).

This construct rarely refers to a specific ethnic group. On the contrary, all ethnic groups become one in the historian Pereira de Sá's discourse. As a consequence, his text does not register difference—or, according to Jitrik (1983: 92–93), he uses a descriptive procedure (with Columbus as its antecedent) that could be called "reduction to unity" ("*reducción a la unidad*"). The passage that follows marks the moment in which all indigenous communities become (for the historian's comfort) members of the same ethnic group, the Tape: "The Minuan Indians dominated the vast shores and the impenetrable continent. The Tape and the Charrúa were inimical to each other. *In bloody wars, the Tape, who destroyed their enemies [the Charrúa], prevailed because they were the bravest and the most powerful. For this reason, they ended up dominating the country and banishing their enemies*" (Pereira de Sá 1900: 16; emphasis added).

As far as I know, the Tape never dominated the region; nor did they extinguish the Charrúa. The Tape were not even of local origin, and the Charrúa, as is well known, were exterminated much later (in 1831) in an infamous ambush conducted by the first president of independent Uruguay.[7] Inaccuracies aside, the description of the Tape Indians in this text has some points of contact with the description that Pereira de Sá offers of the Amerindians in general, with additional data:

> They skillfully use the violent weapons created and inspired by their barbaric ways: two balls tied by a rustic thread, and a leather lasso. . . . The antidote to those weapons is the sword, which they fear as if it were Mars' lightning. They are considerably afraid of firearms, because they superstitiously believe that they were conceived as an artifact to destroy their nation.
>
> After the arrival of the Spaniards, they preferred the javelins and spears to the bows; they always carried them when they fought on horse and became more daring with this change of weapons. On foot, they are weak, timid, and cowardly, . . . they prefer licentious to domestic life. . . . In them, the senses are more important than rationality. (Ibid.: 17)

The Tape are brave and strong, according to Pereira de Sá, but they are also superstitious, licentious, and sensual. For any European (or Occidentalized) observer, these traits characterize primitive and irrational men. For Pereira de Sá, the Amerindians' irrational fear of firearms is sufficient proof of their superstitious nature. The representation of the aborigines offered here is so general that it does not discriminate among ethnic groups; thus, Pereira de Sá is able to attribute the hostilities suffered by the Portuguese at the hands of the Charrúa, Chaná, and Minuan to the Amerindians' alliance with the Spaniards. Blinded by the general description of the Amerindians, he is incapable of realizing that only those from the Jesuit missions—the Tape—collaborated with the Spaniards.[8]

Pereira de Sá gives the last touch to his portrait of the "savages" when he refers to the assault on the fortress by the Spanish, who are reinforced by hundreds of Amerindians from the missions:

> The Castilians and the barbarians wandered along the streets. They saw painful situations in all of them [the streets], but they did not show any compassion for the [victims'] complaints—instead, they hit harder, because their wrath increased when confronted with [the victims'] resistance and desperation. The officials tried to prevent this disgrace, but most people, in fear, did not obey. Meanwhile, the enemy was performing abominable outrages. *Not even the sacred Temple [the church] was spared the fury of the Spaniards.* (Ibid.: 35–36; emphasis added)

In Pereira de Sá's version, cruelty and savagery are not the patrimony solely of the Amerindians; their allies, the Spanish, are also responsible for the massacre. To the lack of legitimation of the Spanish cause, the historian now adds their barbaric and sacrilegious behavior. Interestingly, in this Portuguese account the sacrilege is committed by the most unthinkable agent, the Spanish priests: "Finally, they profaned the sacred [place] without any regard for the images. Some of our Jesuits communicated with their Spanish fellow company men, who did not try to avoid the outrageous defilement of the sacred performed by their Indian companions" (ibid.: 36). Lobo also denounces the Jesuits for their responsibility for the massacre, characterizing them as bloodthirsty, greedy, and despotic ("Carta del gobernador de Rio de Janeiro," in Azarola Gil 1931: 191). As we can see, being associated with the Amerindians is almost a crime. This procedure, which implies a comparison, is an attempt to discredit the European enemy; it is the discursive procedure through which even Christian subjects, such as the Jesuits and the Spaniards, are animalized.

Pereira de Sá is narrating a military defeat, which means that he cannot praise the enemy (a device we saw in Barco Centenera and other chroniclers) to exalt his side's victory. Thus, he demonizes the enemy in order to establish, very clearly, the villains in this story. This occurs frequently in the *Historia,* which also refers to the 1705 and 1735 sieges. The Spanish are portrayed not only as barbaric and murderous, but also as cowardly, because they send the Amerindians to the front line while they stay in the rear guard (Pereira de Sá 1900: 56). To complete the picture, Pereira de Sá tells us that the Spanish fear the Portuguese officials (ibid.: 84). A passage that illustrates this representation well describes the Spanish as fleeing a skirmish for fear of death ("*o temor da morte*"). One fleeing Spaniard leaves his sword and cape behind and must humbly ask for them later: "*E como temia o castigo pela fraqueza, rogava pelo q. nâo podera defender a cobardia*" ("Afraid of the punishment for his weakness, he had to implore for what his cowardice was unable to defend" [ibid.: 105]).

The Portuguese, on the other hand, are portrayed as brave: "*As rezistencias eran mais valerosas, q. os assaltos*" ("The defense was braver than the assault [ibid.: 62]); "The Portuguese troops, fearless before the enemy's bullets, always confronted the numerically superior Castilian troops, making them retreat thanks to their [the Portuguese] valor" (ibid.: 157). They are also benevolent: "After battle, our Portuguese soldiers did not commit any cruelties and showed benevolence toward the prisoners" (ibid.: 105). And they are educated, as the eloquent speeches attributed to Sebastião de Veiga, the Portuguese governor, show (ibid.: 73–84). Not surprisingly, the classical references that fill the governor's speeches are very similar to those Pereira de Sá uses in his text.

This black-and-white picture of the conflict is contradicted somewhat in the account by Ferreira da Sylva, who sometimes acknowledges the honorable attitude of his enemies. For example, he portrays Don Bruno Mauricio de Zabala, governor of Buenos Aires, as a good neighbor and respectful of the law, without failing to defend his monarch's interests. Zabala is even presented as a friend of Vasconcellos, the governor of Colonia do Sacramento (Ferreira da Sylva 1748: 25), a friendship that is confirmed by a text from the Spanish side ("Diario de Cabrer," in González 1882: 1:126).

Ferreira da Sylva's discursive strategies regarding the Amerindians also differ slightly from Pereira de Sá's. Although he uses some of the usual elements in constructing the referent "Indian," such as valor and a barbaric nature, he also praises the libertarian spirit of the Minuan, the only indigenous group he mentions specifically: "These Brazilian people are barbaric and inconstant; they are also rebellious and indomitable: they are not subject to any prince, yet" (ibid.: 12).

The representation of the Amerindian as Other (in the usual way) and the comparison of a European culture (the Spanish culture, a cousin of sorts of the Portuguese) with an indigenous one is the device used to depict human alterity in these texts. The territory, however, is represented in a different manner: as desirable, as worth possessing. Further, Pereira de Sá believes that it is mandatory to populate those lands, which are "asking" to be populated: "A land like that, without a Christian population, is like a body without a soul or a sky without stars. The pleasant air, the temperate climate, the amenities of the countryside, and the fertility of its soils make this land a desirable and pleasant place" (Pereira de Sá 1900: 14). This kind of praise, which at times transforms the land into an avatar of the Renaissance topic of *locus amoenus*, reaches its highest peak in the following passage:

> The Castilians wrongly wanted to usurp Portugal of *the Elysian Fields of this era*, where an eternal, flowery and green spring reigns, countless herds of cattle graze, and infinite numbers of horse roam. The land is very abundant in fruits and vegetables. The trees, showing their gratitude to the farmer, offer their fruits with flowers in the first year of growth. The variety of daisies is a quotidian mockery

> to the eyes. Nature, having forgotten that it had created beautiful spectacles like this for the recreation of its creatures, produced a new wonder in these lands. (Ibid.: 17; emphasis added)

Classical references, then, are the framework for praising the land. The Elysian Fields, the epitome of beautiful and abundant places in the classical tradition, is the other term of the comparison that the Portuguese chronicler proposes.[9] However, in the middle of a eulogy of the land, a mercantile touch taints the idyllic picture when some well-fed cows approach the scene and start to graze. This displacement of the Renaissance topic of the *locus amoenus,* in which "the non-utilitarian space of pleasure acquires a practical virtuality," develops into what Julio Ortega calls *"el lugar de la abundancia"* ("the place of abundance" [1988: 106–7]. According to Ortega, the transformation of the classical topic begins with the production of the first colonial texts (especially Columbus's), which tended to give a utilitarian profile to the merely pleasant place. Although Pereira de Sá wrote his text two hundred and fifty years after Columbus's paradigmatic text started the tradition of the *lugar abundante* (abundant place), the topic's currency in the eighteenth century is more than evident. The late colonization of the lands of Uruguay may have brought about this currency—it took a long time for the European observer to start representing those lands as a pleasant or abundant place. Remember that the first author who mentions the fertility and potential abundance of the lands is Hernandarias—whose assessment was confirmed by his introduction of cattle. On the Spanish side, there are descriptions of similar tenor. One can be found in Francisco Millau's text, which was written in 1772 but collected in the twenty years of his stay in the lands on the River Plate. (His stay began in 1752, when he arrived as one of the members of the demarcation party.) What follow are Millau's opinions of Montevideo and the surrounding areas:

> The terrain of the northern shore of the River Plate is even better than the terrain south of that river, due both to the better quality of the black soil there, which is much deeper than that on the other shore, and its fertility, which makes the soil suited to the production of a higher number of produce and crops. This is so because it is a terrain watered by numberless rivers and arroyos that cover the whole land, and because their shores are populated by thick and tall woods. (1947: 94)

During the century-long dispute between the Spanish and Portuguese empires, the land under study, once considered "unprofitable," clearly changed dramatically as an object of representation. Constructs are not immutable; as noted earlier, they are a product of the interaction between the referential act and its context.

The Portuguese occupation of the San Gabriel area brought on a series of events that helped determine the future development of European-based social life in the territory. However, the establishment of a Portuguese fortress on the northern shore of the River Plate was not an isolated fact; other significant events occurred during this period, including the temporary occupation of the area of Castillos (Department of Rocha, on the east coast of today's Uruguay) by the French. The French and Portuguese incursions drove the Spanish authorities to recognize the need to settle the area—a realization that ultimately led to the foundation of Montevideo. I propose that the Portuguese, French, and Spanish settlements were attempts to appropriate a new referent, a new object of desire—that is, "the (abundant) lands of Uruguay."

According to Lozano, a French fleet under the command of Captain Moreau landed on the coast of Castillos in 1720, intending to trade with the infidels (*"establecer comercio con los infieles"* [1873: 3:472]). Governor Zabala of Buenos Aires could not permit such an invasion, because French presence in the area would be prejudicial to the provinces' trade and to the security of the River Plate region (*"perjudicialísimo este comercio á estas provincias, y espuesto a que los franceses intentasen fundar poblacion en aquellos parajes, que seria mayor perjuicio a la seguridad de la navegación del Rio de la Plata"* [ibid.]). Lozano's words lay bare the precarious geopolitical situation of Buenos Aires at the time. With the Portuguese presence in Colonia do Sacramento, the risk of other rival settlements increased. The most logical move for the Portuguese was to establish another settlement or fortress on the coast of Montevideo or Maldonado. In doing so, they would consolidate their dominion over the northern shore of the river. From a Spanish perspective, the fertile prairies—especially since the introduction of cattle—were vital to the survival of Buenos Aires. Thus, the Spanish crown could not allow Portuguese expansion to continue. The alarm that the French fleet's appearance in the region caused is therefore understandable: It added complexity to the situation and forced the Spaniards to make a drastic decision. The Amerindians were also an enemy, from the Spanish perspective, because of the brief but ceaseless hostilities to which the aborigines subjected them.

The Spaniards had to establish a town (or at least a military camp) on the northern shore to control navigation in the river and prevent communication between Colonia do Sacramento and the Portuguese headquarters in Brazil. Governor García Ros understood the situation and sent a report to King Philip V in 1717 (after the second devolution of Colonia do Sacramento to the Portuguese); in the report, he warns about the danger of leaving the northern shore unprotected ("Exposición del gobernador de Buenos Aires," in Azarola Gil 1931: 214–18). The king, perhaps persuaded by Ros's arguments, sent several *cédulas reales* to the new governor, Zabala, who took office in July 1717. The first of those documents is dated November 1717; others are dated October 1718, May 1723, and December 1723. In the December 1723 communication, the king's impatience is evident: "If you have not executed my previous orders, you must immediately execute them without wasting any time. Otherwise, I will consider it a disservice to me, and you will be prosecuted for serious charges" ("Real cédula al gobernador de Buenos Aires repitiéndole el encargo de fortificar Montevideo y Maldonado," in Azarola Gil 1933: 227). Despite the king's insistence, Zabala was not able to follow these orders: He had neither the money nor the human resources (settlers and priests) to establish a settlement. The situation grew worse for Zabala. On December 1, 1723, the harbor pilot Gonardo arrived in Buenos Aires with news that the Portuguese were building a fortress in Montevideo.

The Portuguese expedition, commanded by Freitas da Fonseca, had orders to establish a military camp in the same zone. Zabala prepared, with great effort (and great expenditure), to evict the enemy.[10] With the collaboration of hundreds of Tape Indians commanded by the Jesuits, Zabala set out to dislodge the Portuguese. The Portuguese, seeing that they were outnumbered, left the fortress without confronting the Spanish troops.[11] Thus, Montevideo was founded thanks to an invasion (Azarola Gil 1933: 85).

After Montevideo was established, the Spanish started to gain the upper hand in the dispute for the lands north of the estuary. The Portuguese continued to conduct hostilities until 1776, however, the year in which they were definitively expelled from Colonia do Sacramento. The brief and occasional skirmishes, and the victory of the Portuguese after the 1735 siege, illustrate the sacrifices that the Spanish side endured in its effort to win possession of the lands north of the River Plate. To make things worse for the Spanish, the Portuguese were not the only threat they had to face: The Amerindians who were not under the Jesuits' influence, such as the Charrúa and the Minuan, were also present in the region, killing the cows and helping the Portuguese. In the war that confronted the Spanish authorities and the Minuan (a conflict known as the Minuan war), the Portuguese and the Minuan joined forces against the Spanish.[12] This can be interpreted as a case in which the Amerindians served as an object of dispute for both empires; at the same time, however, it can be seen as an occasion on which the region's indigenous peoples acted as very significant agents in a complex political and military situation.[13]

This guerrilla warfare, which continued until the wars of independence, took the shape of an open war in 1731 (ibid.: 155), following an incident between some Minuan and a Portuguese from Montevideo: The Minuan tried to steal some of his horses, and in the skirmish, one of the aborigines died. From that moment, the Minuan started to wage war against the city.[14] The clash of cultures took place, again, on the northern shore of the river. From a Spanish perspective, a formal apology for the affront should have sufficed. Blind to cultural difference, they did not understand that European social practices had nothing to do with indigenous practices. But their blindness is not suprising: Many a twentieth-century scholar has shown a similar lack of understanding of indigenous cultures. An example of that ethnocentric perspective can be found in Azarola Gil, who says: "Minuan violence neither admitted investigations, nor extenuating circumstances nor judicial action; they just convoked the tribe and attacked the cattleherd posts that were scattered throughout the countryside, killing the peons" (ibid.: 154). We should ask: What kind of justice is Azarola Gil talking about? All signs point toward a Western notion of justice that, in Azarola Gil's opinion, should be applied in every context. That is, in Azarola Gil's text, a local cultural creation (European justice) is implicitly given a universal reach.

Azarola Gil is part of a tradition that defends the Spanish side in the war. One of the texts in which that tradition was founded is a report by the *cabildo* in which the Amerindians (the Minuan) are represented in a way that does not differ significantly from representations we have already seen. The survival of the construction of the referent "Minuan" is evident in this passage: "They have not only resisted true religion but also have manifested *an immeasurable hatred against the people who populate Montevideo.* Your Highness already knows about the way the Minuans insulted the Spaniards in 1730 . . . [when], *with inhuman cruelty,* [they] killed, violently, more than one hundred Spaniards" ("Informe del procurador José González de Melo," in ibid.: 73). Resistance to religion, evil-spiritedness, and a dehumanizing cruelty are still the characteristics that define the referent "Indian" (or, in this case, "Minuan") in the Spanish texts.

Yet despite this grim portrayal, changes do take place over time in the relationship between the Amerindians and the Spaniards. Although the Minuan do not come to be represented in a better light, the Spaniards are at least forced to acknowledge them as valid interlocutors. In February 1732, Zabala signed a peace proposal that would end the conflict between the Spanish troops and the Amerindians. As Azarola Gil points out, this peace treaty is of great historical importance, because it is the first signed on the northern shore (ibid.: 158). Further, for the first time we are faced with a document that explicitly represents the Amerindians as the Spaniards' equals. A careful reading of the proposal shows, however, that the equality the Spanish are offering is based on European cognitive and cultural patterns. In other words, it is based on the assumption that, to achieve peace, the parties to the agreement must abide by the customs, rules, and laws that organize Western society. Thus, the Spanish attempt once again to neutralize the Amerindians' alterity by assimilating them to the patterns of another (European, as always) culture. An example of this strategy can be found in the Spaniards' demand that the Minuan respect a very Western institution, private property:

> The Indians will not harm any *estancias* [cattle ranches], farms, cattle, and other estates owned by the neighbors of this city [Buenos Aires] and Montevideo. If they should be found robbing or performing other evils, the neighbors are allowed to punish them without taking them prisoners; the Caciques must not interpret this as a declaration of war, since the only purpose of punishing criminals is to secure peace for everybody. ("Tratado de paz," in ibid.: 263)

In this document, the Minuan are asked not only to respect the rules of private property, but also, above all, to accept culture-specific (that is, Occidental) institutions such as justice. Accepting those institutional values involves, among other things, trusting the system and abstaining from appeal to justice by one's own hand: "Reciprocally, if they find a Spaniard disturbing the peace of their tents or robbing their cattle, they must take him to Montevideo, where he will be punished. They will receive total satisfaction of their demands, but they will not be allowed, under any circumstances, to take justice into their own hands" (ibid.).

Even if the Spaniards could make the Minuan accept conditions that had nothing to do with their way of life, they still had a major problem to solve: How could they communicate the proposal to the Minuan in an intelligible way, without distorting its content? The peace treaty is the first colonial document covering events on the northern shore of the River Plate to acknowledge explicitly the problem of translation: "All this is expressed for the deputies' knowledge, knowing that these expressions are impracticable with the Indians. However, they [the deputies] should explain to the Indians these concepts as well as they can" (ibid.). The author of this document seems to be aware of the impossibility of making a literal translation—due less to linguistic differences than to cultural ones. Although the document is not explicit about cultural difference, I see the writer's perception of the problem in the phrase "*se podrá explicar lo que fuere dable a su conocimiento*" ("the deputies should explain to the Indians these concepts as well as they can"), which seems to acknowledge the coexistence of two different universes of meaning.

The existence of two worlds that have trouble communicating with each other is an issue that underlies not only this text but also most of the textual production of the colonial period. However, the majority of colonial texts of

European origin express nothing about this essential conflict. Translating messages between the two European enemies was relatively easy: The Spanish and Portuguese spoke related romance languages, and they belonged to the same cultural matrix. This was not true of communication between the Western and indigenous peoples. An enormous cultural distance existed between the Spanish and Minuan worldviews, requiring the translators to undertake a semiotic operation that has the purpose of translating a worldview into a language (in expressive form) that is not the one in which that worldview was originally uttered. The purpose of translation is, then, not only to make the differences in meaning intelligible, but also to make the sense originally attached to one language as a vehicle resonate in another language, as Joseph Graham states (1985: 25). From this perspective, the miscommunication between the Amerindians and the Spaniards can be seen as a consequence of both sides' misunderstanding of the problem of translation. The incapacity to translate a worldview into a language and a culture that has completely different organizational principles from the one that is the object of translation underlies many of the conflicts between cultures in the colonial era. It is also the problem faced by the naturalists and historians we will see in the next chapter. This misunderstanding is dramatized in a passage of the peace treaty that requires the Amerindians to swear that they will fulfill their obligations: "This was sworn by the two Caciques, who stood up. They grabbed the Commander Captain's right hand, put it on the left side of his chest and repeated the ceremony with the rest of the Deputies" ("Acta de celebración del Tratado," in ibid.: 264). The text takes for granted that the Minuan understand the concept of swearing—which is not an irrational assumption. However, even if they did understand the notion, their failure to comply with some of the treaty's requirements suggests that swearing may have had a very different meaning in their culture.

In order to provide a more complete picture of the discursive practices used during this period, I will study other textual examples that show how the Spanish constructed the referents "Portuguese" and "lands of Uruguay."[15] The Spanish represented their Portuguese enemies as fearful. Take, for example, Lozano's description of the outcome of the 1705 siege: "[The Portuguese escaped] with great credit to the Spanish valor, whose ardor the arrogant Lusitanians feared so much, to the point that they abandoned their very fortified camp and took refuge in their ships in order to return, in fear, to Brazil" (1873: 3:464–65). This image reappears in another text: "The mere appearance of the Spanish troops caused admiration and terror among the Portuguese of Colonia" ("Año de 1762" 1982 [1849]: 13–14.)[16]

The Spanish also portray the Portuguese as malicious by using a range of adjectives that are very similar to those used by the Portuguese to represent the Spanish. For example: "We [the Spanish] have already seen the insolence with which the Portuguese nation has conducted its duplicitous projects" (ibid.: 2). The next text is a poem in *décimas*[17] written by a Spanish sergeant for his beloved girlfriend ("Relación exacta" 1920: 276–94). The sergeant was accompanying Governor Cevallos on his 1778 expedition to recover Santa Catarina and Colonia do Sacramento for the Spanish side. Although the sergeant's *décimas* narrate the entire campaign, I am interested only in the fragments containing information about the reconquest of Colonia and the writer's impressions of Montevideo.

After the punitive expedition returns from Santa Catarina, it makes a rest stop in Montevideo. Unfortunately, immediately after the troops land, they are asked by the city of Montevideo to repress the activities of a horse thief known as Pinto Bandeyras in the countryside surrounding the city. As in Pereira de Sá's text, fertility and abundance play an important role in the sergeant's construction of the referent "territory." The following *décimas* provide an example of that textual strategy:

> The bolas, knife, and lasso, I infer, are more important than money in that country in relation to eating, because if anybody desires to have a cow, he catches her by the legs, lassoes her by the neck, and cuts her throat with a knife, in order to eat her later.
>
> They despise the cow's heads. They throw away some of the other parts. They do not even look at the entrails and dispose of the anterior feet. They are only interested in the ribs, haunches, tongue, and kidneys of the best cows, leaving the rest of the meat to the Cimarrones [wild dogs]. (Ibid.: 289–90)

In these lines, the *locus amoenus* topic again leaves room for a less idyllic and more pragmatic view of abundance—a view in which the European observer's awe before plenty predominates. By this time, cattle have proliferated so extensively in the region that thousands of cows remain as surplus that cannot be sold to the *saladeros* (where the meat was preserved with salt). José Pedro Barrán calls this socioeconomic situation of surplus, to which the sergeant's *décimas* refer, the "economy of abundance" (1991 [1989]: 1:32). Barrán also says: "The abundance of meat—the staple food—, its cheap price in the capital and its frequent low exchange value in the rural areas, made the life of the popular classes much easier because it did not force them—as in other regions of the world—to comply with the biblical condemnation that sounds very much like an employer's dictum: you will work for a living" (ibid.: 32). The cows that are merely a part of Pereira de Sá's landscape are placed admiringly in the foreground by the Spanish sergeant: "They get an entire cow for each platoon. If the first one is thin, they get two that day. You could certainly supply the city of Granada—and, I believe, in excess—with the meat that lies permanently on the streets of Montevideo" ("Relación exacta" 1920: 290). For those Europeans accustomed to different socioeconomic circumstances, the ease with which food is obtained in the countryside surrounding Montevideo—"the site of plenty"—is difficult to understand, and the wasting of parts of the cow almost outrages the observer.

Predictably, the European observers' contact with Montevideo's abundance takes them from awe to greed, and even to envy. The sergeant, who was used to the eroded soils of Europe, marveled at the fertility of the American lands. The images in his *décimas*—like the testimony of Pereira de Sá—convey the results of Hernandarias's political-economic project: a project that, in less than two centuries, changed the referent "*tierras de ningún provecho*" into "*los Campos Elíseos de la edad moderna,*" or "the Elysian Fields of modern times."

These verses present another peculiarity: They leave the human beings who exploit nature in the shadows. I am referring, of course, to the incarnation of alterity that appeared in the texts examined in the previous chapters—that is, the inhabitants of the areas that, with the appearance of cities in the region, could now be called "rural." The texts we have examined so far describe a landscape in which the actors are Spanish, Portuguese, or Amerindian. Now a new human group known as the "gaucho," who are defined in terms not of ethnicity but of lifestyle, starts to take shape in the chroniclers' discourse. In the *décimas* under study, this new social agent, although of Spanish origin (*Mestizo* or *Criollo*), seems to belong to none of the main sides in conflict—indicating, perhaps, that this agent was not easily interpellated by the European empires' "civilizing" projects. One must wait until the wars of independence to see the gaucho as a "patriot" who joins the revolutionary armies.

Although the Spanish sergeant does not dedicate many words to representing the gaucho (or *gauderio*), a silhouette takes shape in the interstices of his text. For example, one can catch a glimpse of the gaucho in the sergeant's description of typical rural activities—for example, when he mentions utensils such as "*Volas, Cuchillo y Lazo*" ("bolas, knife, and lasso") and when he explains the meaning of vernacular words, as in "*y se llaman Simarrones/ por sus libres alvedrios*" ("and they are called 'cimarrones' because of their freedom" [ibid.: 290]). The predominant (European) discourse in the text is contaminated by traces that suggest the existence of a supposedly absent element, the gaucho. One faces, then, a discrepancy between the discourse and the object of discourse—that is, between the traces that represent an American oral culture and a literate culture that registers the former.[18] For example, the poetic form that the sergeant has chosen, *décimas,* belongs to an educated, high register. Paradoxically, when the genre of *gauchesca* poetry consolidates a few decades later, *décimas* will be one of the most popular types of stanza. (The *gauchesca* genre, created and practiced by *Criollo* intellectuals, attempted to capture the image of the gaucho by imitating his voice.[19]) What the sergeant presents instead is a discourse that sees reality through literate eyes and that manifests his wonderment at the strangeness of customs found in oral culture: "In this country, any foot soldier ceases to be such immediately and becomes a mounted one. For the most insignificant chores, the servants, wherever they are, pick a horse in a hurry. The owner does not punish him even if he sees him taking the horse" (ibid.: 289).

I get the impression from passages such as this one that the close relationship between the River Plate region's rural dwellers and the horses tends not only to amaze, but also to annoy, the European observer. Although these verses do not clearly show contempt or disapproval, I recognize in them a reaction similar to one that we will find in texts by travelers (especially the French ones) examined later. In any case, what seems to irritate the sergeant most is the lack of respect shown by the gauchos—not only the "thieves," but also the "owners"—for the notion of private property. In this narrative, the economic system of the rural areas of the River Plate works in an inadequate, non-European way.

After their brief account of the gauchos, the *décimas* continue: "*A la colonia pasemos,/ y su conquista excelente,/ pues es digna ciertamente/ de la mayor atención*" ("Let us move to the issue of the Colonia and its excellent conquest, because it is certainly worth our attention" [ibid.: 290–91]). The final moment of the conflict is narrated from a Spanish perspective that abounds in heroic overtones. As we have already seen, confronting a powerful enemy enhances the winner's victory; thus, the following representation of the Portuguese fortress is not surprising: "Our brave army arrived in the Real de San Carlos that is located in front of the admirable Fortress, which was armed with all the supplies that belong to the sovereign art of war. It was so well prepared that it seemed impossible to defeat it" (ibid.: 291).

In this stanza, the *décimas* disappear, and the martial action is narrated in the *octava real,* a type of stanza that characterizes epic poetry (this one does not fit that description exactly, however, because it has only seven lines[20]). Later, the sergeant provides a step-by-step narration of the different strategies Cevallos used to defeat the enemy. During the action, the Portuguese are portrayed in a respectful way, although it is always clear that the Spanish army caused fear among the enemy: "*acuden al muro diligentes,/ mas confusos, y aturdidos, que valientes*" ("they dutifully come to the walls, with more confusion and bewilderment than bravery" [ibid.: 292]); "*ya estaba en su lugar la Artilleria,/ de cuya vista quedó tan desmayado/ el infeliz Portugués, como admirado*" ("the artillery was already prepared, at whose sight the wretched Portuguese were as dismayed as they were amazed" [ibid.]).[21]

The passage written in *octavas reales* has, of course, an epic hero: Commander Cevallos. His figure is presented in the framework provided by the rules governing the genre—in a fashion that resembles, for example, Homer's presentation of Achilles, whose mere presence dissuades the enemy from fighting: "*digeron, que entregarse pretendian,/ que Quentas con Cevallos no querian*" ("they said that they wanted to surrender and that they did not want problems with Cevallos" [ibid.]). The victory is complete when the Spanish triumphantly enter the fortress. At the end of the epic passage, the *décimas* return, and we find Cevallos willing to go to Rio Grande to continue punishing the Portuguese. But news of the peace treaty between the empires reaches Cevallos at this point in the narration, and he decides to stop his campaign. His brave Spanish troops, willing to keep fighting, regret the decision: "This news, my dear love, may have caused joy in the enemy's hearts, but not in ours. Our choleric, vindictive, and ardent heart wished, with conviction, to conclude the Portuguese problem in a bloody way" (ibid.: 294).

Let us say, for the sergeant's posthumous consolation, that at least in Colonia do Sacramento, "bloody" is the way in which "*la portuguesa cuestión*" ("the Portuguese problem") ended. Further, the bloody ending led to a devastation of the city that lasted for many years, as can be seen in the testimony of the traveler Tadeo Haenke, who described what he saw in 1789 this way: "The settlement is half ruined; its streets host today only a few houses made of stone and many abandoned lots with decaying walls. It is still possible to see some debris [from the final battle]. The bell towers also remain as skeletons of the building that was once the Main Church. It is as if this city is paying the price for Portuguese ambition. It is now poor and devastated and its population is now lower in number" (1943 [1795]: 105).

In sum, the texts analyzed in this chapter register a discursive world in which substantial changes occurred in the referent (or construct) "lands on the northern shore of the River Plate." The ways in which the European subject of discourse represented the referent "Amerindians of the region," however, did not change much. On the contrary, the referent is almost the same as that shown in the previous chapters. Further, in this period a new object of representation—the inhabitant of the rural areas—enters the European universe of discourse and partly inherits the treatment reserved for the Amerindian. As Ayestarán points out, the Spanish describe the transgressor (the gaucho) in a way that is far from anthropologically sensitive, using, as they did with the aborigines, European culture as the standard against which to measure cultural achievement. Thus, in the corpus of eighteenth-century discourse, the gaucho is presented as a lazy, nomadic, riding, brawling subject (Ayestarán 1943 [1795]: 7–8).

These texts also represent the conflict between two decadent European empires that are trying to assert rights of possession over the lands and inhabitants of the region under study. Those inhabitants and lands have become objects of desire that cause the struggle between the European actors in this drama. The Amerindians' agency reaches us through the texts that tell indirectly of their resistance to the actions of the Occidental invaders. Unlike their actions, the Amerindians' opinions are not registered in the texts. They do not tell us their version of the conflict. What remains is only a series of imperfect, incomplete translations, such as the peace treaty that takes the liberty of interpreting the will of the Minuan.

Once again, the Amerindians of the region remain silent.

CHAPTER 5

The Encyclopedias

The histories written in the eighteenth century could be considered the encyclopedias on the region because of their systematic and conscious attempt to account for an object of study with the purpose of gathering all the available knowledge about it. These texts are not letters of relation that intend to prove the author's services to the crown in order to get a pension from the king; rather, they are explanations of a determinate object that could be called "River Plate," understood as a geopolitical region. They are an eighteenth-century phenomenon that reminds us of a moment in the history of the colonization of the Americas that José Rabasa calls "the time of the encyclopedia" (a period informed by the works by Fernández de Oviedo and other sixteenth-century chroniclers)—a time in which the "New World" was represented as a deposit of information (Rabasa 1993: 137).

The texts to be analyzed in this chapter differ greatly in epistemological and ideological background from those studied by Rabasa, however, for a simple reason: By the eighteenth century, the conquest and colonization of America had already been going on for two centuries or more in some regions of the continent. As Mary Louise Pratt points out, the later texts are more concerned with the exploration of the interior of the continent than with the maritime exploration that concerned their sixteenth-century counterparts (Pratt 1992: 9). In this respect, these later texts manifest the knowledge criteria that characterized what Pratt describes as a new European "planetary consciousness" (ibid.: 15); further, Pratt says, one of the main traits of that new consciousness was a systematizing of nature through science (ibid.: 29). Natural history—one of the most important scientific tools available to eighteenth-century men of science—therefore helped give an order to the world (ibid.: 31).

The histories of Paraguay (which was, for the Jesuits, a vast region that comprehended approximately the territories of modern-day Argentina,

Uruguay, Paraguay, and part of Brazil) written by the Jesuits Guevara and Lozano in the mid-eighteenth century present a series of characteristics that are identified with the historiographic and scientific discourses of that era. The rigorous standards that frame Guevara's and Lozano's endeavors make their texts appear more thorough than the texts by, say, Barco Centenera and Díaz de Guzmán. According to Andrés Lamas, who introduces the 1873 edition of *Historia de la conquista del Paraguay, Río de la Plata y Tucumán,* Lozano's was the first of the Jesuits' histories (1745); Guevara's was written between the years 1752 and 1767, according to Rojas (1924: 525). Contrary to Pedro de Angelis's assertions in his introduction to Guevara's history (1910b), Guevara took the history by Lozano, his predecessor in the position of historian of the Company of Jesus, as a model. Lozano, in turn, had taken Father Nicolás del Techo (another Jesuit) as his model. This was a common practice among the Jesuits, who believed in the collective production of knowledge (Rojas 1924: 538). I will not account for the totality of the Jesuit histories of Paraguay (or the River Plate) here; I will only indicate some of the ways in which the Jesuits undertook the imaginary construction of the region. For this purpose, the works by Lozano and Guevara represent this corpus well. Further, I will focus on Lozano's text because it is the most exhaustive.

The inclusion of topics related to natural history is common in the historiographic production of the eighteenth century, because at that time history was not dominated by chronology or narrative temporality.[1] Lozano's history, for example, begins with descriptions of the territory's flora, fauna, and aborigines; only later does it narrate historical events from the "discovery" to 1745 (Lamas 1873: cxlv–cxlvi). For his part, Guevara reflects on the difficulties that confront authors who try to write histories of the new lands—the lack of written records resulting from the oral organization of the region's diverse indigenous cultures, for example, and the lack of rigor of the primitive European historians, who did not record events consistently or comprehensively or were biased in their descriptions of the new territories and peoples (1910 [1832]: 35). Guevara's complaints make one think of the truth value predominant at that time, which was based more on the reliability of the available documentation than on personal experience. The search for historical truth through prestigious sources ("*textos doctos*") was, according to Techo, the first Jesuit historian of the region, a natural trait of religious men (Techo 1897 [1673]: 34). Research, then, replaces personal testimony, which dominated the first two centuries of chronicle writing in the Americas, as the privileged source of historiographic legitimation. Another trait we perceive in Guevara's complaints is the privileged position of writing over oral methods in recording the past. This dichotomy, or hierarchical opposition, of orality and literacy dominated the colonial era, with literacy the privileged term.[2]

In his text, Lozano organizes topics in the following order: geography, flora, fauna, origins of the Amerindians, characteristics of the Amerindians; and narration of historical events. Lozano simultaneously describes in detail the geographic accidents of the region and interpolates historical events that took place on the sites he describes. The same abundance of information can be found in the passages he dedicates to flora and fauna.To describe autochthonous plants and animals, Lozano uses the same device employed in earlier texts: He compares the new species to those known to the European subject. For example, he writes: "The *piña* [pineapple] is a gallant plant, and I call it by this name because its fruit, on its exterior, resembles the fruit of the European pine; but its pulp is very tasty and smells beautiful" (Lozano 1873: 245). Similarly, he describes peanuts (*maní*) as "a type of hazelnut that comes in pairs inside a pod, which is much thicker than a garbanzo's pod. . . . Its oil is comparable to that of sweet almonds, with similar effects for medicinal uses" (ibid.: 251), and says that "the Chinese root about which Dr. Monardes wrote is called *yuapecá* by the Guaraní, in whose country it can be found, and it has two species, one white and the other black" (ibid.: 255). This device is also used to depict animals of the region, such as the llama:

> The animals from these countries are primarily those called sheep or ram of the land, or, in Peruvian language [Quechua], *llama*. They grow in the Tucumán province in the area of the border with Peru. It looks very much like the camel, except that it lacks a hump and is a third smaller, but the neck is very long and very similar. They are of various colors (like horses in Spain), among them white, black, brown, and, many of them, gray. (Ibid.: 278–79)

Lamas describes Lozano's modus operandi as follows:

> He creates his nomenclature by giving a European vernacular name to the vegetables that, in his opinion, resemble the Spanish ones he knows, without forgetting to refer to the indigenous name. He gives indigenous names from the Caribbean or Mexico to those plants for which he finds no similar European specimen. Finally, when he does not find any of these similarities, he accepts the indigenous regional name of the plant. (1873: lxv)

Although Lozano does not always respect this order of nominal preferences, it is the most frequent device to which he resorts. This reveals a need to communicate in a way that makes the New World understandable to the European public. Lozano provides the indispensable elements that will allow the reader to form an idea about how the lands and beings of the River Plate look. The frequent appearances of indigenous names are the traces through which the voiceless Amerindians are registered in the conquistador's discourse. The Amerindians, those silent Others, inform and constitute—that is, they are an integral part of—the discourse that describes them. The indigenous names are quoted by the European subject, however; they are not uttered by the original enunciator. Thus, they are not direct speech but are mediated by the European subject of discourse.[3]

Lozano seems to put some distance between himself and the topic of fantastic entities in the region by simply repeating what previous chroniclers said and making clear that they, not he, put forward the existence of monsters:

> They say the animal that grows the Carbuncle—a very rare and appreciated stone—can be found in the Tucumán province, in the direction of San Miguel, and in Paraguay. Yet I suspect that its fame is as fabulous as the Arab Fenix's, in whose existence everybody believes, although nobody has seen it with his eyes yet. For although I have heard that many declared to have seen its immense glow, . . . I have also heard that nobody had the good fortune to find it. . . . This notwithstanding, the *licenciado* Martín del Barco Centenera, archdeacon of the holy church of Paraguay, who lived for many years in these provinces, says that he saw the carbuncle several times and that he chased after it without capturing it. (Ibid.: 299–300)

Thus, Lozano shows a more skeptical attitude than his predecessors regarding the existence of wonders in the lands of the River Plate. The only fantastic entities that he accepts are, of course, those allowed by the Catholic church—miracles, for example. Lozano, as Lamas points out, was a man of his times (Lamas 1873: cxxxi)—and, we could add, of his church—and he interpreted reality with the help of the critical arsenal available to him. In other words, he judges and knows from his epistemic background.

It is from this cultural positioning that Lozano undertakes the task of elucidating the origin of the Amerindian peoples. In his text, the aborigine is again an object of discourse who cannot say anything about himself or herself. In a long passage dedicated to this matter (two chapters that cover pages 344–77), Lozano examines several theories about the pre- or post-deluge origin of the Amerindians, which also implies that they have Eurasian or American roots. In spite of the prolixity of his analysis, he concludes that none of the narratives in particular should be preferred, because "among so many opinions, each one will be able to follow the most appealing one, knowing that nobody is going to persuade him that he is wrong; in the same fashion, he will not be able to convince anybody else who believes otherwise, because it is very difficult to support with any certainty any of these theories" (Lozano 1873: 377). Yet despite the relativism that is revealed in his reluctance to choose one of the possible versions of the Amerindians' origins, it should be pointed out that all the narratives he offers are produced by the European episteme. This is not the case in Guevara's history, which studies only the narratives of origin produced by the Amerindians themselves (1910 [1832]: chap. 2, 37–39). Although Guevara's versions of indigenous narratives undoubtedly include a high percentage of distorting additions or omissions, as well as a certain contempt for the indigenous narrative imagination, his text does represent the indigenous past in a less Eurocentric way than does Lozano's.

Lozano is more respectful of diversity than is Guevara when it comes to the rites, customs, and character ("*ritos, costumbres y genios*") of the "barbaric"[4] nations, as they are called by both Jesuits, who forget (or ignore) Montaigne's warning about the term.[5] Guevara, for his part, proceeds through a certain reduction to unity that subsumes several ethnic groups into one global description—although it is evident that his model in many cases is a very specific ethnic group: the Guaraní. For strong examples of this, see his chapters about the education of children (ibid.: 46–47) and about their idols and sorcerers (ibid.: 48–52).

Lozano, on the other hand, studies each ethnic group separately. What interests me most is that he dedicates a large part of his eighteenth chapter (pp. 407–12) to the Charrúa. His characterization of that ethnic group generally coincides with the one offered by previous chroniclers, with one exception: Lozano provides more information.

> The Charrúa nation was very numerous in the past. It extended from the coast of the Northern Paraná to the shores of the Northern Sea. Very bellicose, brave and spirited people, they were always the hangnail found by the Spaniards when they arrived—voluntarily or not—on their shores. They are still very brave and show their daring spirit to everybody, and nobody yet has been able to subject them [the Charrúa] to their power. The only recognition they offer to the Spaniards is a very costly friendship, because, shielded by it, they commit their evil deeds more safely. (Lozano 1873: 406–7)

Like Barco Centenera and Díaz de Guzmán, Lozano provides an image of the Charrúa that emphasizes their valor, their cruelty, and, implicitly, their capacity to deceive. (They pretend to be friends of the Spaniards, but at the same time they behave like enemies.) The description also emphasizes the Charrúas' lack of predisposition to embrace the Catholic religion and their unreliability—at least by European society's standards: "They are people of little faith and no word, except when it is advantageous to them" (ibid.: 407). The Charrúas' resistance to Catholicism makes their conversion a very difficult task for the missionaries and preachers who try to "save their souls":

> They convert very seldom, regardless of the constant efforts by the Jesuits to gain their souls; their territory is the haven for those who, yearning for freedom, escape to Charrúa lands—which were the Geneva of these provinces. There, not only indians, but *Mestizos*, blacks and even some Spaniards (a horrifying thought)—who want to live without social constraints or fear of the righteousness of the judges because of their enormous crimes, which they continue and augment in Charrúa lands—live in a fashion that is worse than the pagans'. (Ibid.: 410–11)

We can draw a couple of conclusions from this passage. First, as Lozano was writing his history in the mid-eighteenth century), the Indians continued their tenacious resistance to the Spaniards' attempts to evangelize them. Second, Lozano's attitude toward the Amerindians is illustrated in the horror with which he views the Spaniards who prefer to incorporate themselves into a pagan and, by European standards, primitive society. (Remember that to Lozano, the Spanish are members of a superior civilization.) The opposition that underlies this worldview is a logocentric, binary dichotomy in which the Amerindian is not the privileged element.

Although Lozano's text appears homogenous, there are elements that allow us to detect traces of the repressed element of the dichotomy and deconstruct his discourse. Consciously or not, Lozano's text informs us of an objective fact: Members of diverse cultures and ethnic groups—*Mestizos,* other Amerindians, Spaniards—sought refuge among the Charrúa, a culture considered inferior to the European one. This positive presentation of Charrúa society—as a haven for foreigners who decide to incorporate themselves into it—is something of which Lozano seems completely unaware. That is, he does not appear to be aware that by criticizing the conduct of the Spaniards who seek refuge among the Charrúa, he is also making assertions that do not fit his European worldview. For instance, he compares the Charrúas' territory to Geneva, a city famous for giving sanctuary to runaways. This comparison—a positive one, because of the European and civilized nature of Geneva—and Lozano's use of the word "freedom," which is critical in this fragment, can lead the modern reader to see the role of the Charrúa settlements in a more positive light than the one Lozano intends. Analyzing these contradictions, these cases of ideological blindness, allows us to lay bare the structure of European representations of the Other in colonial times—and attempt a representation of the Other that differs from the "official" one.[6]

In some details, Lozano follows Barco Centenera. This leads him into the predicament of trying to justify the archdeacon's exaggerations. For example, Lozano refers to Barco Centenera's description of the Charrúas' running speed: "At the time of the conquest, when they did not know how to ride horses, they were so fast at running that they were able to catch the fastest deer and ostriches. . . . Nowadays, they are less agile but, in compensation, they are very skillful at riding the abundant horses that populate their land" (ibid.: 407). Thus, Lozano finds justification for Barco Centenera's hyperbole in a very reasonable assumption: the possibility of dramatic changes in Charrúa culture brought about by contact with elements that belong to another culture—in this case, the Europeans' horses.

Finally, Lozano provides more detailed descriptions of the Amerindians' housing and customs than did Barco Centenera, but he follows the archdeacon's narration of the bloody encounter between Ortiz de Zárate's people and the Charrúa very closely. He even reproduces verbatim some of Barco Centenera's most unreliable data—for example, the exaggerated number of Charrúa Indians Barco Centenera claims to have encountered. The same can be said about Guevara's version of the events, although his account is considerably more restrained than Lozano's.

The other history I will study in this chapter is Félix de Azara's *Descripción e historia del Paraguay y Río de la Plata,* written at the end of the eighteenth century but not published until the mid-nineteenth century. Azara came to the River Plate region to direct and take part in a series of activities, the most important of which was the demarcation of the Spanish possessions in the region. Spain's power had diminished dramatically by this time; Azara was thus employed not by "the empire on which the sun never sets," but by a weakened Spanish crown that was about to face the wars for independence. This weakening or perhaps the nature of the mission—to survey every inch of the territory—allowed Azara to interact intensely with all of the inhabitants of the region, regardless of their ethnic background.

Another peculiarity of Azara's account—one that brings it close to our contemporary Occidental episteme—is the historiographic criterion he uses, which differs substantially from that in the other encyclopedias we have examined. The sources he uses are not limited to historiographic texts, as was the case for the Jesuits. Azara also consults texts produced in the framework of other disciplines, such as naturalism and ethnography. The Jesuits generally, although not exclusively, limited themselves to quoting other Jesuits. Remember that Lozano quoted Barco Centenera, but his main sources were other fathers from the Company of Jesus. The fact that the Jesuit histories included some commentaries that could today be considered ethnographic, zoologic, or botanic is not tantamount to saying that their framework was conditioned by disciplinary discourses other than historiography. The intertextual dialogue in those texts more often than not was consituted by nondisciplinary discourses, by isolated commentaries about determinate objects of study. Having said that, one should note that although Azara's discursive endeavor differed from, say, Lozano's, the episteme in which the two authors produced their texts was substantially the same.

Azara's historiographic attitude—which looks so "scientific" and "modern" to us—is reflected in a passage in which he explains his methodological reasons for limiting his object of study:

> Because I was alone and the objects I saw were too numerous for me to examine, I was forced to prefer the description of birds and quadrupeds over the description of lands, stones, vegetables, fish, insects and reptiles. Thus, my observations on the latter are going to look trivial and scarce, as if they were written by somebody who had neither time nor intelligence [to invest] in those matters. With regard to the facts of all kinds I refer to [in this book], I have decided not to exaggerate about any of them, and I do not expect the reader to believe my poorly supported statements about them. (1847: 3–4)

Commentaries like this one can be also found in another book by Azara: *Viajes por la América Meridional,* which differs only in detail from *Descripción e historia.* In this passage from *Viajes,* Azara relativizes his own assertions as well as the truth of the facts to which he refers:

> With regard to the facts, the reader can be assured that I have not exaggerated or conjectured at all and that I do not refer to anything that I did not see by myself. Everybody can confirm what I say by his own observations or by the news he could obtain from the inhabitants of the country. With regard to the conclusions I sometimes deduce from the facts, they must be believed when they are well supported. When they are not, they can be rejected or substituted for better conclusions. I will be the first one to accept them. (1969 [1923]: 48)

Compare this passage with one from *Descripción e historia* in which he explicitly enumerates the sources he has consulted:

> I read many ancient documents from the archives located in the cities of Asunción, Corrientes, Santa Fé, and Buenos Aires. I also consulted the archives from the towns and parishes, as well as *the tradition of the elders.* I also read some histories of the country that did not coincide with these original documents. In all of them, I found that their authors did not have enough local knowledge, that they ignored the numbers of nations and Indians, that they ignored the Indians' situation and customs. All this decided me to write the history of *the discovery and conquest,* correcting, as much as I was able to, the mistakes and errors made—sometimes out of ignorance, sometimes out of malice—by these writers. (Azara 1847: 4; emphasis added)

This passage, which was written in *La ciudad letrada* (The Literate City) discussed by Angel Rama, shows a European author who does not hesitate to use oral sources of information in order to complete his encyclopedia. In this respect, Azara follows the tradition of such compilers of indigenous culture as Bernandino de Sahagún and Juan de Betanzos, who dealt with the Mesoamerican and Andean regions, respectively. The tradition of the elders to which Azara refers is the core of an essentially oral culture. In the pages following this passage, Azara criticizes the chroniclers who preceded him for their accounting of the history and culture of the region, but he also hastens to declare his own limitations as a chronicler. For example, he acknowledges that he ignores the work by Herrera, one of the most prestigious chroniclers of the Indies at that time (ibid.: 6). Some of the authors he criticizes—but not by name—are very likely the naturalists Georges Louis Leclerc Buffon and Cornelius de Pauw, who sought to demonstrate the inferiority of the New World compared with the Old World. Their knowledge of the New World was secondhand: Neither had ever set foot in the new lands he despised so much. From this passage, as well as from the general philosophy that inspires the *Descripción*, one can infer that Azara was closer to the defenders than to the enemies of America—although we will see that his evaluation oscillates between a positive and a negative description.[7]

Azara continues with descriptions of the climate, the geography, the minerals, the plants, the animals, and, finally, the different ethnic groups of the region (Africans, Amerindians, Spaniards, and others). He ends his study with a history of the conquest of the River Plate. In Chapter Ten, "About the Wild Indians" ("*De los indios silvestres*"), he says:

> Although man is unintelligible and the wild indian is even more so, because he does not write, speaks very little in an unknown language—which lacks, perhaps, one hundred times more words than it has—and because he only does what his few needs dictate; regardless of all this, despite the barbaric nature of the indian, because he is the main and most interesting part of America, I must include here some of my observations about several nations of wild—or free—indians who are not, and will never be, subject either to the Spaniards or to any other empire. (1847: 142)

Azara's main focus in this passage is the free, indomitable Amerindian confronting the Spanish imperial power. His respect for the Amerindians' courage and spirit is also clear in his reflections on the customs and spiritual traits of those he calls "*naciones de indios* " ("nations of Indians"): "the most nomadic, lazy, strong, arrogant, and untamable ones were the hunters. . . . The least mobile and most kind and pacific were the agriculturalists. Among the latter, some groups are tall, but there are also some other ones that are short, ugly and cowardly and despicable" (ibid.: 248). This passage shows the importance that Azara assigned to warfare in his descriptive model of the Other in relation to the spiritual traits of the diverse ethnic groups with which he interacted.[8] In his model, those who are knowledgeable in the art of war are better than those who are kind and pacific—a notion that pervaded the literary genre known as the chivalric novel. Thus, at least one of the criteria with which Azara evaluates the Other is of anachronistic, chivalric origin.[9]

The duality of Azara's thought is constant. On the one hand, he constructs the Other based on the assumptions and categories of his episteme; on the other, he is an observer interested in the Other's way of life, regardless of his own assumptions. In other words, he is sometimes a subject of discourse who seeks to discover a radical alterity: the absolute Other. The equilibrium he strikes between these attitudes is quite noticeable in the chapters that deal with the ethnic groups.

One of the issues Azara was most interested in clarifying was that of anthropophagy.[10] On more than one occasion, he stated his distrust for other chroniclers' affirmations regarding the Amerindians' alleged cannibalism:

> The majority of the relations and histories agree that almost all the indian nations practiced anthropophagy and that they used poisoned arrows. Yet, I believe both statements are false, since no member of those nations eats human flesh today and they do not know of any poison. They do not preserve any tradition regarding either anthropophagy or poison, despite their constant wars since the discovery of America and despite the fact that they have not changed any of their other ancient customs. (Azara 1847: 143)
>
> The Charrúa killed Juan Díaz de Solís, discoverer of the River Plate, *without eating him,* as Lozano wrongly states in book 2, chapter 1. (Ibid.: 145)

Azara's emphatic denial of cannibalistic practices among the Charrúa goes hand in hand with his refutation of other chroniclers' affirmations about the Amerindians' "savage" practices. For instance, he notes that the Charrúa do not kill women or children, despite their ferocity in combat (ibid.: 148). He also denies that they flayed the faces of their dead enemies' and that they cut themselves with a knife every time they killed an enemy (ibid.: 149). These clarifications are inspired, as I have suggested, by his intention to construct the referent "Charrúa" in a way that does not differ too much from what he is actually observing. Azara's project is to produce discursively an Other who is different from the Other produced by his predecessors: "Yet, they are not—and they have never been—so fast as to be able to catch deer on foot, as Barco states in canto 10" (ibid.: 150). Remember that Father Lozano reproduced Barco Centenera's description of the Amerindians' speed, explaining it in a way that made it more verisimilar without contradicting it. Azara also contradicts the archdeacon's description of the mutilation rites—cutting off a finger's phalanx—practiced by the Charrúa upon the death of a close relative. "Barco, in canto 10, says that they cut off one of their fingers for each dead relative, but it is as I say," writes Azara (ibid.: 158), going on to explain that the Charrúa cut off one phalanx for each relative of a certain kind—that is, not for just *any* dead relative.

The text also contains passages in which Azara's sympathy and admiration for the Amerindians are evident. His admiration, however, is based on the way the Charrúa fit European codes of male valor and skill at warfare:

> Perhaps the Charrúa have shed more Spanish blood to date than the armies of the Inca and Moctezuma. However, in the present they are not more than four hundred armed men. In order to subject them, they [the Spaniards] many times have sent more than one thousand veteran soldiers. Although the Charrúa have been hit several times, they still exist and give us constant war. They are better than we are as riders and in their economy . . . , in riding horses bareback, in not carrying luggage or provisions—they eat whatever they find—, in spending more time without drinking or eating and in enduring hardships. (Ibid.: 150)

Yet Azara does not praise the Charrúas only for their physical superiority and extraordinary valor; he also commends them for their civic and social virtue on occasion. For example, in discussing the freedom that the Charrúas' captives enjoyed, he says: "This freedom and new life suits the captives so well that they seldom decide to return to their parents and relatives. Ruy Díaz refers to this in book 1, chapter 3, saying that the Charrúa are very humane with their captives" (ibid.: 149). Note that while Azara quotes Díaz de Guzmán, he does not mention the horror that Lozano expressed regarding the adaptation of some European captives to Amerindian society.

So how did the encyclopedists fit into the typology of relations with the Other proposed by Todorov? Lozano and Guevara lean clearly toward the axiological pole encompassing those who consider the Amerindians inferior to the European subject and thus do not express respect for them. Azara's discourse, on the other hand, suggests a more ambiguous axiological positioning: Sometimes he criticizes the Amerindians; sometimes he praises them. At the praxeological level, all of the authors studied in this chapter are located at the pole encompassing people who reject the values of the Other while expecting the Amerindian to be incorporated into European values and society. Azara again does not fit clearly into this classification, however, because he does not express horror over Spanish subjects' acculturation to indigenous values and societies and because he describes these indigenous values and social rules as he thinks they are, without trying to produce a portrait of the Amerindian that resembles the Spaniard—that is, whithout trying to portray the Other by assimilation. Having said that, I should point out that the culture from which Azara writes continues to inform his cognitive framework—and, for that matter, his position at the praxeological level. The epistemic level offers a wider range of positions, partly because the European subjects' knowledge about the Other increased as colonization evolved. It is therefore natural that Azara appears to be more interested in attaining knowledge about the Amerindians than were his precedessors, and that he offers more proof of possessing that knowledge.

On the other hand, there can be no doubt about the position of those Spaniards who joined Charrúa society—that Geneva of the River Plate—at the praxeological level: They privileged the values of the Other and accepted them as their own. These European subjects represent only a small proportion of the Westerners who chose to live among the Amerindians—that is, who decided to migrate to a society that was completely alien to their own. They are part of the corpus of evidence cited by Wilcomb E. Washburn in his attempt to establish a moral criterion for evaluating the cultural clash between Europeans and Amerindians:

> Can one make an objective moral assessment of the clash of cultures in the American forest? I have suggested . . . several measures by which such a judgment could be made. One of these measures is the degree to which those who experienced both cultures chose one or the other when they had the choice. There is a good deal of hard data on this subject, most of it supporting the conclusion that Indian life had an overwhelming attraction for whites while "civilized" life had virtually no appeal to the Indians. . . . From the sixteenth century to the end of the nineteenth, accounts of white captives taken prisoner by the Indians provide an index of morality in Indian–European relations. (1976: 344)

Of course, the meaning of expressions such as "when they had a choice" is open to debate. For example, one might ask: Does any prisoner really have a choice? Or is Washburn referring to a prisoner's decision to stay among the Amerindians even after she or he has been offered freedom? However one answers these questions, the available documentary evidence causes the moral evaluation to lean toward the aboriginal side, according to Washburn: There are many more documented cases of Europeans staying with Amerindians than the other way around. Azara is the only chronicler examined so far to face this evidence without abhorrence—perhaps because he seems to be the only one who is able to represent the Amerindians as equals who have their own kind of social and political organization. His awareness of this basic difference between the cultures is apparent in the following passage: "I will call 'nation' any gathering of Indians that share the same spirit, rules, and customs, with a language that differs from the ones known there, the way Spanish differs from German" (Azara 1847: 143). This concept completes one that Azara discussed in *Viajes por la América Meridional,* in which he introduced an element of the "nation" that recalls Benedict Anderson's imagined communities: "Before I describe each nation in particular, I must say that I will call a nation *any gathering of Indians who consider themselves members of one and the same nation,* who have the same spirit, the same rules, the same customs and the same language" (1969 [1923]: 187). Azara's incorporation of the subjective element into his description of "nation" causes him—perhaps unwittingly—to call attention to the importance of indigenous self-descriptions to understanding who the Amerindians are.

Azara also talks about the Chaná, who, he says, have become as civilized as the Spaniards ("*se han civilizado a la par de los españoles*" [1847: 161). This statement again pushes him toward the European pole at the axiological level. And he describes the Minuan, whose democratic and libertarian society, he informs us, is very similar to the Charrúas' (ibid.: 163). (One should note that despite the alleged similarities in their societies, the Charrúa and the Minuan [or Guenoa] were frequently enemies, as Bracco has persuasively suggested [1998: 14, 106].[11]) Their cultures also differed greatly: They spoke different languages (none of them related to Guaraní) and had different social and political relationships with the Portuguese and Spanish (ibid.: 14, 133). For example, the Minuans had a very good relationship with the Portuguese for a while, as shown in Chapter Four; they also maintained a generally good relationship with the Jesuits (another key player in the region, as we have already seen) by keeping the missionaries' hopes alive regarding Amerindian conversion to the Catholic faith (ibid.: 51). Thus, we have to be careful when we confront texts, such as Azara's, that do not always distinguish between local ethnic groups.

Azara's fragments on the Amerindians show that his discourse alternates between praise and critique: Sometimes he criticizes the Other's customs—for instance, when he qualifies some Amerindians as "barbaric" ("*barbaridades*" [1847: 250]) and when he praises the virtues of the conquest and the benefits it has brought to the aborigines:

> Say whatever you want, but only the Spaniards have produced a code of laws that abounds in humaneness and that *protects the Indians by equating them to the Spaniards*—and it [the code of laws] even prefers them in some respects. Some people will argue that those laws have not been enforced, but it is not difficult to compare the lists of Indians who lived when the colonial towns were founded with the number of individuals who inhabit them today; anyone will find, as I have, that *the number of pure Indians has increased* in spite of the fact that many of them have become Spaniards and Mulattoes due to *mestizaje.* (Ibid.: 279–80; emphasis added)

Leaving aside Azara's arguable statement about the growth of the indigenous population, what is evident in this passage is the ideological position from which the author is writing. Despite his efforts to understand and adequately represent the Amerindian, Azara's ideological matrix always permeates his statements and his general view of the Other. One can always find in his texts some justification of the bloody and rapacious enterprise that was the conquest: "Thinking about the different conquests in history, one will not find another with so few excesses perpetrated, or another which has given so many advantages to the conquered peoples with so little bloodshed [as the Spanish one]" (ibid.: 257).

Azara's representation of the Other is not limited to describing Amerindians. His texts register other Others who have not appeared in the documents studied so far in this book. For example, the *Mestizos* are not an important presence in earlier texts, including those of Lozano and Guevara, perhaps because this group was only beginning to emerge when the early chroniclers were writing. Another group is even more absent in these texts: the African, or *el negro.* Azara records the presence of both the *Mestizos* (or "pardos") and the Africans and reflects on them. In his opinion, the designation "pardo" embraces several possible ethnic combinations:

> If the pardo is a son of an Indian and a European [white], he is called *Mestizo*—and the same can be said about his descendants, provided that in the new generations nobody has African blood—whether a little or a lot. If an African marries a European or an Indian, the result is called mulatto—and the same can be said of the descendants.... In some other parts they receive other names. For example, if the mulatto son of a European and an African marries a European, the descendant is called *cuarterón,* because she or he is only one-fourth black; but if the mulatto marries an African, the descendant is called *"salto atrás"* [backward leap], because instead of getting closer to white, the descendant ends up being three-quarters African.
>
> I will limit my discourse to the *Mestizo*'s and mulatto's physical and moral traits, because it is impossible to know about all the possible mixtures that formed them. (Ibid.: 292)

This passage clearly shows one of the mechanisms for constructing the colonial subject that Iris Zavala has analyzed: By using borrowed language (*"lenguaje prestado"*)—in this case, ethnography—the writer seeks to establish an ethnic typology that gives him or her control over ethnic diversity; at the same time, this typology allows the writer to impose order on a world that does not lend itself to organization in discrete unities (Zavala 1989: 335–36). In Zavala's opinion, the mechanisms proposed to control diversity create a social order that exists only in the discourse of the conquistador. That is, in this case, the typology fragments the colonial subject in order to diminish him or her.

The terms that inform a typology of this kind are neither neutral nor innocent, as Azara's use of "*salto atrás*" clearly shows: That was the way in which the descendant who returned to the ominous African origin of one of his or her ancestors was named.[12] It is obvious that the expression of a "backward movement" (or a relapse) has pejorative connotations, especially when set in opposition to an "evolution" toward whiteness. Similarly, the names applied to others who resulted from ethnic miscegenation not only function to acknowledge their existence; they also function to construct meaning for, or assign meaning to, them. Thus, such typologies are an attempt less to create a neutral classification than a hierarchical organization. As Azara says: "The laws place the mulatto in the lowest class, after the Europeans and their children, the *Mestizo* Indians and even the Africans, but the common folk rank them as equal to the Africans and *Mestizo*s and superior to the Indians" (1847: 295).

In actuality, this passage shows two different hierarchical organizations—the legal one and the popular one (the vox populi). This distinction notwithstanding, there is still an issue in which both organizations coincide: typologies are hierarchical structures. In another passage, Azara makes explicit his hypothesis about the "evolution" of races: "From this argument, it can be deduced that not only do species improve with mixture, but also that the European species is more resistant to change than the Indian one—because the latter disappears in the long term and the former prevails. It is true that because the descendants come from Spanish males and Indian females, there is some doubt about what actually prevails: it could be either the male sex or the [white] species" (ibid.: 292). In this passage, Azara also introduces one of the most overlooked Others in the texts analyzed so far: women. They appear only tangentially in Azara's text, and when they do appear, they function only to provide supplementary information about topics that have nothing to do with woman as an object of representation. The representation of woman *in praesentia* is almost null, almost nonexistent, but she appears in the text in the form of brief traces such as the one to which I am now referring—that is, the inferiority of the female as regards the characters who predominate in the reproduction of the species. The rest of the texts studied in this book give even less space to women; in those chronicles, the references to women often take the form of statistical or tangential commentaries.[13]

It should by now be obvious that a relationship exists in the way the colonial chroniclers dealt with the Amerindian, the *Mestizo*, the African, the mulatto, and the woman. The colonial corpus on the River Plate confirms that colonial discourse used *"reducción a la semejanza"* (reduction to similarity)—that is, the reduction of oppressed groups to certain common traits (Adorno 1988a: 59–62)—to construct those groups as Others in America as a whole. A key element in this operation was the comparison (and assimilation) of any oppressed group to women (or, at least, to feminine characteristics).[14] In the few instances in which colonial authors write directly about women (that is, when women are not merely a statistical element), the image they produce is not positive. For example, Azara says about Amerindian women in general: "Perhaps there is no female Indian over ten years old who had said no to a suitor, be he old or young, free or slave, black or white" (1847: 288). Yet no author in the corpus under study can compete with Barco Centenera when it comes to insulting and discriminating against women:

> Although without justice, ungratefulness, evilness, tears, lies, and vengeance are women's treasure.
>
> Ask Aristotle how he felt about women, since he says in his works that their nature is prone to tears and crying in excess. He also says that envy, laziness, and sloth characterize woman. Yet he says something positive about them: they content and sustain themselves with very little food. (1602: 69v)

What we have seen so far allows us to perceive general trends in the process the European subjects of discourse use to represent alterity. First, the colonial subject produces a stereotypical discourse that reflects the values of masculine, chivalric, and Christian culture (Adorno 1988a: 56). Second, according to Adorno, "alterity in stereotypical colonial discourse is not a mysterious, obscure or occult category. It is visible and known; it is postulated in terms of gender and ethnicity: the Moor, the Jew, woman, children" (ibid.: 66). This construction of the Other by assimilating American subjects to oppressed groups that already exist in Europe and Asia is a variation of the process by which "America" (a lump of land) was constructed via assimilation to an existing stereotype: the unknown lands, or *terrae incognitae*.[15]

These strategies for constructing the Other are simply manifestations of a general uneasiness affecting the Occidental and Christian subject—that is, the subject's desire, or anxiety, for the Other[16] results from the encounter with an alien reality that puts into question the foundations of his or her culture and episteme. In de Certeau's words: "The heterogeneous is for each culture the sign of its own fragility, as well as of its specific mode of coherence" (1989 [1986]: 176). But difference has a parallel function: to contribute to the subject's recognition of his or her limits. In other words, the confrontation with the Other helps the subject to build his or her identity in opposition to alterity (Adorno 1988a: 66).[17]

Moreover, from the perspective of this investigation, the European and Christian world's intelligibility is possible thanks to the Occidental subject's relationship with the Other (de Certeau 1988: 3). By creating a space in which to construct the image of the Other, the European subject provides himself or herself with a locus of enunciation, a space from which to emit—to utter—discourse.[18] This dialectical relationship between the creation of a space that is external to discourse and the creation of a space for the emission of that discourse is the one that informs the discursive strategies under study here. Those discursive strategies belong to what de Certeau calls heterologies—that is, discourses on the Other that are based on a division between a subject of knowledge who emits a discourse and the mute object of discourse that sustains the former (ibid.: 3). The heterologies I have chosen to study dramatize what is asked of the Other in order to be part of the conquistador's discourse: She or he must remain silent forever. This silence has already lasted for more than five hundred years.

CHAPTER 6

The Tentative Gaze of the Traveler

> Los viajeros, respecto de los historiadores son lo mismo que los lazarillos, en comparación con los ciegos. *[Travelers are to historians as blindmen's guides are to the blind.]*
>
> —*Concolorcorvo*

The texts in this chapter belong, in their majority, to the genre of travel accounts. Although many take the form of letters, logbooks, or diaries, all record European visitors' impressions of the River Plate region. Yet despite the travelers' shared Occidental worldview, the homogeneity of their representational strategies is fragmented. By this time, the Spaniards and the Portuguese are not the only ones producing representations of the region; other subjectivities have entered the universe of discourse and are contributing their own versions of the referent "Uruguay" (or "lands of Uruguay"). These new subjectivities include the French, the Italian, the Dutch, and the British.

Not surprisingly, the perspectives of these national groups differ considerably from those held by subjects of Spain and Portugal—the two empires that have struggled to possess the region. For one thing, the new groups belong to interpretive communities that, despite their shared Occidental character, differ from the Spanish and Portuguese cultures; and for another, their respective crowns' interests differ from those of the colonizing nations. That is, their point of view is not that of a master trying to protect the crown's patrimony. Although these travelers may at times yearn for—or envy—somebody else's possessions, they cannot make plans for lands that are not their own.[1]

One attitude toward the Spanish colonies, however, is common among the foreign travelers: greed. Take the case of the British traveler Sir John Constanse Davie. In a letter dated 1797, he praises Montevideo for its fertility (1805: 33), adding that the city's location could make it "a very valuable key to the riches of the southern world" (ibid.: 37) and that it could easily be taken by the British: "The article of navigation alone excepted, I believe the conquest of the Plata might be effected with very little danger on the part of the invaders" (ibid.).

In this chapter, we will also examine the testimony of some Spaniards who did not live in the region and of others who did not even have business in the colonies. As a consequence, they—unlike a governor or any other official of colonial administration—did not have a direct political or economic interest in the lands. Thus, these writers' point of view differs from that of the chroniclers studied in previous chapters.[2]

The point of view of the subject of discourse serves as the criterion for grouping the texts studied in this chapter. To put it another way, what these texts have in common is the traveler's gaze, which both surveys a new landscape and records impressions about it. This criterion is, of course, as arbitrary as any when it comes to organizing a body of works, yet it serves as a temporary strategy. In this chapter, I will focus on the gaze of the subject who does not stay long. I am interested in the angle or direction of that gaze, which distinguishes one traveler from another. This gaze resembles Jitrik's "*mirada tentativa*" ("tentative gaze"), which, he says, is "a trait shared by almost the totality of travel literature which constitutes something like a price paid by discourse vis-à-vis the difficulties faced by the eye at the time of making a synthesis [of the observed experience] with the quickness demanded by the rules of the genre 'chronicle'" (1983: 114). In these texts, the spatial element—the description of the landscape and peoples of the new lands—begins to displace the chronicle's predominantly temporal narrative element.[3]

The earliest examples of this kind of literature are *Corto y verídico relato de la desgraciada navegación de un buque de Amsterdam* by Henrich Ottsen, a Dutch sailor who arrived in the River Plate region in 1599,[4] and the logbook of William Toller, an English traveler who visited the region in 1715.[5] Although these accounts do not say much about the lands under study, they are relevant to reconstructing the story of how the referent "lands of Uruguay" was produced. Very few passages in Ottsen's text refer to the lands and peoples on the northern shore of the River Plate; its most important contribution to the production of the referents can be found in its illustrations—which are among the earliest to represent the territory under study. Ottsen offers what he calls "the whole configuration of the magnificent River Plate region" ("*toda la configuración de la magnífica comarca del Río de la Plata*" [1945 [1603]: 39, plate 3); the illustration shows the region's islands, mainland, sandbanks, and shoals ("*islas, tierras firmes, barrancas de arena y bajíos*" [ibid.: 40]). The book also includes a plate that represents Seawolves Island (*isla de Lobos*) (ibid.: 43, plate 4).

One peculiarity of the book is that it supplements the depiction of landscape features with portraits of two of the region's Amerindians. In the original edition (1617 [1603], plate 4), the aborigines appear standing together, facing each other, against the background of a wild landscape (Illustration 1). In the 1945 reprint, however, a map of the region serves as background, and the Amerindians appear standing on each of the river's shores. The one standing on the northern shore (the Montevideo side) is wearing furs, while the other (on the Buenos Aires side) is naked and carries *boleadoras*. In both editions, a caption accompanying the plate reads:

> These savages that we offer to the friendly reader (two specimens *drawn from real models*) were red, with braided hair and a face disfigured by holes in their chins, in which they had introduced little bones the size of glands. They also had pierced the center of the nose, and its cavities were not distinguishable. They also pierced their ears, which were traversed by pig teeth. A very strange spectacle, indeed. They do not speak very much. In the summer they go naked, but in the winter they make themselves a dress with five or six pieces of wild animals' furs. *They are cannibals* and eat the animals with all their bowels. We do not know anything about their religion, but *it is reasonable to surmise that they live like wild beasts.* Their weapon is a slingshot which they use to throw stones. (Ibid.: 40; emphasis added)

This passage's affirmation that the human figures were drawn from "real models" allows one to assume close contact between Ottsen (or a member of his crew) and the represented Amerindians. This is debatable—in fact, it has already been debated. Rogelio Brito Stífano, for example, doubts that the representations of the Indians are based on a perception of the models in situ by a member of the expedition and considers this plate an "imagined composition" ("*composición imaginativa*" [Brito Stífano 1955: 198]), following the terminology coined by Alejo González Garaño. Strangely enough, the Amerindians are not mentioned often in the remainder of the text—that is, the text does not narrate episodes that include the Amerindians as relevant agents. The few times that they appear, they are presented as collaborating with the Buenos Aires authorities, which makes one think they might have been Christian or "civilized" Amerindians. Perhaps these are the "real models" to which the caption refers.

ILLUSTRATION 1. According to Ottsen, this is a "naturalistic" representation of two Amerindians from the River Plate region. The bucolic atmosphcrc suggcsted by the picture is contradicted by the caption that glosses the plate, which informs readers about the Amerndians' cannibalism and savagery. From Henrich Ottsen, *Iornael oft daghelijcx register van de voyagie no Rio de Plata* (Amsterdam: M. Colijn, 1617 [1603]). Reproduced with permission of William L. Clements Library, University of Michigan.

One should also note that no reference is made to the ethnic affiliation of the models represented in the plate. For this reason, it is fair to say that the illustration offers a generic and undifferentiated portrayal of the region's Amerindians. For its part, the caption looks like a compendium of Occidental prejudgments of several Amerindian ethnic groups. This composite of idiosyncratic traits—cannibalism, pierced ears and noses, *boleadoras* (in the graphic representation, or slingshots, as they are called in the caption), laconism, mutism, to quote just a few—takes its raw material, prejudices and verifiable data alike, from European lore.

It seems reasonable that the representation offered by Ottsen—a European subject who is not very familiar with the region—tends to construct the referent "Indian" or "savage" in a general way, without differentiating among the many groups who populate the area. In fact, he repeats the common pattern and reduces the Amerindians to a generic prototype or stereotype, attributing to them such characteristics as savagery, bestiality, primitivism in clothing or nakedness, absence of religion, and cannibalism.

Ottsen's plate 4 also includes a caption. This time, the object of representation is the *isla de Lobos* (Seawolves Island), and the reader again must interpret messages that include information on both the verbal and iconic planes. This kind of message may be inspired by the need of the utterer to transmit an unknown world to a European addressee—hence, the communicational redundancy that predominates in this type of communicative strategy. Estuardo Núñez points out the importance of illustrations and other graphic representations in travel accounts: "The new mentality of the traveler demands, as a correlate to his spatial conception of the world—and as an auxiliary tool for his interpretation of the [new] reality that surrounds him—, the support of graphic images that confirm what he is describing with words" (1989: xii–xiii). One also finds examples of this communicative strategy outside the corpus of travel accounts—for instance, in the Mappamundi of the Southern Cone of America drawn by Cabot, in which he represents some scenes that depict human beings, amazons, etc. (Medina 1908a: vol. 1).[6]

Another interesting contribution that Ottsen makes to the production of referents in the region is his naming of the area of Montevideo, which he calls "Monte Seredo" in plate 3 and in the text: "Monte Seredo, an elevated mountain" (*"Monte Seredo, que es una montaña elevada"* ([1945 [1603]: 46). This name appears infrequently—mostly in maps and navigational charts of Dutch origin—because it was not popular among the sailors who visited the region.[7]

Toller's logbook also combines verbal and iconic information. The author's inclination toward the natural sciences leads him to record the fauna of the River Plate region—at least, as precisely as his doubtful skills as an artist allow. The pages that he dedicates to the zone he calls "de Castillos" are full of drawings of swans, bulls, ducks, corvinas, armadilloes (Illustration 3), and seawolves (Toller 1955: 232, fol. 17; 234, fol. 18; 236, fol. 19; 238, fol. 20). He draws leopards, snakes, and skunks from the area he calls "de Santa Lucía" (ibid.: 252, fol. 27). There is also a drawing based on a real model that represents the captain of the expedition hunting bulls accompanied by some of his men (ibid.: 238, fol. 20). Maps and charts are also abundant. Among them are two that represent the bays of Castillos, Santa Lucía, and Montevideo (ibid.: 240, fol. 21; 250, fol. 26; 244, fol. 23). The verbal part of the text, however, adds very little information to the graphical representations of animals and landscape features. Toller does confirm—as Hernandarias had pointed out a hundred years earlier—that the zone known as Santa Lucía (*"zona de Santa Lucía"*) is very pleasant. By 1715, Santa Lucía was also heavily populated

ILLUSTRATION 2. America's emblematic animal during colonial times was the armadillo. Other American species and scenes of "savage" life depicted in the background complete the exoticist view of a newly discovered land populated by semiclad Amerindians. From Henrich Ottsen, *Iornael oft daghelijcx register van de voyagie no Rio de Plata* (Amsterdam: M. Colijn, 1617 [1603]). Reproduced with permission of William L. Clements Library, University of Michigan.

with cattle. In some passages, Toller refers to the crew's visits to terra firma to obtain provisions—for example, the expeditionaries' first visit to the lands surrounding Montevideo: "They came off & brought off a Large Bull wch they shot. But there were no Fish near the shoar except a few sprats. They report that the country is very Pleasant, extreamly well stockd [with] Cattle & some Deer, pleasently Wooded. . . . We suppose it to be the Bay of St. Lucia" (ibid.: 251, fol. 25v). In other segments of the text, recounting the expedition's stay on the northern shore of the River Plate, he mentions the beauty of the landscape and the abundant bovine population (ibid.: fol. 17v; fol. 23v; fol. 27v; fol. 29; fol. 29v; fol. 31v; etc.), where he narrates the crew's daily hunting to obtain bulls' meat).

What Toller omits in his account is any reference to the human beings who populated the land. One possible explanation is that in 1715, the lands on the northern shore of the River Plate were not heavily populated by human beings. That is, they did not host any permanent settlements: The Amerindians were either nomads or dynamically sedentary, and the Spanish had not yet decided to settle the area. Even if the expedition had traveled as far as the zone in which the Portuguese had established Colonia do Sacramento, which they did not, Toller would not have been able to record human presence in the fortress, because the Portuguese had been expelled in 1705. Although they recovered Colonia do Sacramento in the Utrecht Treaty of 1715, they did not return until November 1716.[8] What Toller finds instead are traces left by human activities—a bleeding ram, for example, that has been hit by a musket bullet (ibid.: 243, fol. 22v). In Castillos, Toller finds more suggestions of human presence: "We saw no inhabitants here, & very few marks of its being much frequented[.] An Arrow was found, an European Hat and a Case Bottle: probably all left by sailors" (ibid.: 233, fol. 17v). As I said, although the traces are more abundant, they are the only signs of human life and activities in the territory explored by Toller and the members of the expedition.[9]

The next group of texts pays more attention than do Ottsen's and Toller's to the lands on the northern shore of the River Plate. These texts include letters written by the Italian Jesuit priest Father Gaetano Cattaneo, in which he relates the vicissitudes of his trip from Europe to the Jesuit missions.[10] In his first letter, one finds a reference to the name "Monte Seredo": "Monte Video is not usually found in the cartographic charts, and when it appears, it does so under the name Monte Seredo, because it is a new settlement—two or three years old—founded by the Court. Some families from the Canary islands are moving there, 25 or 30 of which under the guidance of our Petacchio" (in Muratori 1752: 262–63). This testimony confirms that the name "Monte Seredo" was used mainly in Dutch cartography; it also suggests that the population was very new to the area: Cattaneo was arriving at the same time as the second contingent of settlers from the Canary Islands. He tells us why the Spanish decided to settle here:

> With this settlement Spain secures all that vast portion of land that lies between the River Plate, Brazil and the Ocean, to which the Portuguese strongly aspired, in order to expand the territory of their Brazil to the Colonia or Island of Saint

> Gabriel—which is located in front of Buenos Aires and is guarded by a solid castle—and to use it as a port of entry that would help them introduce as much merchandise as they wish to smuggle into the states possessed by Spain, . . . with great advantage for them and great loss for the Spanish merchants, who, when they come here with their very loaded ships, do not know how to sell their merchandise, finding a country already abundantly provided with all kinds of commodities, because the French and the English also find a safe haven in that Colonia, which allows them to commercialize their own merchandise. (Ibid.: 263)

In very few strokes, Cattaneo sums up the problems faced by Spain, which has to deal with the commercial activities not only of the Portuguese, but also of the French and the English. In his first letter, he presents Colonia do Sacramento as a kind of cancer in the middle of the Spanish possessions on the one hand, and, on the other, as an outpost that is helping the Portuguese extend their dominion over the region—to expand "their Brazil." Montevideo, therefore, is presented as the Spanish response to Portugal's attempts to expand its dominion.

At first glance, Cattaneo's perspective appears to be distanced and informed—as based on relevant economic considerations. This apparent distance seems evident in his restraint in making comments that favor either side in the Spanish–Portuguese conflict: He reports only what people have told him and what he has seen. He narrates the details of the founding of Montevideo in the same neutral tone. Later, he offers a description of the new Spanish settlement based on the testimony of some of the priests who traveled in another of the convoy's ships:

> Nowadays, *there are no more than three or four brick houses and fifty or sixty huts made of ox leather,* where the most recently arrived families dwell until more houses are built for them to inhabit. The bricklayers are the Indians from our Missions, who came in 1725 at the request of the Buenos Aires Governor, in the number of two thousands, to build—as they have done until now—the fortress under the guidance of our Missionaries, who preach to them, take their confession, etc., in their language, because they do not understand Spanish. These two fathers dwell in one of those huts made of leather, and the poor Indians have neither house nor roof, exposed to the rain and the winds after their labors, without a salary, only with the discount of the tribute that they will have to pay. (Ibid.: 265; emphasis added)

The portrait of the settlement—which can hardly be called a city or town—offered by Cattaneo is both very illustrative and dismal: three or four brick houses and fifty or sixty leather huts. To the lack of settlers, one should add the lack of adequate housing—which depends on the Guaraní labor force, who are also in charge of the construction of the fortress. This is the hamlet Cattaneo presents us with; this is Montevideo in 1729. According to Cattaneo, the Spanish would not have been able to build the settlement—it cannot be called a city or a town—without the help of two thousand Guaraní Indians brought by the Jesuits. As we have already seen, this ethnic group had considerable agency in the disputes between the Portuguese and the Spanish over Colonia do Sacramento. Thus, the founding of Montevideo—a consequence of those disputes—again counts the Guarani as actors in the drama to possess that piece of land.

Cattaneo's neutral descriptions give way to a different perspective, however—one that represents the interests of the Company of Jesus. One can see this shift in his application of the possessive "our" to the missions. This possessive, I believe, suggests the existence of an interest that is specific to the Jesuits, which consists of preserving, improving, and praising their possessions. The Jesuits, after all, established something of a parallel empire that was independent from the political and economic colonial possessions of the Spanish and Portuguese. Defending that parallel empire entailed forming Guaraní militias, which were led by the "soldier priests." It also required a propaganda program. The letters written by the missionaries from America were privileged vehicles carrying messages back to the European public: Many of these letters were compiled and published as books, as is the case with Cattaneo's. Hence, it should not be surprising that Cattaneo, at every opportunity, praises the Guaraní from the Jesuit missions—the converted Amerindians who are the living proof of the magnificent achievements of the Company of Jesus. Besides their craftmanship and industriousness, he most often lauds their religiosity (which manifests itself as blind obedience to the Jesuit priests) and kindness. An event in Montevideo that was reported to Cattaneo by his companions illustrates this point. An Amerindian from the missions, unhappy with the labor conditions, refused to continue working. His response to the Spaniards' attempts to coerce him was to grab a horse and a handful of arrows. Everything seemed to point toward a bloody ending to the story, until one of the Jesuits providentially intervened:

> The father came and, with a few words to the Indian, made him get off the horse and return the bow and arrows. Later, with nice manners and words of love, he induced the Indian to accept any punishment he deserved for his fault: he made him lie on the ground, ordered [the troops] to give him 24 whiplashes before the astonished soldiers, who saw how that Indian who was not afraid of the cannon surrendered so quickly to the Missionary's words. (Ibid.: 265–66)

The priest's magical—or divine—intervention literally pacified the rebellious Amerindian. The implications of this episode are very significant. First, the narrator's point of view presupposes that the Amerindian is at fault. That is to say, Cattaneo perceives the Amerindian's rebellion in response to inhumane work and housing conditions (remember that the Guaraní were roofless) as simply wrong. Second, violent repression or punishment of the fault is presented as an inadequate response to the alleged crime—the practitioners of that method make fools of themselves in the narration. The lesson the soldiers learn is that persuasion through faith and good treatment is more effective than violent repression. The moral of this *exemplum*—a typically Christian pedagogical device—is that obtaining obedience from the Amerindians is what really matters, and that the best method for achieving obedience is dialogue, not violence. At the end of the *exemplum,* the Jesuits' strategy is shown to be the most effective one.

I should note here that the Jesuits' power over the Guaraní was a crucial element in the founding of the settlement that Cattaneo describes. Without the Jesuits' help, the fortress could not have been built. Add to this the Guaraní's fighting on the Spanish side in the sieges of Colonia do Sacramento, and the significance of the Jesuits' help in establishing the Hispanic settlement in Montevideo begins to emerge clearly. The power that the Jesuits exerted on the Guaraní from the missions cannot be exaggerated: Without them, Spain would have had serious trouble countering the Portuguese presence on the northern shore of the River Plate.

Cattaneo's second letter contains no references to Montevideo; instead, it includes remarks about the countryside north of the River Plate,[11] to which I will refer when I discuss the third letter. For the time being, I will focus on one of Cattaneo's statements about Buenos Aires in order to identify his situation of enunciation with more precision. As noted earlier, Cattaneo undoubtedly belonged to an interpretive community—the Company of Jesus—that was independent from the European states dominating the region. One could describe the Jesuits as a transnational community that developed in monumental (as opposed to historical) time, but that also was not independent from another, larger community: European culture. That is, although the Jesuits could view themselves as a different interpretive community from the Spanish and Portuguese (or, for that matter, from the English and Italians), they were still framed by the limits of the Occidental episteme. At this more general level, the "outside" that defines the inside—that is, the community—would comprise other types of communities that are truly different from the Jesuits, such as Amerindians, Africans, and Asians. Thus, the cultural boundaries of the macro-community I call Europe are wider than the boundaries delimiting the communities (Spanish, Portuguese, Jesuit, etc.) that together form that macro-community.

Cattaneo wrote: "Buenos Aires is not only the most populated but also *the best of all the cities in these three provinces*—Tucuman, Paraguay, and River

Plate. And this is so *because it partially resembles European cities,* despite the fact that it has a large indigenous population—hence its excess of majesty and beauty" (ibid.: 283; emphasis added). Buenos Aires's superiority to other cities in the region is based on how it compares to European standards of excellence. Cattaneo's statement therefore provides a more complete picture of the situation of enunciation from which he produces the referents—a situation of enunciation that partly determines the final form of that construct.

The third letter tells the story of the priests' voyage to the missions via the Uruguay River. Cattaneo comments on the most salient features of the "country" in his introduction, then narrates the adventures and hardships of the voyage, which included smallpox epidemics and attacks by tigers and by ants. His gaze scans the river's shores while the raft transporting him advances toward its destination. The missionary uses an unusual spelling for the name of the river, "Uraguai," on some occasions (three times on page 293). Like most first-time visitors, Cattaneo hesitates when he has to write vernacular names. (Notably, however, he does not seem to have any doubts about spelling when he reproduces other local names in his three long letters.)

Descriptions of the region's fauna are treated similarly. Compared with that of other chroniclers (Barco Centenera comes immediately to mind), Cattaneo's gaze distorts what he perceives only slightly. (In his letters, a seawolf is a seawolf, not a mermaid or a monster, for example.) But representational problems do arise:

> The most common animals are the tigers, which often remain seated at the beach, looking at the passing rafts. *These tigers are bigger and more ferocious than the African ones.* About their size I will say only that I saw them with my own eyes and touched them with my own hands. The Indians from the *reducciones* [missions] where I am residing now killed a female tiger and brought the skin to one of the fathers' houses. I wanted to measure that skin because *it seemed monstrous to me.* So I made them place the skin in a position that resembled the one the tiger strikes when it is about to attack a man. Although I raised my hand as high as I could, I was able to reach only the animal's mouth—and I am not a short man. (Ibid.: 298–99; emphasis added)

This fragment makes one wonder whether the region's so-called tigers were really enormous or the priest was much shorter than he claimed.[12] Maybe the beasts activated Cattaneo's impressionable nature. Whatever the case, this exaggerated description of an animal is an exception in Cattaneo's text. He usually describes the fauna in believable terms.

It is in the passages describing the Amerindians that one can see Cattaneo's European cultural biases most clearly. After leaving Santo Domingo Soriano, the Company of Jesus runs into a series of indigenous groups that Cattaneo calls "Bohanes, Martidanes, Manchados, Jarós and Charuas," adding that they "live in an area that extends for almost four hundred miles throughout the country located between the Uruguay River and the River Plate—or Paraná, as it is also known" (ibid.: 303). Thus, Cattaneo locates the Yaro and Charrúa on the western shore of the Uruguay River but says nothing about their presence on the other shore—where they traditionally have been located since the "discovery." This is what he says about the Charrúa:

> The most numerous nation of all is the Charrúa, *barbaric people who live like beasts in the countryside or the woods, without house or roof.* They are very lightly dressed and *always ride their horses,* where they carry their bows, arrows, spears, and clubs. *Their dexterity and speed as riders is incredible.* This is a common trait of most of these nations of Indians. Although the Spaniards are very good riders—probably the best in Europe—, it is very rare to see them catching an Indian on the run or able to attack them with their swords. (Ibid.: 303–4; emphasis added)

This representation of the Charrúa is constructed using familiar elements: The Amerindians are presented as barbaric beings who live like beasts in the great outdoors. That is, they lack houses, a fundamental civilizational element for the European observer. Cattaneo also mentions the Charrúas' "speed," a characteristic that Barco Centenera cited to describe the Amerindians' performance on foot but that Cattaneo's text displaces to their horses—a shift in emphasis that also serves to illustrate the changes brought about by the Europeans' introduction of livestock. The image of the Charrúas as centaurs will occur repeatedly in texts by European travelers, because that relationship between an aboriginal human being and a foreign beast fascinated the Occidental observers. The already familiar picture of the Charrúa as savages continues in other parts of the letter:

> Coming back to the Charrúa, let us say that *they are a truly barbaric people.* Their color is bronzelike, because they walk nude under the rain and the sun. They never comb their hair, which *makes them look like Furies.* The chiefs wear a piece of stone, glass, or tin in their pierced chins. Some of them have only one or two fingers left on their hands because they cut off a phalanx when a relative dies. They are abandoning this barbaric rite now. (Ibid.: 304–5; emphasis added)

To insure that his reader does not forget, Cattaneo repeats the description of the Charrúa as a barbaric people. Moreover, he adds a sinister touch to the already horrifying picture of the Amerindians by comparing them to the Furies, very ugly mythological entities with which educated European readers are familiar—a strategy that we saw in earlier accounts. Cattaneo's completes this strategy by coupling the familiar elements with new elements of horror that are exclusively indigenous—for example, the Charrúas' custom of disfiguring their faces with all kinds of objects and the rite of cutting their fingers after deaths in the family.[13] The Charrúa may have practiced such facial disfigurement, but it is very unlikely that they used glass or tin in 1729 or 1730. Those materials had only recently been introduced into the region by the European visitors, and customs do not change so quickly. Recall also that, according to Azara, the Charrúa used small pieces of wood in their piercings as late as the end of the eighteenth century. The *dispositio* that organizes the data about the Charrúa in this text also allows the reader to surmise the author's objective: to impress the European addressee. With this goal in mind, the texts reiterate images of the Charrúa that resemble the descriptions of other indigenous American peoples—that is, as savage and uncivilized—that have already become popular in Europe.

Cattaneo also makes implicit references to the Charrúas' laziness and unwillingness to exploit the land. In his portrayal of the Charrúa, only the women work, keeping the homes functional and organizing the group's frequent moves (ibid.: 305). This plus their nomadism—which, Cattaneo says, the Charrúas share with the "Guanoas" on the eastern shore of the Uruguay River—made the missionaries' job very difficult: "They do not have a fixed domicile. Instead, they wander here or there. The Guanoas from the other shore do the same. This has always been an obstacle for their conversion, because if they do not stay in one place for very long—if they stay today in one place and tomorrow in another—, it is difficult to administer the sacraments to them" (ibid.). And in the priest's eyes, the failure of his Jesuit brothers' efforts is proof of the Amerindians' rebellious nature. He writes: "The fathers have worked very hard for a long time in order to convert them, but until now that has been impossible to achieve" (ibid.). Those efforts included the creation of *reducciones* not only for the Charrúa, but also for the Yaro and Guenoa (the San Andrés and Jesús y María missions, respectively). Yet one day, the Amerindians confined to the Jesús y María mission disappear, leaving the mission completely deserted (ibid.: 306). Although the tone of Cattaneo's letter reflects sadness, one can also read annoyance and frustration between the lines. Whatever his feelings, Cattaneo's letters seem to point toward the Jesuits' having abandoned the difficult task of "civilizing" the region's most indomitable ethnic groups: "To return to the Yaro and Charrúa, let us say that [we] have not found a good remedy for them yet" (ibid.). Of course, in compensation, the results of the Jesuits' evangelizing in the lands populated by the Guaraní were very different.

The construction of the Amerindian Other by assimilating him or her to repressed or displaced European groups—a discursive strategy seen earlier—

can also be found in Cattaneo's accounts. In his case, Cattaneo compares the Amerindians to the Old World heretics:

> The present freedom of movement they [the Indians] enjoy in the Spanish cities—as a consequence of the peace treaties—has the same effect as the one produced in Europe by the heretics, who, practicing [religion together] with the Catholics, stop seeing as many good people and as many good things as they could. And they do not only observe some defects—which are, after all, inevitable in a multitude—: they use them [those observed defects] as an argument to support their own errors. (Ibid.: 306–7)

This passage makes clear that the correct worldview, in Cattaneo's opinion, is the one proposed by Roman Catholicism. One can also deduce that despite their contact with the Spanish in times of peace, the Charrúa and the Yaro did not adapt to a way of life based on European social rules. In other words, what bothers Cattaneo is that the Amerindians have not reached a high degree of acculturation. This allows one to conjecture that indigenous groups existed who held an axiology in which European culture was not considered superior to their own; otherwise, they would have adopted the social codes and rules prescribed by Occidental culture. Had such an indigenous axiology not existed, the Amerindians would have been less hostile to the Spanish, and they would have incorporated themselves into the region's Spanish or Portuguese populations.

To complete Cattaneo's representation of the Amerindians, let us turn our attention to a passage in which he describes a *cacique* (he is not clear about the ethnic affiliation of the chief, who may have been Charrúa, Yaro, or Guenoa):

> The main cacique's name was Don Simone and he looked like a very ridiculous caricature, because he wore a kind of blanket in the form of a raincoat made of several pieces—among which there were some old furs painted like golden leather—, which he may have found in a secondhand store in a Spanish city. He carried a little black cane with a tin handle on top, and he handled it with great gravity as if it were a scepter—which matched, indeed, his blanket and his hair, as disheveled as the others'." (Ibid.: 307–8)

This fragment provides the one piece that had been missing from Cattaneo's portrait: contempt for, or mockery of, the Amerindians. Of course, the *cacique*'s attempt to imitate power symbols characteristic of Occidental aristocracy may truly have appeared ridiculous. Yet, Cattaneo misses the chance to consider the situation from a different angle, which would allow him to read it under a different light. As a member of both the Jesuit community and the European episteme, he is unable to see the indigenous *cacique*'s translation of European symbolic and behavioral patterns as a metaphor for the enterprise in which he is taking part—that is, the attempt to impose European cultural patterns on indigenous cultures. Cattaneo is so immersed in his own culture's ideological framework that he cannot question it. In other words, he cannot see the epistemic violence exerted by his culture on the region's indigenous groups. The effect of that epistemic violence is illustrated very well by the "ridiculous" behavior of the *cacique* Don Simón.

A few years after Cattaneo traveled to the River Plate region, a number of French travelers arrived in Montevideo and recorded written impressions of the lands they visited. Some of them were members of the expeditions commanded by Bougainville in 1763 and 1767. The 1763 expedition had as its objective the colonization of the *Islas Malvinas,* or Falkland Islands; the second sought the return of the Malvinas to the Spanish and to circumnavigate the globe. Bougainville, a naturalist and philosopher who was known as the "*enfant cheri*" ("beloved child") of encyclopedists such as Diderot, was also a man of action—a sailor, a soldier, and a diplomat—with economic, military, and political objectives, according to Louis Constant (1980: i). Bougainville's voyage of circumnavigation was the first in a series of eighteenth-century European attempts to map the world—that is, a series of European scientific efforts that aimed to acquire knowledge about distant lands and determine what was there to be economically exploited and how this exploitation could be carried out. These voyages (which also include the expeditions led by La Condamine and Malaspina) were part of the new European "planetary consciousness" that Pratt discusses. In that context, "scientific exploration was to become a focus of intense public interest, and a source of some of the most powerful ideational and ideological apparatuses through which European citizenries related themselves to other parts of the world" (Pratt 1992: 23). Travel and scientific (for example, natural history) writing were among those apparatuses.

Abbot Antoine Joseph Pernety, a Benedictine priest, traveled with Bougainville's 1763 expedition as a natural-sciences aficionado. His book contains a detailed description of the trip and of the places that the ships visited; it also includes his comments about other voyages to the Strait of Magellan. Pernety provides an extensive description of Montevideo and an account of what happened to the expeditionaries in that city. His impressions of Montevideo are of particular interest in this investigation, because, unlike Cattaneo's impressions, Pernety's are firsthand and extensive. Several *relaciones* from Bougainville's second expedition survive, and I will use them to supplement Pernety's impressions of the area's Amerindians. My focus will be on Pernety's account, however, because it is exhaustive. I will use the accounts produced by the crew of the second expedition (the one that sought to circumnavigate the world) only to supplement the abbot's impressions about the Amerindians of the area.

At the beginning of his tenth chapter, Pernety writes: "Montevideo is, in a sense, *a new colony.* It is not even twenty-five years old and it does not have more than a few houses. *It is, however, the only site that offers an easy haven for anchoring ships in the River Plate.* Today it is a little village that grows prettier as time goes by. The streets are drawn by cord and are very wide so that three carriages are able to pass" (1769: 270; emphasis added). Two characteristics attract the Frenchman's attention: the city's youth and the virtues of its harbor, which is the best in the region. This also marks a turning point in the history of travelers' representations of the region. When Ottsen and Toller sailed along the coasts of the lands north of the River Plate, they did not find any European settlements there. For this reason, their impressions were limited, mainly, to descriptions of the geography (in the case of Ottsen) and the fauna (in the case of Toller). The only testimony of those travelers about the human beings who inhabited the area are occasional, brief, and very vague references to the Amerindians in the text by the Dutch sailor. Cattaneo, for his part, records not only his impressions of the territory and its fauna but also his views on the diverse indigenous groups of the region. The Italian Jesuit could not talk about Spanish settlements, however, because of their incipient nature and scarce number. Now, with Pernety's account, European villages begin to appear in the accounts of Occidental travelers. The "lands of Uruguay" are no longer the wasted, deserted lands described by previous chroniclers; these lands now include Montevideo, which has changed from being just a geographical reference point into the best harbor in the region. Yet the urban setting is still precarious, according to Pernety: The houses are only one story high (except for one belonging to the engeneer who designed the main square) (ibid.: 270). To enlighten readers about the interior of the houses (which he calls bourgeois houses), Pernety describes the one owned by the governor at the time of his visit. "Its entire decoration consists of three bad paintings and a few big, half-painted, half-colored blueprints, which were even worse than the paintings. The seats for the men occupied the two other sides of the room. These are chairs made of wood, with very high backs, in the form of our chairs from the time of Henry IV" (ibid.: 272). The poverty and modesty of the governor's home helps the reader surmise the kind of houses in which the subalterns lived. Later in the text, Pernety continues his description of the modest house.[14]

Pernety also describes physical features of the city and surrounding areas: "The land that surrounds Montevideo is an extensive plain. The soil is black and strong and produces abundantly even with the lightest cultivation. *The only thing the land is missing, in order to become one of the best countries in the world, is farmers.* The air is healthy, the sky is beautiful and the heat is not excessive. There is still a scarcity of wood, which can be found only along the shores" (ibid.: 275). Once again, fertility is one of the elements of the construct "territory" as produced by the European observer. Fecundity, healthy air, a beautiful sky, and a temperate climate make the land a serious candidate for recognition as the Elysian Fields of the modern era, as Pereira de Sá would have it. Yet it is not "one of the best countries in the world," according to Pernety, because it lacks farmers to exploit the soil's fertility and make the land produce up to its natural potential. As in many other testimonies by European observers, this portrait of a wealthy land goes hand in hand with a reproachful attitude—or, better yet, the praise is accompanied by amazement and frustration over the underexploitation, or entropic waste, of the land's economic and productive potential.[15] For Pernety, this underexploitation is due less to the lack of dwellers than to the idleness of the people who already live there. He informs us about this character flaw among the Montevideans in 1763: "The Spaniards from Montevideo are very lazy. They do nothing but talk in groups, drink *mate,* and smoke cigars" (ibid.: 273). It is interesting that the custom of drinking *mate* all day existed this early in the city's life; the same can be said about the Montevideans' penchant for conversation. The cigars are a more complicated issue: Pernety includes a footnote explaining what cigars are and how they should be smoked, so one can surmise that he (and probably a good portion of his European readership) was unfamiliar with that kind of object. The three social activities that Pernety sees in Montevideo complete a picture of a *dolce far niente* of sorts that seemed to be the rule in the Montevideo of 1763.[16] The picture of that way of life is completed by a reference to the Spaniards' traditional siesta, which he blames for the high cost of the labor force: "This good part of the working day is lost. This is the cause both for the little work they do and the high cost of the labor force" (ibid.: 284). Finally, Pernety writes:

> The Spaniards' way of life is very simple. The men who do not work in the trading business wake up very late—and so do the women. They stay at home with their arms crossed until they feel like going out to smoke a cigar with their neighbors. They can often be found in groups of four or five, at the door of a house, smoking and talking. Others jump on a horse and take a ride—not on the plains, but in the streets. If they feel like it, they step down from the horse, join the people they encounter, talk for a couple of hours without saying anything, smoke, drink *mate,* and return to their horses. *It is very rare that a Spaniard promenades on foot—in the streets it is possible to see as many horses as men.* (Ibid.: 282; emphasis added)

Besides Pernety's gift for description, what strikes me in this passage is his obsessive reference to the relationship between the Montevideans and their horses. This description is important because it is the first to represent the inhabitant of Montevideo as a centaur—an image that will enjoy currency in the future. This text shows a somewhat ethnocentric attitude in that it censures and ironizes customs that are alien to the author's cultural background—in this case, the habit of riding horses all the time, which does not cease to amaze the members of the Bougainville's second expedition. A young "volunteer" aboard one of the ships on the circumnavigation voyage also left testimony of his astonishment—and annoyance—over the equestrian and smoking habits of the Montevideans:

> *People are extremely lazy.* For them, every day is a holiday. They can be seen, very bored—with themselves, I believe—, at their front doors, with a cigar in their mouths. They can also be seen promenading on a horse, to and fro. *They are not able to do anything without being mounted on a horse*—they must ride their horses—all of which are saddled and reined, ready to receive their horsemen—to get firewood or any other thing at the house next door. This is not a story [that is, it is true]. (Duviols 1975: 12; emphasis added)[17]

Despite such resentments, Pernety is able to advance a reasonable hypothesis that could explain the causes of the locals' indolence: "It is not surprising that they [the Montevideans] are so indolent: food does not cost them but the time they spend in the killing, the flaying, and the cutting of the bull for its preparation [as food]" (1769: 284). Abundance, then, may be causing the Montevideans' idleness. This explanation would become very popular—even in the twentieth century, as Father Furlong's testimony suggests: "The[ir] easy, untroubled subsistence, the abundance [of cattle], was a disgrace because it gave way to laziness, lack of planning, and no sense of responsibility" (1969: 471). Members of the second expedition also emphasize the abundance of cattle in their testimony. The young volunteer, Fesche, declares: "I am going to talk about the oxen. These animals here are bigger than the strongest ones in France. *Their number is infinite.* An individual is not considered a rich man if he does not own at least thirty or forty thousand head" (Duviols 1975; emphasis added). In another passage in his diary, Fesche expresses his annoyance over the waste of cattle wealth in Montevideo, a complaint that is similar to Pernety's regarding the waste of agricultural wealth: "They do not get [from the entire cow or bull] but the leather and the tongues, which they leave to dry under the sun" (ibid.: 14). A similar assessment can be found in the diary of François Vivez, a surgeon aboard one of the expedition's ships and one of Fesche's companions: "Every year, they kill many cows in order to stop their high reproduction rate. They only take, in order to commercialize them, the cows' leather and tongue. One of the inhabitants [of Montevideo] killed an ox only to get the sirloin and left the rest in the street" (in Taillemite 1977: 196). These representations of the lands on the northern shore of the River Plate resemble a version of the Elysian Fields, but one that is overpopulated with cattle and inhabited by lazy men who do not know how to exploit them.

Another aspect of Pernety's text is that he pays more attention to women than do the other texts we have seen so far, perhaps because the number of women in the region had grown by 1763, or because they played a more central role in Pernety's interpretive community than in the Spanish one. Whatever the explanation, his references to this previously almost absent Other deserve analysis. What strikes the reader immediately is the imaginary scheme of binary oppositions that Pernety proposes: He speaks of men first and of women later. From this perspective, gender appears as an element that organizes the social world. Thus, alongside the first description of the customs of the "Spaniards of Montevideo," one finds its correlate—the customs practiced by women: "The women's height and shape are very pleasant, but it could not be said that their skin has the color of lilies or roses: their faces are dark. It is common for them to have missing teeth—and their teeth are not white" (1769: 276).

This description shows Pernety writing from a rather ethnocentric perspective: In his interpretive community, white or pink skin and a perfect shape are the standards of beauty against which real flesh-and-bone women should be judged. Missing teeth are not, of course, a sign of beauty for the European observer. Fesche, a member of the same interpretive community as Pernety (although he was not a religious man), praises the women he sees in Montevideo: "*Touts leurs femmes son très jolies, fort aimables et extrêmement polies*" ("All their women are very pretty, very friendly, and extremely educated" [in Duviols 1975: 12]). And Philibert Commerson, another expedition member, compares the women of Montevideo favorably to those he saw in Buenos Aires: "*En général, les femmes de Montevideo ont plus des mœurs qu'à Buenos-Ayres, vrai séjour de la galanterie*" ("In general, the women from Montevideo have better manners than the ones from Buenos Aires—[which is the] true home of gallantry" [in Taillemite 1977: 449]). In these cases, these positive portrayals of local women do not depend on the coincidence of their beauty with the European model, whereas Pernety compares the women to a standard (or reference framework) brought from Europe. He does, however, leave some room in his descriptions for the acknowledgment of difference.

The same strategy of using comparison to record difference can be found in Pernety's accounts of women's clothing and their social behavior: "The women [in Montevideo] have at least as much freedom as the women in France.

They gracefully receive visitors and are willing to sing, to dance, and to play the harp, the guitar or the mandolin [in public] without much ado. They are much more complacent than our women in France" (ibid.: 277–78). This portrait also includes a description of the local dances the "Sapateo" and the "Calenda." In general, the role of women in dances—except for the aforementioned ones—is the following: "The way the ladies dance matches the indolence with which they spend their days, although they are naturally very lively. In the majority of their dances, they let their arms hang or keep them under their mantillas—which they call rebos" (ibid.: 278). Two of the local dances are livelier, he notes. While dancing the Sapateo, the women must raise and clap their hands, as in the French Rigodón (ibid.). But it is another dance that really calls Pernety's attention: "A very lively and lascivious dance is sometimes danced in Montevideo. It is called Calenda, and the blacks as well as the mulattoes—whose character is ardent—love it with passion" (ibid.: 279).[18]

In this fragment, another displaced Other makes an appearance: the African. Rarely mentioned in the texts studied so far, the black—and the mulatto—is represented in some detail by Pernety, who paints a picture of a vital and lascivious being. Moreover, the African is made responsible for introducing distorting factors—that is, some of the lascivious dances—into Montevideo's social life:

> *This dance has been brought to America* from the kingdom of Adra—on the coast of Guinea—*by the blacks.* The Spaniards dance it like them [the blacks], without the slightest scruple, in all of their settlements in America. Its indecency is such that it amazes those who have never seen it. Its popularity is so great and enthusiastic that the children dance it from the time they reach the age they are able to stand on their feet. (Ibid.; emphasis added)

That evil dance, brought by the wanton Africans, was so embedded in Montevideo's culture that children danced it from a very early age. From a European perspective, this situation could not but provoke amazement and rejection from the observer; Pernety's "civilized" sensibility could not tolerate cultural manifestations such as the Calenda. According to Barrán, this civilized sensibility (*"la sensibilidad civilizada"*) is none other than the one imposed on American societies by the European bourgeoisie. In Barrán's scheme, however, the civilized model proposed by the Europeans and transplanted to the lands of Uruguay was not adopted immediately by the incipient society—that behavioral model became predominant only in the second half of the nineteenth century (1991 [1990], vol. 2).[19] It should not be surprising, then, that Pernety shows a society that is not yet dominated by the civilized, European sensibility. Unruliness and freedom of the body, the free expression and practice of sexual appetites, and their sublimation through public rituals (such as the Calenda) are manifestations of a sensibility that Pernetty could not but condemn. The carnivalesque side of the dance allows one to consider it a manifestation of the civilized sensibility's opposite—that is, what Barrán calls the "barbaric" sensibility. (For a description of its distinctive traits, see vol. 1 of his book.) The dancers' rubbing their bellies and kissing each other in public violates all of the rules of educated, or "civilized," behavior, which require the repression of such instincts and drives.[20] The abbot's outrage over the public dance points up his situation of enunciation (European, civilized, Christian, etc.), as can be seen in the following fragment: "Let the reader imagine *how shocking such a lecherous dance might be to our French education*" ("*On peut juger* combien notre éducation françoise seroit étonnée *d'une danse aussi lubrique*" [Pernety 1769: 280; emphasis added]).

Pernety's outrage reaches its highest peak when he describes the conduct of the local priests vis-à-vis the Calenda: "They dance it in church and in their religious processions. The priests themselves dance it on Christmas night in a theater over the choir, facing the grille—which they leave open in order to show the spectacle to the people. This sacred Calenda differs from the profane one only in that the men do not dance with the priests" (ibid.: 280–81). For Pernety, it is inconceivable that the church, a place from which civilization and discipline should be promoted, could become a haven for the most objectionable social practices; such disorder and indiscipline are the consequence of a "barbaric" culture. This qualification implies a value judgment, of course—that is, if "barbaric" culture promotes chaos and unruliness, it must be inferior to a "civilized" one such as French society.

We have yet to examine Pernety's treatment of the Amerindian—the Other par excellence—as referent, which has been the main focus of this investigation. The Amerindian does not appear often in the abbot's text. In fact, the proliferation of human groups brought about by the development of European settlements on the northern shore of the River Plate has displaced the Amerindian as an object of representation. By 1763, the Others have multiplied; instead of Amerindians, the travelers' gaze sees *Criollos* (Spaniards from Montevideo), Africans, and women. Amerindians are seen by the European travelers only when the Amerindians visit the Spanish settlements. In Pernety's description, the Amerindians appear as dirty and smelly: "They exhale an odor that sticks to the walls. This odor comes from an infected oil they apply to their bodies to repel the insects" (ibid.: 295). This statement fits Barrán's scheme, in which strong odors appear as traits typical of a barbaric sensibility, whereas the repression or elimination of such odors is undertaken by the civilized sensibility (1991 [1989], vol. 1). Pernety's views on the Amerindian partly coincide with the picture offered by Bougainville, the commander of the expeditions:

> The Natives who inhabit this part of America—north and south of the River Plate—are still free of the dominion of the Spaniards and are called Indios Bravos [wild, or brave, Indians]. They are medium-size and *very ugly. Almost all of them are mangy.* Their color is very bronzelike and with the lard they apply to themselves constantly, they look even darker. They do not have clothing other than a big blanket made of deerskin which covers them to their heels—in which they wrap themselves. (1980: 35; emphasis added)

Bougainville's representation of the region's Amerindians does not add new information (except, perhaps, his reference to mange) to the descriptions that we have already examined. What it does is remind us that the construct "Indian" has not changed much, even though two-and-a-half centuries have passed since the "discovery." Thus, it is not surprising that one finds the same kind of representation of the Amerindians in other texts by the expedition's members. They present the Amerindians as thieves and as cruel, savage, and irreducible to civilization ("Journaux de Philibert Commerson," in Taillemite 1977: 448). Although Charles-Othon de Nassau-Siegen, another member of the second expedition, also cites some of these traits in his account, his description of the Minuan draws a more complete picture than those produced by his companions. While Bougainville visited Buenos Aires, Nassau-Siegen was sent to survey the interior of the country. Thus, he describes what he sees not in Montevideo but in Maldonado, which is east of the territory and near the Atlantic Ocean:

> They live an errant life around the woods and rivers. . . . These Indians are of the color of bronze, marked with more or less pronounced stains. They seem to be very sensitive to the death of their relatives, in which case they rip their bodies with the use of arrows. Women mourn their dead husbands by cutting off a phalanx of their fingers. . . . Still without a cult of established religion, they can be seen, in the great occasions, martyrizing their bodies with arrows until they see an ostrich coming—which, according to their dogma, announces God's will. The Minuan do not cultivate the land and they feed themselves with ox, ostrich, and roe deer. They hunt the latter very skilfully, mounted bareback on their horses. *This nation is very lazy by nature. The elderly recommend that their children not become Christians so that they are not forced to work.* ("Journal de Charles-Othon de Nassau-Siegen, passager sur la Boudeuse," in Taillemite 1977: 386; emphasis added)

Almost all of the elements Nassau-Siegen uses to represent the Minuan coincide with those used by Barco Centenera, Lozano, and Azara to portray the

Charrúa. (Azara also used these traits to describe the Minuan.) Thus, Nassau-Siegen's text looks like a synthesis of the earlier authors' descriptions, although it is very unlikely that he has read those accounts, because he presents the Amerindians as bronzelike, nomadic hunters who practice funerary rites of mutilation; they are also presented as lazy, incapable of cultivating the land, and very irreligious. About the last issue, it is interesting that Nassau-Siegen attributes the Amerindians' lack of religious inclinations to their innate idleness, as represented by the episode in which the elders recommend that their children not convert to Catholicism. A new element in his description is the ostrich superstition, which has not appeared in the texts studied thus far.

Let us return to Pernety's representation of the Amerindians. Although he does not distinguish among ethnic groups, Pernety does refer to the Amerindians' ignorance of the Spanish language (1769: 384) and to their many visits to the city to trade wild-animal furs for wine and liquor ("*aguardiente*") (ibid.: 385). He also mentions a few indigenous social customs—among them, hunting techniques (ibid.: 388–91). These descriptions do not add much to what we have already learned about the Amerindians, partly because Pernety's information about indigenous practices is secondhand, and partly because he does not tell us to which ethnic group he is referring.

In sum, the representation of the local Amerindians in the texts by these French visitors does not mark a significant change in the history of the construction of the referent "Indians." On the contrary, these texts are more interested in depicting the economies, societies, and customs of the European settlements. Further, the proliferation of new Others (at least in the context of the corpus of European texts about the region) diverts the attention of the French observers away from the Amerindians. From this moment on, the aborigines not only lose their voice (which they never had, in any case); they also lose the attention that they once received from European observers.

As noted earlier, these texts were produced by travelers from European countries that were not involved in colonizing the River Plate region. Thus, one could say that their gaze is even more alien (if foreignness can be measured) than that of the Portuguese and the Spanish, who were, after all, active parties in determining the region's present and future. As observers with little commitment to these lands, these foreign travelers were able to take a more distanced view of the region (perhaps because they did not have to make plans to improve the social organization, or defend the territory, of the colonies), and their situation of enunciation—compared with, say, that of Diego García or Ferreira da Silva—can be measured according to the degree of their commitment to the referents they produced.

Another group with a different situation of enunciation comprises subjects of the Spanish crown who for many reasons had to live on American lands without settling there. Although it is reasonable to assume that their texts about America were imbued with a patriotic interest, it would be an exaggeration to attribute to them a devotion and commitment similar to that seen in the texts by the conquistadors and by the public officials who lived in America. Some of the authors discussed in the rest of this chapter were travelers; others were on official missions that forced them to live temporarily in the River Plate region. But regardless of their origin or business, all of them present the region as a wasted, unexploited promised land. They also suggest measures that can be taken to change this situation.

Once again, the tremendous fertility of the lands on the northern shore of the River Plate is the first thing to call the visitors' attention. Andrés de Oyárvide, a member of a party whose mission was to demarcate the boundaries of the Spanish possessions between 1783 and 1801, emphasizes the fecundity of the soil: "The quality of the terrain is beautiful, fertile, and abundant, missing only cultivation in order to produce rich results" (1865: 49). His opinion coincides with that of José María Cabrer, another demarcator: "The weather is peaceful and temperate, and the country is very healthy—no diseases are known there. Its terrain, substantial and well watered by diverse big brooks which are full all year, is very adequate for agricultural production" (1882: 157). Cabrer also writes: "The situation is the best—as if engineered by design—in such an extended countryside; the quality of the terrain is the most substantial, fertile, and pleasant" (ibid.: 138). Yet another demarcator, Fernando Borrero, expresses this opinion (1911: 802). And Cipriano Melo, who did not belong to the demarcation party, offers a similar view in a report addressed to the king. In his report, esthetic evaluations again predominate—reminding one of the Renaissance topic of the *locus amoenus:*

> The fields north of this river cannot be described adequately by the most lively imagination. *A wonderful extension of very pleasant valleys,* interrupted by pleasant elevations from which water falls, forming innumerable brooks, lakes, and great rivers that run in all directions, covered by strong and aromatic pastures as well as medicinal herbs and flowers which call for agricultural exploitation and cattle ranching. At the beginning of this century, they [these fields] were inhabited only by the Indians and the beasts, because domestic cattle did not exist in the Indies. (1865: 276–77; emphasis added)

An anonymous memoir about the "question of the countryside" ("*arreglo de los campos*") in the Banda Oriental, dated 1794, says: "More than once I have heard serious men, tired of traveling all around Europe, say that *only paradise on earth would surpass in beauty and fecundity the meridional part of our America*" (in Brito Stífano 1953: 345–46; emphasis added). In other passages of this text, reference is made to the immeasurable fertility ("*imponderable feracidad*") of the terrain and the fecundity of "our" cattle ("*fecundidad de nuestro ganado*") (ibid.: 342). And according to an earlier account (1749) by the Franciscan friar Pedro José de Parras: "The fields of this city [Montevideo] are very good and they abound in bovine cattle. A few days before our arrival in that harbor, the priest and vicar of that city had sold twelve thousand cows for two *reales*" (1992: 7). The most frequent observations by the members of the demarcation party, in fact, relate to the extraordinary abundance of livestock in the region: The European observers had never seen such overpopulation, and perhaps for this reason they tended toward exaggeration, as in the passage by Cabrer: "This entire peninsula is populated by a multitude of *estancias* [cattle ranches] in which innumerable cows, horses, sheep, and mules are raised. There are *estancias* that own from 20,000 to 40,000 head of cattle; some even own as many as 80,000 or 100,000." ("*Toda esta península está poblada de multitud de estancias en que se crian un sin número de animales vacunos, lanar, mular y caballar. Hay estancia que tiene 20.000, 30.000 y 40.000 cabezas de ganado, y aun las hay de 80.000 y hasta de 100.000*" [1882: 141]). Compare this with the testimony of Francisco Aguirre, another demarcator, dated 1783: "I marvel when I witness the ease and abundance with which these fields are managed, because I believe there are no others—and perhaps there will never be—in such a situation in the world" (in Groussac 1905: 151).

Precisely because they come from an overpopulated continent (compared with America) with food-production problems, these visitors appreciate the land's enormous potential value for exploiting cattle. Thus, in a discursive register that mixes envy with outrage, they continually lament the waste of the region's riches—riches that are

> not only capable of making their inhabitants happy, but also of *sharing their abundance with the peoples of the other hemisphere.* For the time being, it is notorious that what is exploited of the country's produce is some cows' leather. I say "some" because the quantity is very small in comparison to what is killed and lost—without including the females, because with respect to these, the waste is total. (Oyárvide 1865: 50; emphasis added)

In another passage, Oyárvide offers a detailed description of how the locals waste the meat, because they already know that everyone will kill daily his or her own cow ("*ya se sabe que cada persona ha de matar diariamente la suya*" [ibid.: 351]). An indignation similar to Oyárvide's is apparent in the Frenchman Fesche's testimony and in the anonymous *décimas* examined earlier. Aguirre also tells about irrational exploitation of cattle in the region (in

Groussac 1905: 144). In Oyárvide's opinion, Europe needs the productive surplus of the lands of Uruguay, and this worries him. His gaze appears, then, not as that of the colonizer who tries to improve the productive conditions and standard of living of his or her colony, but as the greedy gaze of an imperial subject who is trying to figure out how to appropriate America's wealth. Consequently, he proposes a method for doing so:

> If all that variety of abundant produce and primitive wealth—which they have in excess in this country—could be exported to those who, if they do not lack all of them at least have need of some of them, what kind of comfort would not come in return to the farmers, among whom it is not rare to see, nowadays, their children—of both sexes—dressed almost like savages? (1865: 50)

If I am not mistaken, the expression "primitive wealth" ("*primitivas riquezas*") can also be translated as "raw materials" ("*materias primas*"). With regard to "comfort" ("*comodidades*"), one can surmise that it would be generated not only by the benefits of commercial exchange, but also—and mainly—by the arrival of European manufactured commodities. Thanks to this reading—which is simply a translation of Oyárvide's words—we realize that the trade the Spaniard is proposing is simply the classic model of colonial exploitation—embellished slightly by the writer's alleged good intentions—which involves extracting raw materials from the colonies in order to return them in the form of manufactured goods. This characterization establishes with precision the situation of enunciation from which Oyárvide produces his discourse: imperial Europe's episteme. His goal is simply to increase the profit margin in an unequal commercial exchange.

In addition to pointing out the land's fertility and abundance of cattle, the Spaniards who lived temporarily in the lands of Uruguay recorded their impressions of the region's social and cultural life. The judgments of the Spaniards and of the foreign visitors examined earlier coincide almost completely, especially when they refer to the existence of a barbaric culture that is unacceptable according to their European standards. Azara's description of the state of affairs in the countryside provides a good example. Throughout his texts, Azara presents a rural situation in which disorder, chaos, and the indiscriminate slaughter of cattle, together with a lack of churches to provide spiritual nourishment—and discipline, I would add—for the peoples of the region, results in a situation that the European observer does not hesitate to qualify as barbarism. One sees this perspective clearly when Azara writes about the inhabitants of the rural areas: "With regard to their clothes—or better said, their nudity—and with regard to their furniture and comfort, they are not much more advanced than the infidel Indians. Their disgusting houses are always surrounded by piles of bones and rotten meat, because they waste four times the meat they consume" (1943: 5). Comparing the inhabitants of the rural areas to the infidel Indians is the worst accusation of barbarism that a European subject can utter.

The "civilized" sensibility also sees other areas of social life in which symptoms of barbarism predominate, including not only chaos, disorder, waste, and licentiousness, but also idleness. Its opposite, work, is one of the gods—as Barrán would have it—of burgeois sensibility. Indolence and sloth, then, are attitudes as negative as the indiscriminate killing of cattle, in the European observer's eyes. This is so because, according to the "civilized" Europeans, idleness promotes depraved and lascivious behavior. As Cabrer writes: "All the neighbors have their own piece of land, which they cultivate with idleness. In those countries, indolence and laziness reigns, and that is the cause of their corrupted customs—they love to play cards and indulge in other vices" (1882: 140).[21] In the European and Christian world, work is the antidote to that kind of conduct: "The priests should incessantly denounce those pestiferous vices, as well as attempt to persuade [their congregations] that work is a virtue that makes men happy" (Azara 1943: 5). Thus, one of Azara's suggestions for improving the state of affairs in the countryside is to establish parishes to prevent the moral corruption of the population (ibid.: 6). Another suggestion he makes is also common among the demarcators: promoting the founding of towns to establish centers of civilization that can reduce the unruliness of rural social life (see, for example, Oyárvide [1865: 351–52] and Aguirre [in Groussac 1905: 152]).[22] All of these strategies, as the reader may already have surmised, are framed by the domination enterprise conceived in Europe, and of which the emerging bourgeoisie is the principal agent. The coincidences in diagnosing the situation of rural areas and the solutions proposed in the demarcators' texts show a view and a discourse that results in the production of a rather homogeneous referent, as we will see later.

Let us turn now to another Spanish author: Concolorcorvo, or Alonso Carrió de la Vandera, second commissioner for the improvement of postal services between Montevideo–Buenos Aires and Lima.[23] In November 1771, Concolorcorvo departed for the River Plate region to fulfill his duty. His book, *El lazarillo de ciegos caminantes,* is a travel account of his return to Lima. To supplement his impressions, I will examine this text alongside José de Espinosa y Tello's "Estudio sobre las costumbres y descripciones interesantes de la América del Sur" (1938). Espinosa y Tello, a member of the scientific expedition led by the sage Alessandro Malaspina (1789–94), recorded his views on the Banda Oriental and its inhabitants (1938: 276–342).[24]

Concolorcorvo's perspective is undoubtedly Spanish, although his situation of enunciation is slightly different from that of the demarcators analyzed earlier. Although Concolorcorvo lived in America and was a public official, his position caused him to deal in services, not commodities. In other words, he was a bureaucrat. More concretely, his job itself was part of a strategy through which the literate city tried to impose order on the vastness of the American territory—especially on the rural areas.[25]

About Montevideo, Concolorcorvo wrote: "barbaric word, or at least corrupted from the Castilian *Monteveo,* or Portuguese *Monteveio* or the Latin *Montemvideo*" (1985: 20). His attitude toward the city's name already attests to his positioning as a subject of discourse. According to his implicit narrative, an original name existed in a romance language or in Latin, and it was corrupted by a barbaric—or barbarizing—linguistic agent. The derogatory tone of his comments can also be seen in his description of the fortress: "It [Montevideo] has a fortress that serves as a citadel, but it is so poorly built that it threatens to fall apart" (ibid.: 20). The general feeling his discourse transmits is that we are looking at a poor, barbaric, and disorganized city. He also cites Montevideo's low population and lack of census-taking and registration (ibid.)—elements that contribute to his portrayal of the city and its social life under a grim light.[26] Yet his most negative observation concerns an element that is found not within the citadel's walls but outside, in the surrounding areas: "lazy *Criollos*, who with great precision are called *gauderios* [gauchos]" ("*holgazanes criollos, a quienes con grandísima propiedad llaman gauderios*" [ibid.]). Here is his description of these people in its entirety:

> These are young men born in Montevideo and surrounding areas. *They try to hide their bad shirts and worse dresses with one or two ponchos,* which they make with the skin of horses. They use the saddle as a pillow. *They get hold of a little guitar, which they learn how to play very badly, and they sing out of tune various "coplas" which they ruin* and many more that they compose—which regularly talk about love. They promenade freely throughout the countryside and, with notable complacence from *the semibarbaric colonists,* eat at the latter's cost and *spend entire weeks lying on a piece of leather, singing and playing.* If they lose their horse or if it is stolen, they take—or somebody gives them—another one from the countryside. (Ibid.: 22; emphasis added)

The first thing one notices in this passage is Concolorcorvo's description of the gauchos' poor appearance: In his opinion, their habits and style of dress do not reach the civilizational standards of European culture. In other words, clothing serves to signal the gaucho as an Other.[27] Their musical skills also transgress Occidental standards of beauty. Concolorcorvo does not portray the colonists who own the lands through which the gauchos perambulate under a favorable light, either: He sees them as semibarbaric because they do not enforce the laws of private property—foundation of European economic life—strongly enough. But the worst thing he sees is the gauchos' vagrancy and lack of productivity, which are an unforgivable sacrilege against the new capitalist god, labor. This rounds off a highly negative construction of the referent "rural-area dweller" from a European perspective. This is not surprising, however, because we have already seen Ayestarán's description of how European subjects created the referent "gaucho" during the eighteenth century: In that century's corpus of discourses, the gaucho is portrayed as a lazy, nomadic, riding, and brawling subject (1950: 7–8). And Josefina Ludmer (1988) analyzes the negative connotations of the word *gaucho* up to the appearance of *gauchesca* poetry, at which time the referent evolves into the "patriotic gaucho" (*"gaucho patriota"*). Until then, however, the gaucho is presented as a "wanderer without property and without a job or a known domicile; this is the known equation the dispossessed [equals] the criminal (Ludmer 1899: 16 and *passim*).[28]

The final touch in Concolorcorvo's portrayal is his reference to the gauchos' scarce or absent notion of private property, which the author infers from their attitudes toward horses—that is, when they lose their horses, they take another one from the countryside's vast plains. At this point, I should note that the character who is presenting this dismal description—Concolorcorvo—defines himself as a "pure Indian" (*"indio neto"*) from Cuzco (1985: 13). However, as Stolley points out after analyzing other fragments of the text in which Concolorcorvo talks about himself, the narrator's ethnic identity is not so clear: He could also be a *Mestizo* (Stolley 1992: 104–5). In any case, Carrió de la Vandera's strategy of putting this diatribe in the mouth of a member of an ethnic group regarded as inferior by Western subjects—be that group Indian or *Mestizo*——aims to make the gaucho look even less civilized than educated *Mestizos* or Amerindians to European readers.

Espinosa y Tello offers a more comprehensive description of the gauchos, which does not stop at enumerating their most irritating social practices (by "civilized" standards). His account also investigates the rural way of life. Not only their clothing but also how the riders spend their time draws his attention:

> *His [the gaucho's] monotonous life is limited to going out to the countryside, always mounted on a horse, and running from ranch to ranch,* without caring about his own sustenance—sure to find it in the first place he stops, as anybody receives candid hospitality without having to give thanks for it, because the ranches are always stocked with jerky—a kind of meat dried in the sun and cut in thin slices that can be barbecued in four minutes. (1938: 288; emphasis added)

Espinosa y Tello also records the relationship between the gaucho and his horse—that is, the gauchos' centaur-like condition as described earlier by the French travelers. Another familiar element in his text is the amazement of the European observer vis-à-vis the ease with which the gauchos take care of their basic needs in the countryside of the Banda Oriental. The friendliness Pernety saw in the inhabitants of Montevideo becomes a characteristic of the rural proprietors, who generously feed the errant gauchos. What makes this hospitality possible in the countryside, of course, is the extraordinary abundance of both equine and bovine livestock.[29] Espinosa y Tello writes:

> Many of these libertine *guasos* or *gauderios* abuse the hospitality that is so generously offered to them. All of them sleep together in the same house. The size of the small rooms does not allow for the separation required by decency and order. When everybody is asleep, some of the men crawl in silence and assault the beds of the women they desire—who suffer—if they do not agree to have sex—the outrage of their virtue, in order to avoid a scandal that would also embarrass them in public; yet, they defend themselves as best as confusion and violence allow them to. (Ibid.: 291)

That Espinosa y Tello notices ungratefulness and licentiousness among the gauchos tells us less about their way of life than about the European observer's worldview. First, Espinosa y Tello gives the reader an approximate idea about the prevailing of instinct over reason in rural society—a typical trait in barbaric culture, according to Barrán. He completes that picture when he says: "The simplicity of these people develops amid their passions and vices; the way in which they fall in love is very singular" (ibid.). Second, Espinosa y Tello emphasizes the civilized perspective from which he accounts for the situation, especially when he calls forth such disciplining notions as "order" and "decency" and when he mentions the outrage to women's virtue. All of these characterizations reveal the author's position as a member of a "civilized" interpretive community. This "civilized" perspective is pervasive among the texts under study in this chapter, as can be seen in that anonymous 1794 memoir (in Brito Stífano 1953: 360–62), which portrays the gauchos' excessive freedom, lack of religiosity, and skimpy clothing as deviations from a social ideal—or what Barrán calls "the disciplining of society" (*"el disciplinamiento"*). Thanks to the background against which it is compared—"civilization"—the referent "gaucho" does not differ much from the referent "Indian," constructed as a barbaric and uncivilized Other. Yet there is a major difference between the referents in Espinosa y Tello's text: He presents the gaucho as a speaking subject, whereas in the European representations we have examined so far, the aborigine has remained a silent creature. Espinosa y Tello narrates with amazement—and even with a little irony, which is typical of "civilized" observers—the gauchos' communicating practices:

> They ride their horses to the door of the owner of the *estancia* [rural establishment] and stay there. The master says:
>
> "God protect you, fffriend"—pronouncing the words very slowly.
> "Sa-me for you."
> "Step down, if youuu wish."
> "It is not necessary."
> "Come on, do not be si-lly."
> "I will accept your hos-pi-ta-li-ty."
> "Leave the horse the-re, please."
> "De-o gratia"—and he comes in.
> "Gentle-man, sit the-re, please."
> "Do you happen to ha-ve a fi-re?"
> "Please, help your-self. It is right there.
>
> With these formulaic words, they sit and start eating on footstools shaped like shoe-repair seats—if they have any—or on cows' skulls. . . . If it is summer, they go to the shade behind the ranch and lie down there. If it is winter, they play or sing, out of tune, strange *seguidillas* [a kind of stanza] they call "chained *seguidillas,*" or they sing or play the *pericon* or *malambo* [two different dances], accompanying them with a small, out-of-tune guitar—which is always a soprano [or treble]. The talent of the singer is one of the best safe-conducts to get hospitality anywhere—that is, to get food and housing. (1938: 289)

This is one of the first texts to describe the gauchos' vocabulary and intonation. The suprasegmental elements of discourse in this text, which are so difficult to reproduce in writing, represent one of the strongest traces of the repressed Other. The logocentric play between absence and presence that dominates the relationships between literate and oral cultures (at least in the Americas) leaves an interstice in the text for the gaucho's (albeit filtered) voice to surface in the European subject's discourse. The textual elements that contribute to this are the dramatization of the dialogue (for example, the use of hyphens to indicate each speaker's elocution in the Spanish original, which signals direct speech) and the use of graphic devices to give an idea of the tone and speed of the original utterances. Still, Espinosa y Tello—the subject who makes room in the literate city for these oral performances—is too alien to the cultural framework of the gauchos' utterances. That is, he does not know anything about the social rules that determine oral performance in the rural areas of the territory. Only with the emergence of *gauchesca* poetry will the *Criollo* and European subject make an attempt to understand the voice of the gaucho in context. But even then, the Other's voice will be mediated by the Occidental subject.

When Espinosa reproduces the courtesy forms in a distanced and ironic way, he shows us his lack of awareness of the structural similarities between the gauchos' rules for courtesy and those of his own European culture. The scene depicted may have been a formulaic performance typical of the rural areas. Occidental etiquette was equally or more ritualized by then, however, and I doubt that Espinosa would have laughed at or criticized it. His cultural bias also shows in his description of the gauchos' leisure activities. His description of rural riders lying in the shade evokes that familiar representation of the gauchos as lazy centaurs. The understanding—or lack thereof—of such social practices seems to be shared by the Spaniards, *Criollo*s, and other European subjects. A similar contempt is evident in Espinosa y Tello's description of the gauchos' singing and playing; his description, in fact, reminds one of Concolorcorvo. Interestingly, the "out of tune, strange *seguidillas*" that Espinosa observes will, with the advent of nationalist *Criollo* discourse a few years later, become one of the region's most celebrated manifestations of patriotism. Take, for example, the case of the *pericón,* the national dance of Uruguay. Even today, schoolchildren are forced to perform the *pericón* (to their chagrin) during patriotic celebrations. Something similar can be said about the *malambo* in modern-day Argentina.

The gauchos' distinctive traits—the same ones denounced in the hegemonic discourse—are what allow us to infer approximately how these people lived. The chronological proximity of the gaucho culture's heyday and of the *gauchesca* literature that attempted to represent it contributes to such a modern-day imaginary reconstruction. This holds true despite the allowances one must make for the mediation of the educated Occidental writer when he (the authors of *gauchesca* literature were all male *Criollos*) reproduced the gauchos' language and worldview.

Let us return now to Concolorcorvo to examine his opinions of the abundance and prodigality he saw in Montevideo:

> They get together to eat part of a young cow or bull. They lasso it, bring it down, and, after tying its feet and hands, they take its coccyx, with its leather—while it is still alive—and make some cuts to the meat and barbecue it. They eat the meat almost raw, with only a little salt, if they happen to have any. *Sometimes they kill a young cow or bull only to eat its matahambre,* the meat between the ribs and the skin. *At other times, they kill an animal only to eat its tongue*—which they barbecue in the embers. (1985: 22; emphasis added)

Again, we face the outraged gaze of the European subject—this time a resident of American territories—as he views the uneconomical practices of the region's rural inhabitants. Such are the abundance and waste in the countryside, in Espinosa's opinion, that: "In the surrounding areas of Montevideo, the alkaline in the meat can be smelled. Animal bones and carrion, over which dense clouds of voracious birds of prey—*caranchos* [a local bird of prey], seagulls, buzzards, and many others—obscure the scene, offend the eyes" (1938: 279).[30] Other texts emphasize a different kind of waste—that is, the lack of exploitation of the land's wealth (see, for example, Brito Stífano 1953: 344). Despite this waste and prodigality, Concolorcorvo occasionally shows his Hispanic pride in the region's wealth: "Let the journalist from London try to impress us with the pieces of beef they eat there. If there the biggest piece of meat weighs 200 pounds, of which 200 lords eat, here 500 pounds feed only seven or eight *gauderios*—who once in a while share the cow with its owner." (1985: 23)

In sum, the texts by Concolorcorvo and Espinosa y Tello—like the other texts examined in this chapter—take a European perspective that sees the lands and inhabitants of Uruguay as alterities. The new element Concolorcorvo appears to contribute is a view of the gaucho—that is, of an Other that did not appear often in the records produced by the literate city.[31] In actuality, however, there is another text that predates Concolorcorvo's (by only a few years) in describing the gauchos:

> A few years ago, north of the river, a tribe of bandits formed which may become dangerous for the Spaniards if they do not take quick measures to destroy it. Some criminal fugitives have retired to the north of the Maldonadas. Deserters have joined them. Little by little, their number has been augmented; they have taken some women from the Indians and started a race that does not live but by pillage. They steal animals from the Spanish possessions in order to take them to the border with Brazil, where they exchange them with the *paulistas* for arms and clothes. . . . It is said that they now number more than six hundred. (Bougainville 1980: 36)

Notice that Bougainville assigns responsibility to the gaucho for contraband—a practice that was highly noxious to the economic system of that era.[32] His passage also refers to the ethnic miscegenation that was taking place at that time (the 1760s) in "the north of the Maldonadas" (the easternmost part of today's Uruguay) and to the high number of bandits (six hundred). And for his part, Espinosa y Tello provides the first transcription of an oral exhange between gauchos. Thus, what distinguish these texts are the new referents they produce. Unlike the texts by the other travelers, these texts do not limit their representations to urban areas; they include the opposite—that is, the rural areas, or the gaucho countryside. Thus, these texts mark the start of the process that culminated in the opposition of city and countryside, a crucial dichotomy in the construction of alterity through the ultimate, and most often used, logocentric pair: civilization–barbarism.

The authors examined in this chapter add to the production of referents that we saw in Chapter Four. To the fertility of the land and abundance of cattle that were registered during the establishment of Colonia do Sacramento—which continue to be structural elements of the construct in this chapter's texts—they add representations of the region's incipient urban centers, including Montevideo and Maldonado. This discursive record gives way to the production of a new referent that we could call "society" or "urban society." Society, of course, implies the existence of a culture. The same can be said about the emergence of a rural culture in the region. The depiction of these two emerging cultural forms by Pernety and Concolorcorvo accounts for the complexity of the referent that these authors produced, which is far more complicated than the one offered by Ottsen.

From the travelers' perspective, the social practices and customs of the new cultures are barbaric. Therefore, according to the axiological axis, or level, that measures the relationship between the Self and the Other, these cultures are considered inferior to the European societies from which those travelers came. But in these texts, that alterity appears as a more complex construct than the construct proposed in earlier texts. For instance, the representation of human alterity is not limited to depicting the few Amerindians who peopled the northern shore of the River Plate; now, the perceived and constructed Other is a whole society, with ethnic, class, and gender differences. And another Other is presented as the opposite of urban life: the gaucho, the mortal enemy of the literate city and the Occidental civilizational project. As I noted earlier, the abundant textual evidence about the gauchos' way of life would make producing an approximate reconstruction of their culture a difficult but possible task. Evidence of African culture, on the other hand, is scarce. Only a few references to this culture survive—in Pernety's and Concolorcorvo's texts; in the persistence of their musical tradition of *candombe;* in the texts by Medina (written approximately in 1830); and in a few poems (most of them by Acuña de Figueroa) that imitate the Africans' speech—and very little more than that. Descriptions as detailed and lively as Pernety's imply that African culture must have had an identity and personality that was totally different from that of the other cultures with which it shared the territory. That is, the African culture must have represented yet another interpretive community. From this perspective, one can regard the few texts that record the existence and vitality of African culture in the territory as written residue of an oral culture,[33] residue that was not produced as self-description but appropriated by literate culture. The indigenous societies fare even more badly in terms of potential retrieval from oblivion: Not only are there no self-descriptions by the Amerindians, but the Amerindians themselves have disappeared—

exterminated in genocidal fashion. Moreover, because no Occidental literary tradition took the Amerindians as an object of representation (unlike the situation of the gauchos and *gauchesca* poetry), the region's Amerindians could not leave even that kind of residue.

One might say that Juan Zorrilla de San Martín's long poem *Tabaré* (1956) could be considered a literary manifestation that attempts to recapture Charrúa culture. I cannot take that argument seriously. First, the poem's main character, the so-called Indian Tabaré, is in fact a *Mestizo:* His mother is of Spanish origin.[34] Second, Tabaré does not show any cultural traits that modern ethnography considers typically Charrúa. Finally, the poem's intention is to create a negative image of the Amerindian (wantonness, animalistic behavior, etc.) compared with European civilization—that is, Europe again appears as the positive pole in the poem's logocentric opposition, as Javier García Méndez (using a different theoretical framework) points out (1992: 15–17).

A few more recent literary works have undertaken a recovery if not of the culture, at least of the image, of the Amerindian. The most notorious examples are the novel *Bernabé, Bernabé* by Tomás de Mattos (1989) and the play *Salsipuedes* by Alberto Restuccia (1985). From a critical perspective, both deal with the abhorrent extermination of the Charrúa—an issue I will discuss briefly in the Conclusion.

Conclusion

The Territory as the Stage for the Drama of Difference

I have thus far limited my analysis of colonial times to texts. But written (and oral) discourse was only one of the means through which European subjects imagined and described the American territory. Their descriptive arsenal also included a tool for representing and controlling the lands they possessed: geography and its privileged form, cartography.

In the language of geography, the American territory was imagined as a blank page waiting for European subjects to leave inscriptions on it. European cartography from the sixteenth and seventeenth centuries is early testimony to that conception when it represents inhabitable American space through a theoretical and conceptual apparatus of Occidental origin. The territory of the state known today as Uruguay, as a part of the continent, is no exception to this way of "seeing." As the land is represented through cartography, the Ptolemaic conception—that is, the geographic gaze—imposes its rules upon the represented object. In other words, the process begins by drawing an uninhabited lump of land that lacks traces of the aboriginal peoples. That, in general, holds true for the first two centuries of European presence in the region: Although a few seventeenth-century maps show Amerindians in the territory, most drawn during this period systematically neglect the aborigines' presence. Although the Occidental observers were well aware of the Amerindians' existence, the representational techniques available to the cartographer made recording indigenous signs and activities difficult.

As more expeditions arrived in the region, the maps' uninhabited mass slowly began to take shape, and toponyms started to proliferate. The land's topography gradually aquired names of European or Guarani origin, some of which disappeared over time (Monte Seredo, Solís River, Jordán River) while others persisted (Uruguay River, Cape of Santa María). By replacing indigenous names with Christian names ("Terra Nova" or "of the Holy Cross"), Occidental cartographers were making a political move that erased the indigenous presence and inscribed the new lands in European history and culture (Mignolo 1993: 233). This political–discursive operation must be taken into account whenever one imagines the American territory as a "natural" part of Western culture: It will remind one that this way of imagining is simply the consequence of an ideological operation and that this America is nothing but a cultural artifact.

The early maps of American territory exemplify the Ptolemaic gaze, which homogenizes space (Rabasa 1993: 199) and standardizes the territory in a way that produces an illusion of sameness (Harley 1990: 113). Using these procedures, cartography is able to silence difference—that is, the idiosyncratic—and via euclidian geometry, it produces a uniformity that denies the particularities of the territory it attempts to represent (Harley 1988: 65).

Unlike the geographic gaze, however, the land keeps records of some of the activities of its original inhabitants. Even the conquistadors' chronicles contain relevant information about the actions of the so-called Indians of historical time. A study of these sources reveals that, despite its prevalence over the centuries, the image of America as a blank page waiting for inscriptions was not the only possible one—even in the narrow ideological framework provided by the Occidental worldview and episteme.[1] The geographic gaze understands the world as a totality whose center is Europe, which is presented as the privileged agent on that continuum known as "world history." This historical agent exerts his or her dominion over the world through—among other things—cartographic activities. Mapmaking visually organizes lands in order to demarcate and possess them; it also names, or renames, areas of the world to make them meaningful to the European subject.

In these pages, I will propose an image that differs substantially from the one created by the geographic tradition. That is, I will provide an alternative history of the territory's occupations, conceptions, and practices in an effort to change the Occidental way in which its modern-day inhabitants perceive it. And, if possible, I hope to help these modern-day dwellers to relate in a different way to the lump of land on which they stand.

Ten (or Eleven) Thousand Years of Human Activity in the Territory

A few decades ago, it became clear that humans have occupied the territory under study for millennia. Archaeological excavations in today's departments of Artigas and Salto, Uruguay, have revealed the existence of a series of cultures—of which the *catalanense* and *cuareimense* are the most studied—that developed approximately 10,000 to 11,000 years before the present (B.P.).[2] Today, the territory's inhabitants seem to be largely unaware of those human predecessors. In fact, a systematic obliviousness pervades Uruguayan society, reaching not only the common citizen and the state authorities, but also the educational system and other state apparatuses. The excavations in the Department of Rocha, which started in 1986, are changing this situation. The area being investigated holds a large number of mounds, or *"cerritos de indios"*; according to numerous sources,[3] the present inhabitants (*Criollo* and *Mestizo*, as a rule) continue to use these conical, elevated earthworks for flood protection and to obtain better visibility of the area. This continuity of use does not, however, presuppose awareness of the earthworks' original purpose. That is, it does not create a historical consciousness allowing those users to conceive of themselves as a link in a long chain of human actions in that territory.

The culture that constructed the mounds has been (and still is) intensely studied, and many hypotheses have been developed to explain its organization and cultural traits. The most interesting theory states that the resources the landscape offered to those prehistoric peoples were more abundant than was once believed. This representation of the land has changed the region's archaeological panorama substantially, the archaeologists say. Under the new proposed model, the region's hunter–gatherers inhabited and exploited a highly productive territory, as measured by the return value equal to the difference between investment and benefit of the available resources. Combining the large number of mound structures found in the region with this new economic picture allows the archaeologists to hypothesize a high population concentration, contradicting earlier ideas about the territory (López Mazz and Bracco 1992: 277).[4]

Another hypothesis advanced by the archaeologists leading the recent investigations posits that the prehistoric peoples exploited (and therefore occupied) the land in annual cycles. This leads them to conjecture that the mound builders had a certain degree of sedentism. The annual cycle presupposes exploitation of different regions in different seasons of the year; the evidence from the mounds points toward spring–summer occupation (López Mazz

1995b: 94). By contrast, the traditional model presents these hunter–gatherers as small nomadic groups (some one hundred men and women) who fought for survival in a very hostile, natural-resource–poor environment (López Mazz and Bracco 1989: 111).

The discovery of human bones in some of the mounds suggests that they had a funerary function. During study of those cases, evidence was found of combustion testimonies associated to other materials, which suggests a correlation between both series of elements (Femenías et al. 1990: 348). Interestingly, the combustion structures do not present characteristics suggesting that they were used in home heating or for cooking. On the contrary, the relics suggest a ceremonial or ritual function. In addition, the archaeologists have found holes in and traces on the ground made by small branches, which seem to be vestiges not of housing but of activities related to funerary rituals. Researchers believe that such ritualized treatment of the dead suggests a complex society with a rather sophisticated organization of communal work (López Mazz and Bracco 1989: 111). Further, the archaeologists have found evidence of different treatment of individuals buried in the mounds, which allows one to hypothesize the incipient emergence of a non-egalitarian society (López Mazz 1995a: 71).[5] According to Joseph Tainter, differential treatment of the dead indicates social stratification (1978: 107). He also says that ritual as a system of communication reveals information about the status of the dead individual (ibid.: 113).

Some investigators working before 1986 believed that the mounds had a housing or protective function—a very reasonable hypothesis, given lowlands' tendency to flood.[6] The current archaeologists propose yet another function: The mounds could have been territorial markers. One of the first articles by this group of archaeologists presents the mounds as elements that promoted social cohesiveness, allowing their builders both to demarcate territory and to construct their identity (Femenías et al. 1990: 352). The most interesting hypothesis, however, may be the one put forward recently by López Mazz, who believes the mounds' strategic location could be related to a communicative function—suggesting a possible relationship between the mounds and an exchange network among indigenous groups (1996: 4, 9).

Everything we know about the mounds points clearly in one direction: The prehistoric inhabitants left traces, marks, and footprints that reveal their activities in the territory and the environment. This allows us to represent the activities that gave birth to the mounds as part of the history of human practices that developed later in that same space. That is to say, these activities are antecedents to—and a legacy for—the human groups who have succeeded the mound builders in occupying that space. The Amerindians of historical time must have perceived the traces of activities that the mound builders left. The "*bichaderos*" (or "*vichaderos,*" the stone pyramids built over hills or other elevated areas), which served as tombs for the Charrúa (Pi Hugarte 1993: 117–18), are an interesting case suggesting this. Although it may be mere coincidence that Amerindians in historical time used elevated areas for funerary ends, it may also be a case of imitative or acculturated use of space. Apart from textual sources' attribution of their use to the Charrúa, little is known with certainty about the *bichaderos.* We do not, for example, know whether the Charrúa built the pyramids themselves or the pyramids were constructed by another ethnic group.[7]

Like the Indians of so-called historical time, the rural inhabitants of modern-day Uruguay seem to have perceived those prehistoric earthworks. Indications of this can be found in an article by Carlos Ferrés, who recorded such testimony from rural dwellers as, "There was a time when the neighbors found refuge in those ancient cemeteries, transforming them into real dwellings" and "If one has to send a party of rural workers to those fields for a while, they will choose as a campsite the same places on the creek's coast where the Indians built their platforms" (as quoted in Vidart 1996b: 54–55, 60). It is our duty as scholars to continue studying how those ancient, human-made structures were used and represented in order to preserve that knowledge as landscape capital.[8]

Ethnic Groups of So-Called Historical Time

Very little is known about the cultures that existed in the region before the Spanish arrived, and despite the large number of chronicles produced after the Europeans arrived, little reliable information can be found about indigenous ethnic groups. Leaving that aside for the moment, one can say that the majority of those who have studied this issue have identified three clearly different ethnic groups living in the territory at the time of the "discovery": those of Guaraní origin, the Chaná-Begua, and the Charrúa. Since the founding of the modern state known as Uruguay, the Charrúa have received by far the greatest amount of attention from chroniclers, as well as from educational and state institutions. Although a fair amount is known about the Guaraní (including the very extended Tupi-Guaraní culture), common citizens usually relate these indigenous peoples to the history of other modern-day states, such as Paraguay and, in some cases, Brazil.[9] Thus, the Guaraní are generally perceived as alien to the course of human history in the territory north of the River Plate. As a result, contemporary citizens forget about the permanent and continuing presence—from prehistoric times to the present—of this ethnic group in the lands under study. Recall that the founding of Montevideo was made possible by the participation of several platoons of Guaraní Indians, who, on more than one occasion, expelled the Portuguese from Colonia do Sacramento. Many of these Amerindians stayed in Montevideo practicing trades and crafts that the city, lacking a specialized labor force in the first years of its history as a Spanish settlement, needed desperately. This settlement would eventually become the capital of the modern state of Uruguay. The Guaraní's agency in and importance to the development of European-based societies in the territory is confirmed by genetic studies of Uruguay's current population: These studies show a very high percentage of indigenous contribution—mostly by those of Guaraní origin—to the global numbers, especially outside Montevideo (Sans 1992: 32–36).

Most of the early documentary sources confuse the Chaná-Begua and the Chana-Timbú, and recent academic investigations of the subject do little to elucidate their ethnic differences—or their possible kinship, which would justify the similarity in the names assigned to these groups (see Pi Hugarte 1993: 61–62; Vidart 1996a: 14–16). The only thing we know for sure is that there are no documented references to Chaná-Timbú presence in the territory (according to Barrios Pintos 1991: 38), whereas some texts record the presence of the Chaná-Begua.[10] The consensus on this group is that they made pottery, navigated in canoes, and probably had rudimentary agricultural knowledge. Because of the strong influence of diffusionist theories on the development of both Uruguayan and Latin American archaeology and anthropology, scholars have generally believed that the Chaná-Begua learned agricultural techniques from the Guaraní, who—according to numerous textual sources—mastered some techniques for exploiting the land.[11] Ana Inés Fregeiro contests this generally accepted hypothesis, arguing that the Tupi-Guaraní possessed one particular technique for exploiting the land—the *roza*—before the European explorers arrived.[12] Her argument, however, suggests that it is unclear whether the Tupi-Guaraní were the sole agents responsible for introducing agriculture into the territory (Fregeiro: 1966: 90). Because the *roza* is an agricultural method applied to the rainforest, the argument that posits continuity between possession of that technique and the practice of agriculture on the northern shore of the River Plate—a temperate region where the prairie, not the rainforest, predominates—looks rather weak. Thus, Fregeiro proposes, speculatively, a possible inverse path for agriculture: that the Guaraní may have acquired the agricultural practices of the Chaná-Begua (ibid.: 90).[13] This alternative hypothesis is interesting in that it questions diffusionist theories presupposing the need for a "most advanced" group to exert influence over less sophisticated groups. Besides, it is a good example of how little knowledge we possess about the life, culture, and social interactions among groups of Amerindians in historical time.

The Charrúa, as is well known, are the territory's most studied indigenous group, commanding the focus of most of the historical and ethnographic investigations. Moreover, the Charrúa are considered an emblem of national character—take, for example, the national soccer team's absurd "*garra charrúa*" (Charrúa courage). Finally, the social imaginary attributes to the Charrúa the assassination and subsequent deglutition of Solís and some of his companions. A description of the role that these Amerindians play in the social imaginary of modern-day Uruguay would not be complete, however, without mentioning their extermination at the hands of the president of the country's first independent constitutional government. The Amerindians who feed nationalistic sports pride were, ironically, ambushed and exterminated more than a century and a half ago. For the *Criollo* elite who ruled the brand-new republic, the Charrúas' unforgivable sin lay in the fact that they never adapted to some of the main tenets of capitalism, such as respect for private property. They were therefore an annoyance and an obstacle to "progress" and "civilization."

In 1831, Fructuoso Rivera, the first constitutional president of the independent republic of Uruguay, organized a gigantic barbeque to attract the highest possible number of Charrúa. Once the Amerindians were drunk, Rivera's men began massacring the guests. Although Rivera orderered this criminal act, attributing it only to him would be naive: No one in the *Criollo* ruling class protested the massacre. To use Vidart's metaphor, Rivera was only the trigger on a firearm that had been loaded for a long time (1996a: 93).

Unlike other extinct indigenous groups throughout the Americas, the Charrúa did not die from the hardships of forced labor. They were not inclined to do agricultural tasks; moreover, there were no silver or gold mines on the northern shore of the River Plate. Neither did they die from foreign bacteria or viruses: They did not interact much with the European settlements beyond visits to obtain alcoholic beverages and tobacco. It took a cowardly ambush to destroy this ethnic group. Only in the 1990s, however, did some intellectuals start to talk openly about the darkest moment in the history of Uruguay as an independent nation. Until then, silence and dissimulation had been the most common postures among historians and educators.

Some of the myths about the Charrúa are as old as the (European) history of the territory. From the earliest chronicles, the Charrúa are described—as the reader may remember—as brave and savage warriors, a characterization that has been reproduced ad nauseam by the ideological apparatuses of the modern state. The Charrúas' defensive reaction to the Occidental invaders is also part of the national folklore. Along with these characterizations of the Charrúa, one must consider all kinds of confusions and distortions that survive in the social imaginary—for example, their alleged cannibalism based on the events surrounding Solís's expedition, despite the almost unanimous rejection of this hypothesis by Luis Rodolfo González, Susana Rodríguez Varese, José Toribio Medina, and other scholars who have studied the event, not to mention the complete absence of references to the Charrúa in all chronicles narrating the "discovery" of the River Plate region. Our late–twentieth-century image of the Charrúa is based only in part on those first chronicles. Most of what we believe about them is grounded in myth.

It is interesting to examine the problems posed by the chronicles and other colonial documents that represent that episode. As we have seen, the most popular version of the event narrates the killing of the Spaniards and presents them as victims of the Amerindians' cannibalism. The chroniclers do not, however, identify this group of cannibalistic aborigines. A key element in assigning an ethnic affiliation to them involves identifying where the episode took place: If this can be established, the reasoning goes, the Amerindians' ethnic origin will be easier to decipher. It is not my intention in this book to support any of the multiple speculations about the geographic location of the "discovery." Rather, I am interested in calling attention to indigenous behavioral patterns, such as nomadism, because they lie at the core of the confusion over where the episode took place: Indigenous mobility provides one of the reasons that scholars have not been able to agree on a specific location. That nomadism is also the main cause of the doubts about whether the Guarani or the Charrúa attacked Solís and his crew members.

One can deduce from the chronicles about the region that the Charrúa occupied the area covering today's departments of Colonia and San José during the summer, but one could also find the "Guaraní from the islands" ("*guaraníes de las islas*") there (Barrios Pintos 1991: 37).[14] These assumptions may be valid roughly for the sixteenth century; in the years that followed, some ethnic groups were displaced, and some disappeared. For this investigation, it is most interesting to examine the reasoning of scholars who seem unaware of methodological problems that their investigations should overcome. An illustrative case is that of Barrios Pintos, who uncritically accepts the account of the anthropophagic episode (ibid.: 47). He argues that the territory in which Solís's expedition landed fell in a zone inhabited by both the Charrúa and the Guaraní. The former were never considered cannibals, whereas the latter were famous for being so. Thus, Barrios Pintos simultaneously acknowledges that the act of cannibalism took place and attributes it to the Guaraní. One must remember here that Barrios Pintos draws his conclusions from secondhand narrations—no eyewitness accounts of this episode exist. And even if such testimony existed, it would not, by anthropological standards, be considered valid ethnographic proof. (The trusting reader should recall that many eyewitnesses "saw" sirens and men with dog heads in America.) Attributing this practice to the Guaraní is also problematic because the cannibalistic ritual, as described by Jean de Léry, Hans Staden, and Roger Barlow—takes a long time. This contradicts the most widely accepted version of the event, which presents the Amerindians' eating the Spaniards ipso facto.[15]

The lack of ethnographic information about the territory's indigenous groups before the Spanish arrived also has important consequences when it comes to identifying (and naming) those different groups. Traditionally, for example, the Minuan, or Guenoa, have been regarded as having cultural traits that were very similar to those of the Charrúa, as Azara's text demonstrates. Recent investigations by Diego Bracco, however, show not only that the Minuan/Guenoa were a different group with a different language, but also that they were occasional enemies of the Charrúa (1998: 14, *passim*). Moreover, despite the lack of interest they have engendered among Uruguayan scholars, the Minuan/Guenoa were one of the largest indigenous groups in the territory on the northern shore of the River Plate throughout the colonial period, Bracco says (ibid.: 141).

Another example of the difficulties inherent in identifying Amerindian groups can be found in the case of the Chaná-Begua. Eduardo Acosta y Lara identifies the Chaná-Begua as navigators, for example, and regards the Charrúa as a group that did not navigate (1961: 11). His certainty notwithstanding, it is possible, if one looks carefully, to find documents that contradict his assertions. Among these are the report by the expedition treasurer Montalvo (1915: 297); Lopes de Souza's diary (1926: 47–48); and the *relación* by Hernandarias that states: "I found some of the local Natives' canoes there" ("*alle alli algunas canoas de los naturales de aquella costa*" [Azarola Gil 1933: 209]). It is not easy to establish a relationship between the canoes and the Charrúa, however: How does one know who the canoes belonged to? In the best-case scenario, with confirmation and support lacking in the remainder of Hernandarias's document, one can give such an assertion the value of mere conjecture—as I propose to do with Acosta y Lara's rival hypothesis. In this regard, contemporary scholars studying the region's indigenous past are in a situation of uncertainty: The documents in general contradict one another, which makes creating a hierarchy of truth value—for example, determining that document "Z" has more value than document "Y"—a very difficult enterprise. The lack of such criteria exposes scholars to the same perils threatening those who identify indigenous groups based on what is known about them—"what is known about them," after all, comes from chronicles that in turn validate themselves using other chronicles of similar nature. To make things worse, those chronicles are usually written by European subjects who ignore the aboriginal languages and have little knowledge of the territory and peoples they are describing. One can therefore see, I hope, how arbitrary it is to favor the testimony of one chronicler (say, Lopes de Souza) over that of another (say, Montalvo) when it comes to describing and identifying the ethnic affiliation of indigenous groups.

These problems multiply when one tries to account for ethnic groups whom the chroniclers ignored. A good example of such a culture is that of the mound builders, who are not mentioned at all in the available colonial documents,[16] even though some Carbon 14 datings suggest that the mound-building culture coexisted with the Spanish explorers. The approximate date of 370 B.P. is corroborated by the discovery of material attributable to European culture in the higher levels of a mound known as site CH1E01 (R. Bracco 1992: 12, 15).[17] One of the questions that arises from this evidence is: Why do some sixteenth- and seventeenth-century chronicles discuss the Charrúa and Chaná—and some nonexistent groups, such as the Arachan—but make no reference to the mound builders? Another pertinent question is why they suddenly disappeared from the site. According to Bracco, the answer to the latter question can be found in the dramatic changes brought about by European subjects after they arrived in the region (Bracco 1990: 71, *passim*; Cabrera Pérez 1992: 116). The Spanish did not go alone to the territory occupied by the mound builders; they took with them their culture and their utensils, their technology and their social practices. It is possible, then, that the first contact between the prehistoric Amerindians and European culture was made through animals and objects, not human beings (Bracco 1992: 71, *passim*). Such indirect contact could explain why the mound builders are absent from the European chronicles produced in the sixteenth and seventeenth centuries: Their territory—the lowlands of today's Department of Rocha—was perhaps too far from the Spanish crown's bureaucratic centers to be recorded by European observers (Bracco 1990: 15). It is also possible that the mound builders' culture had been exposed to processes of transculturation with other indigenous groups. This interaction may have affected the different groups that were in contact (the Charrúa, the Guaraní, and the mound builders)[18] in ways that are totally unknown to us as modern readers—modifying diverse aspects of their respective cultures (for example, clothing, pottery, etc.). Last but not least, the changes in the region—cultural and otherwise—may have forced the local Amerindians to move to the western part of the territory (Cabrera 1992: 114, 117).

The European Presence in Colonial Times

This was approximately the population the Spaniards found when they arrived in the lands north of the River Plate. They met with ethnic groups who were not always hostile to them. Those groups, in general, were nomadic, organizing their societies in ways that did not depend on the existence of a state or of urban centers. In addition, the Amerindians did not have well-organized agricultural systems—unlike the Andean and Mesoamerican groups encountered by the armies of Cortés and Pizarro. The lack of organized land-exploitation systems made it difficult for the Spanish to survive in what, from their perspective, were inhospitable lands. Their abandoning of the city of Buenos Aires, which had been founded by the Adelantado Pedro de Mendoza, provides an example of the starvation invaders could suffer if they did not find a way to sustain themselves. Moreover, as we saw in Chapter One, the first expedition that set foot on those lands was expelled in a very summary way. Those who followed were also attacked by the locals, as we saw in the testimony left by members of the expeditions led by Cabot and Ortiz de Zárate. Barco Centenera, the archdeacon who traveled with the latter expedition, left a clear and vivid picture of the Charrúa attacks that forced the Spanish to leave the area. For these reasons, and because of the European empires' initial lack of interest in the newly "discovered" territory, settlement of the region progressed very slowly. Only after Hernandarias introduced equine and bovine livestock on the northern shore of the River Plate did those lands become an object of attention for the Spanish crown. The introduction of cattle brought about several changes: Some of them made European and *Criollo* settlement easier, but some of them made it even harder. On the one hand, the abundance of meat eliminated the sustenance problem. On the other, it gave the Amerindians the same benefits, making their own sustenance easier. The introduction of equine livestock also made indigenous resistance more effective: It gave them even greater mobility than they already had (as the frequent reports about their raids show), thus making their subjection by force a very difficult task for the invaders.

So difficult was their conquest that the first permanent European settlement in the territory, Colonia do Sacramento, was not founded until 1680, by the Portuguese. Before 1678, the Portuguese crown did not object to Spanish possession of the territories in the area known as San Gabriel—they had been granted to Spain by the Treaty of Tordesillas. But in that year, Portugal's prince regent sent Manuel Lobo to populate that area. As we have already seen, legal justifications for Portuguese possession of the area were much less important than the recognition of the fertility and potential wealth of the lands in dispute.

Portugal also planned to consolidate the Paulista *Bandeirantes'* frequent incursions into the territory so that the crown could make more comfortable usufruct of the northern shore of the River Plate. Recognizing the potential productivity of the land was not new, as the reader may remember: Hernandarias had already introduced cattle to the region. The changes in the territory that this move brought about included partial modification of the area's ecology and the transformation of its potential economic wealth. From 1680 on, then, a new actor becomes evident in the territory—one who joins the Amerindians and the fluctuating presence of the Spanish. This new scenario reveals the true nature of American and Uruguayan lands as an object of dispute.

For a century, armed conflicts and diplomatic struggles between two contending empires—Spain and Portugal—dominated the history of the region. It is in this period that an image of the territory that has been erased by the hegemonic, or official, historical accounts starts to take shape. The territory as an object of dispute, as a stage where difference was dramatized, is at odds with the official narrative, which conceives the history of the region as the pacific development of a single, homogeneous Spanish culture. Yet historical investigation shows a different situation. For example, it tells us that Montevideo was founded in 1724 as protection against perils that seemed imminent even to the indolent and slow-minded Spanish administration. One of these perils (added to the frequent incursions of the *Bandeirantes* and the threatening presence of Colonia do Sacramento) involved the landing of French pirates, who tried to settle on the coasts of Castillos in 1720 (Lozano 1873: 3:472). Thus, Zabala decided to solve the problem by founding Montevideo, because the northern shore of the river was a key element in the survival of the people of Buenos Aires—the closest Spanish settlement. Because he lacked the people and supplies to undertake the mission, however, his efforts were in vain until 1723. In that year, Gronardo informed him of the Portuguese's intention to settle in Montevideo in order to secure their absolute control over the northern shore of the river. This scenario—the stage on which several actors struggled to possess a territory—would continue until 1776, the year in which the Portuguese were expelled definitively from the area. The struggle did not end after this Spanish victory, though. The ethnic groups of historical time—the Charrúa and the Minuan—refused to surrender or assimilate to an alien culture. And a new social subject—a product of miscegenation and cultural hybridity—entered the scene in this era: the gaucho, a human type who forged a culture on the pampas that was as alien to the Occident as was Amerindian culture.

The visits by other European subjects added even more complexity to the multiethnic nature of the territory's population. During a period that covers approximately two centuries, many travelers (usually businessmen, priests, and naturalists) left their impressions about and on the land they visited. They reproduced, with only slight changes, the same kind of representation of the Amerindians that the region's first chroniclers produced. Recall that Ottsen, for example, attributed anthropophagic practices to the Amerindians but, like the Spanish chroniclers of the colonial encounter, failed to inform the reader of the cannibals' ethnic affiliation. When these travelers contributed new information toward the construction of the referents "lands of Uruguay" and "inhabitants," it had to do with the city of Montevideo, which began to take shape in the eighteenth century. Cattaneo, for example, described Montevideo as a small village. According to Cattaneo, the city was founded in response to Portuguese attempts to control the territory and in response to dangerous incursions by French and English pirates. At first glance, his account—written from the perspective of a traveler who was not a subject of any of the nations at war in the area—appears to be more distanced and dispassionate than the chronicles produced by the parties involved in the conflict. Yet, this "distance" is illusory. In actuality, as a Jesuit, Cattaneo was also an interested party in the conflict. As is well known, before it was expelled from America, the Company of Jesus built a powerful empire based not only on the wealth that it was able to generate, but also on the strength of the armies of Guaraní Indians who blindly followed and obeyed the priests. This is not an irrelevant detail: The Guaraní frequently intervened on behalf of the Spanish crown during the century-long struggle over Colonia do Sacramento—for example, by actively collaborating in the founding of Montevideo. The scarcity of soldiers (and people in general) that Zabala confronted makes the Guaraní's contribution appear fundamental. Thus, Cattaneo's view of the state of affairs on the northern shore of the River Plate was not objective at all—hence, his permanent praise of the Guaraní from the Jesuit missions, whom he offered as living proof of the greatness and achievements of the glorious Company of Jesus (remember, for example, the passage on pages 265–66). Through his testimony, one sees entering the scene another European historical agent (the Jesuits) who is distinguishable in some respects from the subjects of the empires in conflict, but whose role in the region's geopolitical drama is equally important.

Pernety also described Montevideo as a village and recorded his views on another social group that was forming in the city: the Africans, whom he depicted as lascivious and primitive. The same reaction to the African subject can be found in the text by Concolorcorvo, who also left his "civilized" impressions of yet another human type: the gaucho, or *gauderio.* And the reader may recall that Concolorcorvo expressed outrage at the culture of waste that was predominant in Montevideo and surrounding areas. He was not the only one to do so. Another Spanish traveler, Espinosa y Tello, recorded negative judgments on the issue. In the testimony of these travelers, the territory once again is presented as an abundant place—so abundant, in fact, that its inhabitants dissipate its wealth.

At the beginning of this chapter, I declared that the idea of the American territory as a blank page is a fallacy. The form in which residents of modern-day Uruguay imagine their land, however, owes much to that fallacy: The indigenous presence is never a relevant element in the national narrative. Moreover, the indigenous element is never present in the ways these residents imagine their territory. This means that the Amerindian is also absent from the narratives through which the history of human activities in the territory is conceived. In these pages, I have tried to propose a different way to understand both territoriality and its historical correlate. To begin with, as we retrieve the memory of indigenous practices as part of the history of human activities in the territory, we should complement it with an awareness of the limits on our knowledge of the salient characteristics of the different ethnic groups—historic and prehistoric. We know very little about how those Amerindians perceived themselves; we also know almost nothing about how their social life was organized and about the beliefs they held, among other elements crucial to understanding any culture. The textual sources' lack of reliability and the scant (though growing) body of archaeological evidence make it impossible to describe, with honesty and certainty, what the Charrúa, the Minuan, the Chaná, and the mound builders were really like. Keep in mind that we do not even know what these people called themselves. The names with which we are familiar were given to them by the Guaraní, the interpreters and guides of the Europeans who arrived to populate the area. It may well be time to acknowledge our precarious gnoseological situation and warn against the perils of uncritically reproducing an image of the Amerindians that is nothing but a cultural artifact.

Further, the value the European observers assigned to, and the images they produced about, the lands of Uruguay varied greatly over time. They were, after all, considered "unprofitable" until Hernandarias introduced livestock—at which point they became an object of desire and greed. The territory also became an object of dispute, with an increasing number of actors on the stage: In addition to the Spanish and the Amerindians, the Portuguese, French, and English played a role in the struggle to possess the land. That struggle did not take place exclusively on the battlefield; it was also fought in the legal arena and in the discursive realm, as numerous colonial chronicles and documents show. Whether we are aware of them or not, the consequences of those struggles are still alive. Whenever one imagines the territory as a place where only one cultural tradition and an exclusive historical project developed, one is taking the side of one of the many narratives about the appropriation of the territory, all of which represent, fatally, a single cultural tradition.[19] The interaction of several historical and cultural agents presents a view of the history of human life in the territory that looks more like a Tower of Babel than like the monolingual and homogenous image offered by "official" history and the encyclopedias.

In sum, my goal in this book is to call attention to the constructed and prejudiced nature of the imaginary representations of the territory and its human history. This goal is motivated by the belief that human beings have a special relationship with the territory they inhabit, and that the way in which they imagine this territory has important consequences for how they organize their social and cultural life—as well as for how they imagine and plan their future as a collective body. For this reason, I believe that it is necessary to call attention to the cultural differences that underlie the illusion of homogeneity promoted by the modern national project. If one does not acknowledge that repressed difference—that marginalized diversity—one will forget about the strategies and devices through which difference has been repressed. Exerting epistemic and physical violence upon the Other has been one of the most popular strategies. One way to stop exerting this violence on the Occident's Others (from the past and in the present) is to oppose the oblivion to which they have been condemned.

Final Words

Throughout this book, we have examined texts that largely have not been regarded as objects of study by specialists in Uruguayan literature or scholars of colonial Latin America. The latter have focused on texts produced by Columbus, Cortés, Guaman Poma, Garcilaso Inca, and Bernal Díaz, among others—leaving the majority of the texts studied in this investigation outside the colonial canon. I agree with Mignolo when he says that the canon of colonial Latin American studies should become a corpus—that is, it should encompass all extant texts rather than a selective list. At this moment of transition in the discipline, it seems opportune to include the texts studied in this investigation in the corpus of colonial studies; failing to do so will deprive the discipline of a series of documents that account for and refer to not only Uruguay, but also a region that extends over half of the continent. In addition to texts about Mesoamerica and the Andes, the discipline should incorporate those that refer to the River Plate area. They are also a product of the colonial encounter. In addition, they use discursive and rhetorical strategies that are similar to the paradigmatic ones. Although they share the general coordinates of colonial discursive production, however, these texts should also be distinguished as a subgroup of this production because they create different referents. These are the texts that produce the referents "Uruguay," "River Plate," and "the Charrúa", unlike those that produce "Peru," "the Inca," and "the Aztecs." To be complete, the study of European subjects' construction of America needs to take into account this group of forgotten texts, because they challenge what I call the predominance of the three cultures.

The reasons for the neglect of this region may be many, but two are very likely to explain it: the peripheral status of the region during colonial times and the lack of prestige—in the Occidental world—of indigenous cultures known as hunter–gatherers. Without temples, writing systems, or state organization, the lands populated by the Amerindians on the northern shore of the River Plate were not interesting enough to the Occidental episteme. However, I believe that the margins of the Spanish empire deserve as much attention as its bureaucratic centers, because, among other reasons, they show us one of the different ways in which the appropriation of indigenous lands by European subjects took place. They also remind us that hunter–gatherers—and sometimes early agriculturalists–were not easy prey for Western military and administrative means of control.

Throughout this investigation, I have focused on one of the discursive aspects of the texts that form the corpus: the production of selected referents. I have tried to offer an overview rather than an exhaustive reconstruction of the formation processes of the referents "lands" and "peoples" of the northern shore of the River Plate. Examining the history of the representations of a reality that was new to the European subject of discourse has allowed me to study the ways in which these subjects constructed their Others—that is, the dichotomies and logocentric pairs that they used to produce the referents. Through this process, the marginal communities that opposed the soon-to-be-hegemonic European project were represented through discursive strategies that devalued and repressed them—sometimes by comparing them unfavorably to a model of excellence that was based on European patterns ("civilized man"); at other times, by neutralizing their differences via assimilation (real and imaginary) to European standards. This strategy played yet another role: At the same time it allowed the European subjects to construct the Other, it also fostered their construction of European identity. This led to a tautological result at the axiological level: the European subject, by comparison, was better than the Other. This Other multiplied and became more complex as time passed. To the Other of the time of the "discovery"—that is, the Amerindian—the texts record the representation of Africans; *Mestizo* groups, such as the gaucho; women, an almost nonexistent Other in discourses referring to the beginning of the conquest; and, finally, colonial society, as represented by cities and villages—the most complex, stratified alterity.

Logocentrism was exerted from an axiological framework that privileged writing over orality and the city over the countryside. In the texts analyzed in this book, the subjects of discourse constantly have to translate one culture for another—that is, they need to transmit to their own people (or community) the cultural alterity they have confronted. Although one can detect traces of the cultures repressed by the logocentric axiology in those translations, one cannot find the voices of the devalued communities. Literate culture silences its Others—that is, oral cultures. As a result, we are left without self-descriptions produced by the displaced communities. In other words, we do not know whether the Minuan called themselves Minuan, or how the gauchos sang their songs, or how the African perceived their own dances. All that remain of those cultural manifestations are traces. In some cases, one can find discursive (textual) manifestations of more recent origin—for example, *gauchesca* literature and the documents of the African Medina—but they play by the rules of the triumphant literate culture.

Examining the traces of the Other in the *Criollos'* and conquistadors' discourse will not allow us to reconstruct the cultures that have disappeared, but it will give us at least a retrospective approximation of them. These traces also show the modern reader that those silenced Others did not remain passive before the conquistadors' aggression. They fought tirelessly to defend their territory.

The main obstacle to reconstructing extinguished—or in some cases, assimilated—cultures is that, as members of a literate culture, we stand on the other side of the line. Our discourse is already contaminated, because we are incapable of seeing without the prejudices of the Occidental literate episteme. Faced with the impossibility of reconstructing the discursive and cultural polyphony that characterized human interactions in colonial times, I have tried to propose an alternative path: to show how the Other poisons the discursive structure through which he or she is being constructed via repression or devaluation. In other words, I have tried to show how the Other's traces call into question, and lay bare, the mechanisms the European subject used to construct reality.

This project is inspired by the belief that through the study of the European strategies for the construction of alterity (which takes the shape of, for example, the referents "territory" and "peoples"), we learn something about the interpretive communities that partake of the Western episteme—the framework that shapes the cognitive patterns of the potential addressees predicted by colonial texts. Moreover, we—modern-day scholars, modern-day Latin Americanists—can also be conceived as the implicit readers of the texts produced by some of the practitioners of humanistic disciplines, such as "national" historiography, whose representatives are, among others, Francisco Bauzá, Enrique Azarola Gil, and Emilio Coni. Their texts reaffirm the axiologies inherited from the colonizers and therefore present the repressed, colonized communities—the gaucho, the Amerindian, the African—as inferior beings compared with the "civilized" European or *Criollo* subject. The hierarchy established by those texts, which presents Occidental culture as superior to oral societies, is inherited and brilliantly summed up by the political class of the post-emancipation, or post-independence, era, who developed the civilization–barbarism dichotomy in order to explain the history of the region.

This dichotomy still has currency today—a time in which, thanks to the hegemonic discursive tradition, the Amerindian, African, and gaucho have become the modern-day citizen's Others. Latin American subjects see the world with a borrowed gaze and describe reality using a discourse that depends on the strategies prescribed by the Occidental nations and their cultural traditions. However, although we are part of the European episteme, some international organizations (such as the IABD, IMF, and GATT[20]), remind us—by treating us differently—that we are not really European. It follows that if we are something different, our worldview and our discursive strategies should also be different. These pages are intended as a contribution toward that end.

Notes

Preface

1. I understand that field of studies as the one in which humanists trained in language and literature departments produce scholarship on the colonial era.

2. In another passage, Zamora states that "geographical space is always constructed discursively" (1993: 130).

3. To give the reader an idea about the power of official discourse in Argentina, suffice it to say that many people believe that there are no Amerindians in that country today. This false image of a country without aborigines (a modern byproduct of the image of the blank page that I will discuss later) is testimony to the power of Argentine and *Criollo* discourse to silence alternative histories.

Introduction

1. I should point out that even in some regions of the Andes and Mesoamerica, the Spanish gained control over the territory only after a long struggle. For detailed accounts of those slow processes of conquest, see Spalding (1984) and Stern (1982) on the Andean regions of Huarochirí and Huamanga, respectively, and Lockhart's seminal *The Nahuas after the Conquest* (1992) on Mesoamerica.

2. Something similar may be happening in the present, according to Pierre Bourdieu, who says that the collective productive forces that are resisting neoliberal globalization (a program of systematic destruction of collectives) may also be feeding and sustaining the new world economic system: "It is in reality the permanence or the survival of institutions and agents of the old order now being dismantled, and all the work of the different 'social workers,' and also all social, familial and other solidarities, which prevent the social order from collapsing into insecurity" (Bourdieu 1998: 103).

3. Effective occupation of the land was made possible by the introduction of these European species. The livestock not only provided sustenance for the Spanish (and later, the Portuguese); it also brought about dramatic changes in the native biota. For a study of this topic, see Crosby (1996 [1986]) and Verdesio (forthcoming).

4. In a different work (Verdesio 1995), I address the issues of what should be studied and why in the corpus as a whole. I cannot go into detail here. Suffice it to say that a very large number of texts register the history of representations of the territory and its inhabitants, and that the investigation of that corpus transcends individual efforts because we are facing a new sub-area of colonial studies: that of texts that have the lands and people of the northern shore of the River Plate as referents.

5. Rolando Laguarda Trías (1982) attempts to demonstrate that Vespucci was the first explorer to land in the region under study, in 1502. Even if this is true—which is a moot point—Vespucci's expedition produced no written references to the River Plate region, which renders this voyage insignificant for the present investigation.

6. Francisco Cevallos defines European Renaissance teleological history as a constant linear progression that begins at the moment of creation and ends on Judgment Day. The world moved, in this conception, toward a *telos* defined and organized by an almighty God (1986: 57).

Johann Gottfried von Herder, from his own romantic perspective and in an attempt to defend his people's national spirit, denounced the European pretense of being the privileged agents of universal history (1968: 78). This evolutionist model, which conceives of European civilization as the highest point of human development, also exists in the disciplinary field of anthropology, as many authors have pointed out. See, for example, Sambarino (1969: 12) and Fabian (1983).

7. For a discussion of the need to include texts written in languages other than Spanish in order to achieve a better understanding of the colonial encounter, and for a survey of the linguistically diverse nature of the colonial semiosis in the region, see Verdesio (1995).

8. "The desire to explain might be a symptom of the desire to have a self that can control knowledge and a world that can be known" (Spivak 1988a: 104).

9. On this issue, see Spivak (1988a: 105–106). She offers an interpretation of some of Derrida's ideas about explanation through the elimination of the margins.

10. The exclusion of Otherness always and by necessity implies the negation of difference. In this respect, Homi K. Bhabha proposes a view that relates the denial of diversity and the affirmation of the same in the colonizer's discourse to both the Lacanian mirror stage and the Freudian notion of fetish. In Bhabha's opinion, the narcissism of the imaginary that denies the difference evident at the symbolic level and the negation of sexual difference through fixation of desire on a fixed object have something in common with the mechanisms that operate in the discourse of the European colonial subject (Bhabha 1983: 18–36).

11. Numerous works deal with this issue. Good summaries can be found in Godzich (in de Certeau [1989]) and Adorno (1988a: 63).

12. In Jameson's opinion, however, texts attempt, at an imaginary level, to solve a contradiction that exists in the real world (1981: 77).

13. The existence of gaps or silences in a text and their relevance to reading processes has been studied by numerous scholars, one of whom is Wolfgang Iser (1974: 58).

14. As Derrida himself says, accepting for once the term "deconstruction" to refer to his own practices: "Deconstruction does not consist in moving from one concept to another, but in reversing and displacing a conceptual order as well as the

nonconceptual order with which it is articulated. For example, writing, as a classical concept, entails predicates that have been subordinated, excluded or held in abeyance by forces and according to necessities to be analyzed. It is those predicates . . . whose force of generality, generalization, and generativity is liberated, grafted onto a 'new' concept of writing that corresponds as well to what has always resisted the prior organization of forces, always constituted the residue irreducible to the dominant force organizing the hierarchy that we may refer to, in brief, as logocentric" (1988: 21).

15. I understand polyphony as a notion equivalent to multiplicity or heterogeneity in the structure of any society, not in the sense that comes from M. M. Bakhtin's studies on the novel (1981: 259–263). In actuality, what Bakhtin talks about cannot be understood as polyphony in the sense I give it here, because the novel always has a single voice, regardless of the literary tricks a skillful author can perform. In order to be polyphonic, an author must share the writing of the novel with his or her Others. According to Edward Said, the Bakhtinian notion of polyphony is a laboratory creation that hides the true nature of the "real" historical crisis that forced the academic world (Bakhtin included) to pay attention to marginal interlocutors (Said 1989: 205–25, esp. 210). A notion closer to the one I propose is that advanced by Antonio Cornejo Polar (1989b: 23).

The discursive plurality that Jean Lyotard (1981) proclaims as the trademark of the postmodern era can be found in any place at any time, regardless of which master narrative predominates, as long as more than one group shares the territory. Despite my reservations about Lyotard's theoretical system, I believe that some of his ideas coincide with the theoretical framework of this investigation—notably, his respect for alterity and his belief in the right of every group to express its own narrative (Lyotard 1977: 28, quoted in Carroll 1987: 72). In this framework, denying the right of expression to any group is already an injustice (Carroll 1987: 75). As a consequence, the "natural" state of a society should be polyphonic.

Regarding plurality, a critique of Habermas's ideas can be found in Brenkman (1987: 49–50).

16. For a treatment of these topics, see Mignolo (1983a: 7, 18–19). There is yet another possible step, but Mignolo does not take it: to propose the study of theoretical practices in order to produce knowledge about them. Said proposes something like this when he argues in favor of a study that contextualizes the disciplines in historical terms (1989: 213, *passim*).

17. Theories account not for a referent but for a theoretical object, according to Mignolo (1983a: 26). It can be said, however, that a theory *constructs* its reference (because it deforms it) by giving a form to its object of study—that is, a *construct* can at best be considered a map of the referent, but it can never be its exact duplicate. On the ways in which theories construct their referents, see Mignolo (1989b: 64). On pages 61–63, he introduces the concept of "ontological compromise" (taken from Quine), which operates as a key to elucidating the questions presented by the problem that is known in the field of philosophical semantics as "on denoting" or "on referring"—that is, the problem that involves the relationship between "reality" and the propositions that attempt to describe it. On the construction of the object of study in the field of literary studies, see Cornejo Polar (1989b: 23).

Chapter One

1. Michel Foucault describes his inquiry as one that wants to discover "on what basis knowledge and theory become possible; within what space or order of knowledge was constituted; on the basis of what historical *a priori,* and in the element of what positivity, ideas could appear, sciences be established, experience be reflected in philosophies, rationalities be formed, only, perhaps, to dissolve and vanish soon afterwards" (1970 [1966]: xxi–xxii). What he is studying is therefore "the epistemological field, the episteme in which knowledge, envisaged apart from all criteria having reference to its rational or to its objective forms, grounds its positivity and thereby manifests a history which is not that of its growing perfection, but rather that of its conditions of possibility; in this account, what should appear are those configurations within the space of knowledge which have given rise to the diverse forms of empirical science" (ibid.: xxii). Episteme is thus the system that makes the discursive practices of a given culture possible.

2. Some versions, of course, have opposed the hegemonic one. A couple of good examples are the *indigenista* novel and the dependency theory, whose most popular version is the one offered by Eduardo Galeano (1997 [1971]).

3. Although my perspective on colonial issues differs considerably from Murena's, I use his metaphor because of its undeniable suggestive power.

4. We are therefore examining texts that can be viewed as foundational narratives. I do not use this term in the book, because I do not want the texts under study to be confused with those that Doris Sommer calls "foundational narratives"—that is, the Latin American novels that propose an ideal national project (1986: 47–73; 1990: 71–98).

5. In the first volume, Medina discusses the documentary proof that supports his thesis (1516); in the second, he reproduces the original documents.

6. Although Lozano believes that the 1508 voyage took place, he also thinks that Solís did not stop at the estuary. This voyage took place, but, contrary to what Lozano believes, it never reached such a southern latitude, as Medina (1897) points out.

7. Other secondary sources, such as *cédulas reales, asientos,* and *capitulaciones,* have helped some authors to rule out the dates 1508 and 1512. I refer the reader again to Medina and Madero.

8. All translations are mine, unless indicated otherwise.

9. The Caribs' animal condition, or their lack of "civilization," is a permanent presence in Columbus's diary. On the relationship between anthropophagy and the animalization of the Amerindians in the discourse of the conquistadors, see Bolaños (1994: 137–38).

10. Rolena Adorno (1988a: 64) talks about the defeminization in some texts produced by members of colonial oppressed groups as a response to the feminization they suffered at the hands of the oppressors' discursive practices.

11. Eating human flesh, according to Anthony Pagden (1982: 83), was compared to eating filth—an association that adds darker overtones to the representation of the Amerindians as cannibals.

12. Given the form in which educated people followed the colonization of the Americas, this is a plausible hypothesis. In his private letters, Peter Martyr himself

propagated stories about the "discovery and conquest" of the Indies. See Mártir de Anglería (1990).

13. Fernández de Oviedo believed that the discovery took place in 1512 and that the 1516 voyage was the second to the region: "He brought information about those shores. And in order to get there with more people the King himself made him his captain and conceded him the right to populate that great river. *And he [Solís] returned to those lands* with three very well-armed ships, provided with people and victuals, in order to discover and to know the secrets of the land, the year of one thousand five hundred and fifteen years" (1959 [1535–47]: 352; emphasis added).

14. Díaz de Guzmán, Barco Centenera's contemporary, does not say anything about the 1516 events because he ignores their existence. For that matter, he also ignores Solís's death at the hands of the Amerindians. The date of the "discovery," for Díaz de Guzmán, is 1512 (1882: 7).

15. Medina, for example, pays special attention to the information Fernández de Oviedo claims to have gotten from Alonso de Santa Cruz, a sailor and cosmographer in Cabot's expedition, on the River Plate (1959 [1535–47]: 355–59).

16. Medina advances the hypothesis that the specific site of the landing is the place on the Uruguayan coast known as Martín Chico.

17. The already familiar account of feigned indigenous hospitality precedes this quotation, as does an account of the different names of the river (Mar Dulce, de Solís, de la Plata) throughout history.

18. Actually, Azara's speculation on Solís's confusion regarding the region's ethnic groups is based on the assumption that the 1512 voyage took place. If the existence of that voyage is not accepted, the hypothesis stating that Solís found two different indigenous groups in his voyages is not possible. As a curiosity in the history of attributing the massacre to various indigenous groups, a twentieth-century critic, Andrés Saumell, attributes the killing of Solís to the Guenoa in a footnote (in Ulloa 1990: 2:205).

19. I refer readers to the passages in volume 1 in which Azara denies the cannibalism of the Charrúa.

20. This version has been so persuasive that Medina, for example, dedicates several pages to demonstrating that the banquet took place. It is noteworthy that Medina declares explicitly that he will not try to identify the ethnic group to which the cannibals belonged; he will only establish the precise site at which the encounter took place. His strongest argument, in my opinion, is the testimony of Cabot (which appears in the caption to his map), who allegedly learned about the massacre directly from its only survivor, Francisco del Puerto (Medina 1897: cclxxx–cclxxxvii). Madero believes, however, that all the versions that refer to cannibalistic acts are part of a European imaginative tradition and that we should refrain from reaching a conclusion until we have access to more reliable documents (1892: 28–29).

21. Columbus's discourse, which described the Arawaks—who neither had writing nor built monuments—was far more paradigmatic for those chroniclers describing hunter–gatherers or early agriculturalists than for those who had to depict highly complex societies, such as the Inca or the Mexica. That is probably why the portraits of the Amerindians produced by the chroniclers of the River Plate region owe more to Columbus's discourse than do, say, those produced by Hernán Cortés or Bernal Díaz.

22. Beatriz Pastor reaches this conclusion at the end of her analysis of Columbus's discourse from the second voyage on (1988 [1983]: 20).

23. For Pastor, Columbus's discourse is also a mystifying one, but (with good reason, I believe) she does not consider it one of the founders of the epic model. Hernández Sánchez-Barba, for his part, adheres to a critical tradition that can be traced to books such as Ida Rodríguez Prampolini's *Amadises de América* (1948). Rodríguez Prampolini associates the epic hero in the strictest sense with the heroes of chivalric novels and considers the discourses structured around the adventures of the epic–chivalric hero as Hispanic American epics of the conquistador experience.

24. Hernán Vidal talks about the epic as a legitimating ideological instrument (1976: 35–43).

25. I am paraphrasing Lucía Invernizzi Santa Cruz (1986: 100). Something similar can be seen in Cabeza de Vaca's *Naufragios,* the text that Invernizzi analyzes. In Pastor (1988 [1983]), *Naufragios* is the counterpart to the mystifying epic of Cortés.

26. Frederic Jameson argues that history presents itself in a textual form that implies a narrative. In the master narratives that underlie any text, a subject of history and a telos, or an end, is present (1981: 28–29, 49).

27. This gaze is therefore similar (although with variations) to that of the eighteenth-century voyagers who will be studied later. The differences result, of course, from the historical stages of the epistemes—that is, the fifteenth and eighteenth centuries—in which the groups of voyagers were operating.

28. For a historical study of the evolution of the Patagonians (whose possible origin could be found in the chivalric novel) in the European imagination, see Duviols (1985: 55–71).

29. On the name "Montevideo," I refer readers to Buenaventura Caviglia's ingenious *La etimología del nombre Montevideo* (1925), which proposes dozens of possible etymologies, including *Monte Vireo, Monte Violo Ioan Diaz Yolis, Monte sexto destas Indias,* and the well-known *Monte sexto de este a oeste.*

30. For a study of clothing as a rhetorical instrument that represents and organizes power relationships, see Meléndez (1995), in which the author analyzes a range of colonial texts, from Columbus's diary to Concolorcorvo's *El lazarillo.* In these texts, European subjects present clothing as a sign of civilization that distinguishes dressed, "civilized" Occidental subjects from the naked, "barbaric" indigenous subjects (Meléndez 1995: esp. 411–18).

31. What follows is a synopsis of the itineraries of these two expeditions. Cabot, who was heading toward the Maluco, lost a ship in Brazil (Santa Catarina island). While he was there, he met two former members of Solís's crew, who told him about the presence of silver in the River Plate region. Based on this new information, he decided to change the course of his navigation to explore that region. At the same time, García was commanding an expedition to the River Plate. He departed some time after Cabot and ran into problems in the Canary Islands. When he finally reached his destination, he discovered, much to his surprise, that Cabot was already there. In the meantime, Cabot had founded a small settlement and fort at Sancti Spiritu, on the shores of the Paraná River. From that vantage point, he was planning to travel upriver to find the promised silver and was preparing to leave when García arrived. As a consequence, the captains came into conflict over who had the right to command the exploration. After

a few discussions with Cabot, García decided to return to Spain. For more details about these episodes, see Medina (1897; 1908a; 1908b) and Madero (1892).

32. In another *relación,* dated 1537, the river is called "of Silver." By that time, however, calling the river "of Silver" had become customary (Andrés de Urdaneta, "Relación escrita y presentada," in Medina 1888: 3:387).

33. Madero also believes that the survivors of Solís's expedition were the first to give the river its current name (1892: 303).

34. These companions are mentioned by Luiz Ramírez ("Carta de Luiz Ramírez," in Madero 1892: 1:333); they are also mentioned in, among other documents, the records of the suit against Cabot ("Interrogatorio presentado por Sebastián Caboto," in Medina 1908a: 1:462).

35. It should be noted that, in the questionnaire presented by García, he uses the name "Silver River" to refer to the estuary (Medina 1908a: 2:165).

36. As noted earlier, Madero shares the thesis that the process that changed the river's name started in Santa Catarina. But he differs with Medina in that he believes the diplomacy of the Portuguese and the indifference of King Charles V were the main reasons for the change (1892: 305).

37. It is possible that these Amerindians were the Charrúa, because San Salvador seems to have been under their territorial influence at that time. According to Cabrera and Femenías (1990: 13), all of the available documentary evidence suggests that this area was inhabited by the Charrúa, at least during the sixteenth century. However, judging from the investigation of these issues conducted by Diego Bracco (1998), which will be examined later, this is not a proven fact.

38. Of course, Cabot's declaration about the events differs dramatically from that of the other witnesses, who accuse Cabot of not having worried about the fate of Montoya's men. Fortunately for Montoya's men, another ship in the armada got lost and found them by chance, making their return to Spain possible.

39. Incorporating another voice into a discourse does not cause that discourse to lose its monologic status, because its subject can filter or modify the Other's voice to the point of distortion. Michel de Certeau thinks in similar terms when he argues that discourse quoting the discourse of the Other cannot ever be the discourse of the Other itself (1989 [1986]: 78).

40. Cristobal Jaques, a Frenchman in Portugal's service, had briefly explored the estuary, but little else is known about his expedition, as Medina rightly points out (1908a: 1:141). A document survives in which one of the sailors on Loaisa's voyage tells how he and some of his companions were taken prisoner by Jaques' armada ("Declaraciones que algunos marineros de la nao San Gabriel dieron en Pernambuco," in Medina 1888: 3:157). Ramírez also mentions the French captain: "We feared that the armada of Cristobal Jaques, captain at the service of the King of Portugal, who had visited this Solís River, and promised a certain Francisco del Puerto we found there that he would return. If it was that Cristobal Jaques who entered the river, our ships would be in great trouble" (in Madero 1892: 348). Little information is available about the date of Jaques' voyage. The only sure fact is that it took place after 1521 and before 1525, as Felipe Bosch suggests (1971: 21).

41. The importance of naming as an act of possession and of referring as a performative act will be discussed later in this chapter.

42. For a discussion of the sources that refer to that episode, such as Francisco de Xerez, Cristóbal de Mena, and many others, see MacCormack (1989).

43. We will see that Barco Centenera tells a story about Spaniards who are taken prisoner by the Charrúa, but he provides no information about the captives' lives among their captors.

44. For a critique of some of the Todorov book's shortcomings, see Clendinnen (1993: *passim*) and Adorno (1989: 203–207).

45. One of the best-known exceptions to this attitude is the *Naufragios* by Alvar Núñez, who was a captive of North American Indians for many years.

46. To date, no documents have come to light recording the experiences of captives among the Amerindians of the northern shore of the River Plate.

47. The same device was applied to the region's flora and fauna, as will be discussed later. A peculiarity of naming as an act of possession in the lands under study is that the act was often mediated by the Guaraní interpreters to whom Schuller refers. It should be pointed out that Jitrik's words should not be interpreted literally: The land already had owners. Although they did not count as owners in the European imaginary, they did exist outside the Western subject's mind.

48. See also Jitrik (1983: 101). Fernando Aínsa describes the Europeans' modification of the observed reality as a selective reorganization of reality. In his view, naming and possession are descriptive: They selectively enumerate what the author arbitrarily chooses (1977: 97–98).

For the ceremonial aspect of possession throughout the conquest period, see Greenblatt (1991) and Seed (1995).

Chapter Two

1. After Schmidel escaped from the terrible situation in Buenos Aires, he went to Asunción, where most of his narrative is set. His stay on the lands north of the River Plate was very brief. For this reason, his gaze tends to resemble that of the traveler (of which the documents from the Magellan's and Loaisa's expeditions are good examples). Schmidel, however, seems a little more prone to describing details than were his predecessors.

2. *La Argentina* offers a history of the River Plate region that includes a detailed narration of the events that occurred during the Ortiz de Zárate expedition. It also narrates events that have very little or nothing to do with the main topic: for example, the adventures and misdeeds of the British pirate Drake. This has brought about the severe criticism the poem has suffered from scholars who expected Barco Centenera to respect the thematic unity typical of classic epic poems. For a review of some of those critiques, see Verdesio (1993a). Some portions of that article—especially those that deal with Barco Centenera's poem—are reproduced here.

3. See, among others, Canal Feijóo (1984: 131); Coester (1938 [1916]: 16–17); Rojas (1924: 194–201); de Angelis (1910a: i).

4. For a complete panorama of the critical production on Spanish-language epic poetry, see Pierce (1968: 31–51).

5. For a study of these criticisms, see Verdesio (1993a).

6. No page number is given in the original. The writer positions himself as the carrier of a new knowledge that deserves to be propagated throughout the world. We will later see that this situation of enunciation (shared by most European explorers and chroniclers) identifies the world with Europe.

7. This is the Ciceronian notion of history as a teacher for one's life (*magistra vitae*), as a summa of universal knowledge (Mignolo 1981: 361–62).

8. This characterization of the gnoseological attitude of the European subject vis-à-vis America can be traced as far back as the works by Alfonso Reyes, who even considered the new continent to be a creation of Europe. His approach, unlike Pastor's, was devoid of any critical edge regarding this European gnoseological attitude—to the point that his text sometimes sounds like a celebration of the "creation" of America by the European subject (Reyes 1942: 10, 16, 37, 65). The production of America as a construct is the thesis that inspires Edmundo O'Gorman's *La invención de América* (1958), and it informs some passages of Enrique Pupo-Walker's *La vocación literaria del pensamiento histórico en América* (1982: 38–64). It is also mentioned by Angel Rosenblat, who, in turn, refers to other authors who have studied the European attitude that consists of verifying more than "discovering" the New World (1977: 160). Another author who says that the European subject classified American reality according to a pre-existing system before actual observation took place is Anthony Pagden (1982: 2, 10–11).

9. Reyes (1942: 58–65) and Rosenblat (1977: 141–51) write about the influence exerted on Columbus and the early explorers by the literary corpus on *terrae incognitae*.

10. In this article, Mignolo enumerates the different sources of information and their truth value, basing his classification on the historical metatext of the historiography of the Indies: 1) direct access to the information (produced by eyewitnesses or agents); 2) indirect, immediate access (produced by those who lived in the Indies in a later historical moment or by writers who lived in Spain but were contemporaries of the events narrated); and 3) indirect, mediated access (written from Spain at a chronological moment after the events). Among other authors, Mario Hernández Sánchez-Barba states the importance of personal experience for the legitimation of the discourses produced by the first chroniclers of the Indies (1978: 31–32, 47, 52, 58).

11. At that time, the name "Carib" was applied not only to the ethnic group from the Caribbean, but also to cannibalistic peoples.

12. He is referring to the mythological animal that carried the magic, homonymous stone.

13. Anagpitan, according to Barco Centenera, is the name given to the carbuncle by the Guaraní: "*diablo que reluze como fuego*" ("a devil that shines like fire" [1602: 21v).

14. On the distortion of reality through the use of strategies of identification and verification, see Pastor (1988 [1983]: 6–7).

15. See Pastor (1988 [1983]: 7–18). The irruption of "fable" that Alfonso Reyes discusses results in a representation in which fabulous visions take the place of realities (1942: 62). The monsters of the unknown lands lived in the popular fantasies of Europe as a whole (Rosenblat 1977: 148). One can confirm this statement simply by looking

at the age of "discovery" maps on which monsters appear in the margins (Harley 1990: *passim*).

16. Jitrik studies this Columbian strategy, although he does not use these examples (1983: 125–28).

17. On the diversity of spellings with which Columbus attempted to account for the new objects he observed, see Menéndez Pidal (1968: 9–46).

18. On representing the colonial subject using borrowed languages, see Zavala (1989: 332–33).

19. On the role of binary hierarchical relationships used by European subjects to represent the American Other, see Adorno (1988a: 62).

20. This is the definition Meltzer (1987: 71) offers: "The person who regards the sentence about Odysseus as either true or false is attributing a nominatum to the name 'Odysseus', but cannot, in Frege's view, ascertain truth-value. In other words, because fiction has no nominata, it is incapable of signifying truth. But the person reading the sentence about Odysseus clearly understands to whom the name 'Odysseus' refers, creating what we may call a 'cognitive nominatum.'" This notion is related to some of the ideas at play in this book, especially the one postulating that "true" objects are identifiable not as simple "presences" (independent from the lucubrations of the observer) but as products of an activity—that is, as a result of a process that constructs true objects less than discovers them (Lewis 1979: 461).

21. "All can be referred to, providing we have the necessary context, in the make-believe mode (just as all qualities can be referred to in a non-fictional mode by our speaking about them)" (Whiteside 1987: 200). Although these concepts come from Whiteside's analyses of literary texts, they are also useful in studying nonfiction, or serious (in Searle's terminology [1975: 619–32]), discourses. White, de Certeau, and many others have shown that historical discourse uses the same rhetorical devices found in fictional discourse.

22. Lewis (1987). Whiteside talks about a tension produced by the dialectics between text and reader (1987: 203); Meltzer presupposes these dialectics when she proposes the "cognitive referent."

23. The European man of letters was the archdeacon's ideal reader. According to Abdul Jan Mohamed, imperialism has two stages: the dominant (the earliest, when conquest and colonization are achieved by coercive means), and the hegemonic (where domination is exerted through the ideological apparatuses). During the first stage, the discourses produced by European subjects about the colonies are addressed to a European readership; in the second, those discourses are addressed to a colonized subject (1985: 61–63). Barco Centenera writes for an audience in which the ideal reader is a European-educated subject, so his text is produced *for* and *by* that reader. Peter Hulme, too, discusses the domestic scope of some European discourses on the New World (1986: 7).

24. I use quotation marks in this way—despite the critique in Searle (1973) of Russell's quoting practices, and despite Rubén Tani's ideas on the subject (1982)—so the non-specialized reader will not be confused. Tani would use the quotation marks in the following way: 'northern shore of the River Plate,' 'Charrúa' (1982: 262).

25. *Insidiosæ* (sly, treacherous) was the adjective Peter Martyr used, although it is not clear whether the Amerindians he was talking about were the Charrúa.

26. I refer here to such factors as the lack of ongoing indigenous agricultural practices that could sustain the Spaniards and the absence of an indigenous population concentrated in urban centers, which could have made controlling the land easier for the invaders.

27. It should be noted that the Spaniards also encountered considerable resistance in several regions of Mesoamerica and the Andes outside Cuzco and Tenochtitlan, the capitals of the Inca and Mexica states. For a study of a conflict between the Spaniards and indigenous groups not organized around a state, see Bolaños (1994).

28. In his *Institutio Oratoria* (X. 1. 31), Quintilian says that history and epic are closely tied. G. Pontano also called attention to the relationship between these two types of discourse (as quoted in Mignolo 1981: 374).

29. Although I agree with Adorno's objections to Todorov's *The Conquest of America*—notably, that he studies only texts written by the conquistadors (Adorno 1989: 203–207)—I cannot analyze texts produced by the American Other in this investigation. Unlike the corpus from the regions studied by Todorov, the corpus that has the lands of the northern shore of the River Plate as its referent does not include texts produced by indigenous groups.

Chapter Three

1. The date 1576 is proposed by both José Guevara and Father Pedro Lozano. Azara, on the other hand, proposes 1584, although he does not offer any proof, as Bauzá points out (1965 [1880, 1895–98]: 137). Bauzá presents as fact that the Amerindians who harrassed the Spaniards were the Charrúa (ibid.: 135–37).

2. Coni quotes a document dated July 12, 1628, in which Hernadarias claims that he owns the cattle populating the northern shore of the River Plate, because he brought them from his *estancias* (ranches). The witnesses' depositions confirm Hernandarias's claims.

3. For more information about Hernandarias's life, see Molina (1948) and Guastavino (1928).

4. Some groups of Charrúa moved to the shores of the Paraná because, as Sallaberry (1926) demonstrates, they were lured by the meat of the cattle that proliferated on the Santa Fe and Entre Ríos *estancias.*

5. Hernandarias, a pragmatic man, obtained a positive result even out of the failed expedition: He was able to explore the unknown lands south of Buenos Aires. For a detailed account of the expedition and its itinerary, see Molina (1948: 146–55) and Aranguren (1963: 65–68).

6. On his talent as a statesman, see Tiscornia (1973).

7. Molina uses this appellation in the title of his book and on many occasions in the text. Madero praises Hernandarias for his contribution to the development of public instruction in the region (1892: 286). Another celebration of the governor can be found in Aranguren (1963).

8. Lozano (1873: 3:305).

9. For a detailed biography of Hernandarias, see Guastavino (1928) and Molina (1948).

10. See Molina (1948), Madero (1892: 284–90), and Lozano (1873: esp. passages in vol. 3 that refer to Hernandarias).

11. Coni made this statement in a conference speech. Menéndez does not mention the date and place of the conference.

12. The second *reducción* is named San Juan de Céspedes in another document ("Carta del gobernador Céspedes," in Azarola Gil 1933: 214).

13. Aranguren says that one of Hernandarias's concerns was to control the illegal butchering of cows by fugitive Spaniards, Amerindians, and wanderers (*vagos*) on the lands that he had populated with cattle, including the eastern shore of the Uruguay River (1963: 139–44). The abundance of cattle, then, prompted the creation of a new social type.

Chapter Four

Epigraph: Cielito or *cielo* was a popular musical genre that originated in the gaucho culture of the River Plate.

1. The Portuguese made an even earlier incursion into the land under study. In 1673, Portuguese sailors took possession (symbolically, of course) of the Montevideo area by sculpturing the crown's coat of arms in the *Cerro* (hill) (Azarola Gil 1933: 47).

2. I assume that the translation of the Portuguese text was done by Azarola Gil, because he does not name a translator.

3. The *Bandeirantes* were groups of people from São Paulo who made their living by capturing Indians to sell as slaves and by looking for sources of precious metals. Their expeditions to the continent's interior were called *bandeiras*—hence, the name.

4. For a detailed account of the reconquest of San Gabriel, see Azarola Gil (1931: 45–57).

5. Apart from Hernandarias and Garay, few European leaders excelled as conquistadors or warriors in the history of the territory.

6. For the record, regardless of whether this expedition took place, Cabot was not at the service of Spain in 1496.

7. Most of the time, the Tape came to the territory following their spiritual (and military) leaders, the Jesuits. I will say more about the end of the Charrúa in the Conclusion of the book.

8. Confusion of ethnic groups is a trait that this text shares with the early chroniclers' texts. It is surprising, though, that an educated eighteenth-century European subject was not able to fare better at the gnoseological level—at least, compared with his contemporaries (for instance, Lozano, as we will see later).

9. Eneas had to cross the famous Elysian Fields on his way to Hades. According to Curtius, the origin of the expression *locus amoenus* can be found in Eneas's itinerary (1975 [1948]: 275–76). He also affirms that some Christian poets used the Virgilian image of the Elysian Fields to describe Paradise (ibid.: 285). On the treatment of this topic (the abundant and pleasant place) by the chroniclers of the Indies and its identification with paradise on Earth, see Duviols (1985: 19–42).

10. This episode is narrated in detail in Azarola Gil (1933: 81–87). It is also documented in "Diario del gobernador de Buenos Aires," in *Biblioteca del Comercio del Plata* (1982 [1849]: 1:100, *passim*).

11. See Zabala (1982 [1849]). For an account of the events after the foundation of Montevideo, see Azarola Gil 1933: 90–151, 163–98).

12. This ethnic group has been called by many different names, but the most common, apart from Minuan, has been Guenoa. For more information about this group and its history on the northern shore of the River Plate, see Bracco (1998).

13. For an account of the logistical help that the Amerindians received from the Portuguese, see Azarola Gil (1933: 156).

14. A detailed account of this war can be found in Azarola Gil (1933: 151–62).

15. One can replace the referent "lands of Uruguay" with "north of the River Plate" or "Banda Oriental of Uruguay" (as it was sometimes called).

16. On this issue, see also Schiaffino (1928: 206). It is interesting that, while the Spanish side viewed the enemy's retreat as a cowardly action, the Portuguese represent it as a triumph of their own shrewdness—a matter of perspective, of course.

17. In actuality, not all of the stanzas in this poem are *décimas,* despite what the title and first verses say: *"En décimas te he de hacer/ de toda la expedición/ una plena relación/ de sumo gusto y placer"* (In *décimas* I will relate/ the expedition with great pleasure" ["Relación exacta" 1920: 276]).

18. Cornejo Polar calls the situation in which a cultural system is dominated by a discursive form belonging to a different culture a heterogeneous text (1980: *passim*).

19. Some scholars prefer to define this text as a poem written in the gaucho style instead of qualifying it as *gauchesco* because it shows some aspects of Uruguayan lands and some activities typical of the area (Becco, "La primitiva poesía gauchesca," in Becco and Weinberg 1977: 12). Lauro Ayestarán also considers this poem an antecedent to the *gauchesco* genre and published it in his *La primitiva poesía gauchesca en el Uruguay. Vol. 1 1812–1838* (1950: 65–84). Although *gauchesco* poetry is a type of literature in which the literate subject creates a language (which shapes itself partly through the appropriation of stylistic devices that existed in the oral genres of the illiterate countryside), and although the gaucho is constructed from outside, it would not be fair to say that one faces a representation of the gaucho that resembles later literary experiments, such as Sarmiento's *Facundo,* or the portrait offered by hostile observers such as Concolorcorvo. On this issue, see Ludmer (1988: 27–31) and Rama (1982 [1976]: 179–211). In fact, the *cielitos* by Bartolomé Hidalgo (who fought for the Banda Oriental independence circa 1812), dating from the beginning of the genre, praise the gaucho enormously and present him as the epitome of patriotism. See Hidalgo (1979).

20. This can be observed in the original in Spanish (which is not included in this book due to lack of space). In it, the first line of this *octava real* rhymes with the last line of the previous one, which says: *"fue de la forma siguiente"* ("it happened as follows"). Other irregularities that should be pointed out are that some verses in the poem are not endecasyllables and, in some cases, four rhymes are paired, a disposition that is not very common in this type of stanza.

21. The last verse has twelve syllables.

Chapter Five

1. This accounts for the abundance of texts with "natural history," "history of plants," and so on in their titles. On this subject, see Mignolo (1981: 368).

2. On Europe's position regarding the orality–literacy dichotomy and the need to use writing to produce true history, see Mignolo (1982; 1986a; 1989a). For a similar attitude regarding the history produced by European subjects of Africa, see Gates (1985: 2–20, esp. 11). A general treatment of the dichotomy in Latin American history, colonial and otherwise, can be found in Rama (1984: esp. chap. 2).

3. Bakhtin's notion of polyphony also describes discourse in which a single enunciator filters—and appropriates—the Other's discourse at the time he or she quotes it. That is why the reader should not interpret my use of the term "polyphony" in a Bakhtinian way.

4. In Aristotle's system, the barbarian was an irrational and bestial being (Elliott 1974: 103–4). Pagden mentions the same traits and says that the term "barbarian" is the opposite of the notion of "civilization"; he also says that the term "barbarian" is loaded with negative connotations that indicate inferiority. In the ranking of humankind constructed by the European episteme since the hegemony of Greek culture, the barbarian occupied the last place (Pagden 1982: 15, 18, 20). Hulme also traces the origin and connotations of the term since its first uses by Greek authors, especially Herodotus (1986: 20–21). The construction of the Amerindian as a barbaric and savage being is a strategy used by colonial writers of Christian and Occidental origin, all of whom are part of a tradition that began in America with Columbus.

5. According to Montaigne, all human societies are "barbaric" in the eyes of other human societies: "We call barbarism all that differs from our mores and uses; it seems that we have a definition of truth and reason that is solely based on the ideas about the opinions and uses of the country we are from" (1979: 254).

6. This picture of a "democratic" indigenous group cannot be found in chronicles describing areas dominated by the Mexica or the Inca, where a pyramidal and authoritarian social structure was the rule.

7. For a thorough analysis of the "polemic on the New World," in which Buffon's and de Pauw's doctrines are described, see Gerbi (1960 [1955]).

8. For an analysis of the role that notions of warfare played in the construction of the Amerindian Other during colonial times, see Adorno (1989: 216–18).

9. It should be noted that, although Azara resorts to the chivalric model, the description that he offers of the Amerindians he sees in the region (early agriculturalists and hunter–gatherers) differs considerably from the ones found in earlier chronicles describing the states of the Inca and the Mexica. Some of these earlier writers resorted more to Western literary tradition (the epic model, in Cortés's case) in order to praise the complex organization of societies that resembled, in more than one respect, those of the West.

10. Since Columbus's first voyage, cannibalism had been a permanent concern for the conquistadors. Europeans were obsessed with finding Amerindians who fit one of the stereotypes of the unknown lands—that is, savages who ate human flesh. Hulme offers a reconstruction of the history of the terms "cannibal" and "carib" as well as of their ideological and psychological connotations (1986: 45–87).

11. Bracco presents two documents written by witnesses, not historians, that he rescued from oblivion showing that the names Charrúa and Minuan (Guenoa) were

used interchangeably: "Guenoa infidel Indians (or as they are called in Buenos Aires: Minuan)" (quoted in Bracco 1998: 110), and "the Guenoa nation, called Minuan by the Spaniards from Santa Fe and Buenos Aires, who corrupt the word" (quoted in ibid.: 111).

12. In the typology by León, which is reproduced in Zavala (1989: 336–37), two different terms are used to refer to the same concept: "*salta atrás*" (jump backward) and "*torna atrás*" (comes back). Both are defined as the result of a marriage between a Spanish man and an Albino woman ("*español y mujer albina*"). Albinos, in turn, resulted from the mixing of a Spanish man and a Moorish woman ("*español y mujer morisca*"). Azara's and León's denominations have basically the same derogatory overtones.

13. Women do appear as subjects in colonial texts about other areas of the River Plate. Further, one very early text (1546) that has survived is a letter written by a woman: Isabel de Guevara, who lived in the River Plate region. For a study of the letter, see Lopreto (1996). However, women are not a common presence in the texts that make up the corpus that I have chosen to study.

14. For a discussion of the recent body of works about the feminization of the indigenous Other (and other marginal groups) and the reasons behind it, see Bolaños (1994: 138–49). One of those reasons, according to Bolaños, was the European subject's need for free (or slave) labor: By representing the Amerindian as effeminate (and often as a sodomite) against the patriarchal European framework, which regarded the feminine as inferior to the masculine, colonial authors proposed the moral (and legal, in the case of sodomites) condemnation of the Amerindians. At the same time, they offered a justification for their economic exploitation (ibid.: 145).

15. Colonial authors did not use the strategy of feminizing the Other only for human beings. On the contrary, the process started with feminization of the land—of America itself—as de Certeau (1988) shows in his analysis of Stradanus's engraving representing a civilized and fully dressed Vespucci awakening a naked woman who represents America. Other critics who have since studied the engraving include Louis Montrose (1993: 177–83) and Rabasa (1993: 23–48).

16. Spivak uses the term "desire" (1988b: 203); I prefer "anxiety." The concept—but not the expression "anxiety for the Other"—can be found in Gossman (1986: 25).

17. Adorno's article represents an outstanding application of de Certeau's categories and ideas to the area of colonial studies, which is why I quote from it rather than cite de Certeau directly. On the construction of the same in opposition to the Other, see Brennan (1990: 59), in which the author emphasizes the impact that the European presence in foreign and unknown lands had on the posterior formation of those lands' national narratives.

18. On this procedure, see de Certeau (1989 [1986]: 67, 73).

Chapter Six

1. For a perspective similar to the one proposed in this chapter, see Duviols (1985: esp. 14). For an overview of the interests of European nations that did not possess vast lands in America, especially in the eighteenth century, see Meyer (1982: 17–39).

2. Recall that some of those earlier chroniclers had direct interests as governors or colonial officials. The Spanish writers' lack of direct interests in the Americas puts

these travelers in a category similar to that of the historians. They differ, however, in that the historians' discursive production took place within the framework of a disciplinary practice. In other words, travelers and historians produce classes or types of texts that belong to different discursive formations.

3. According to Estuardo Núñez, this tendency appears as early as the seventeenth century in European texts about America (1989: x–xi). Further, Aínsa points out the travelers' constant mobility and their tendency to produce inventories of what they see (1977: 99).

4. Ottsen was in charge of the *Silver World,* one of the ships that was heading to Buenos Aires, via Guinea, to establish commercial relations with that city. The tough conditions that Spain was imposing on Holland at the time account for the long expedition. It was financed by the Company of Distant Countries, which specialized in finding new commercial routes to replace the forbidden ones. Ottsen's text recounts the misfortunes (shipwrecks, storms, and kidnapping and arrest at the hands of the Portuguese) that the convoy suffered between its departure from Amsterdam and its arrival in the River Plate. It also narrates the capture of the ships by the Portugese at Bahía de Todos los Santos. Because the governor of Buenos Aires refused to allow the Dutch to do business with the city's people, the sailors spent most of their time in the River Plate region at anchor in the port of Buenos Aires.

5. Toller's text is written mostly in English, though it includes fragments in French and Latin. It relates the itinerary of an expedition that aimed to open a British commercial establishment in Buenos Aires that would be dedicated to the legal traffic in slaves. A peculiarity of this trip is that the crew had very little contact with the shores of the River Plate. The folios of the mansuscript that narrate the negotiations in Buenos Aires are missing.

6. In Medina, Cabot's map is reproduced only in part, and is inserted in a pocket on the last page—a kind of *hors texte.* The Mappamundi in its entirety is reproduced in Duviols (1985: 45). The same strategy of combining verbal and graphic representations to convey perceptions can be found in texts such as the *Nueva Corónica* by Guaman Poma. (On the interaction between verbal and iconic messages in Guaman Poma, see Adorno 1986). And, as we will see later, the interaction between the two semiotic systems is one of the most remarkable characteristics of Toller's text.

7. On the possible origin of the name "Monte Seredo," see the speculations by Buenaventura Caviglia (1925). Mario Buschiazzo cites another document registering "Monte Seredo" and declares that he has not seen the name in other chronicles or documents except in the navigational chart of San Bruno and other maps from the seventeenth and eighteenth centuries (1941: 32).

8. To give an idea about the Spanish crown's lack of interest in the territory, Rogelio Brito Stífano notes that no documents of the period contain testimony of anyone having seen the expedition while it was in the region from June to September (1953: 197).

9. Toller's account, together with other documents that offer graphic representations of the referent "Uruguay," deserves a separate study that records and analyzes iconic representations of the territory throughout colonial history. This kind of study could be called "the *mapping* of Uruguay." Collections of colonial maps and portulans of the River Plate already exist, among them the one compiled by Father Furlong.

An analysis of the impact of maps and geographic charts on the construction of the referent "Uruguay" can be found in Verdesio (1997a) and in the Conclusion of this book.

10. In Muratori (1752: 220–323). Cattaneo's first letter, written from Buenos Aires in 1729, narrates the journey from Cádiz to the River Plate. In this letter, he also dedicates a few pages to the history and natural history of the territory.

11. Cattaneo wrote this letter, dated May 20, 1730, from Santa María de las Misiones del Paraguay. It includes a brief account of the preparation—in Buenos Aires—of priests who were heading to the missions and a short description of the province in general.

12. Today, we not only know that those animals were not so big; we also know that they were not tigers.

13. I will not comment on the "truth" of these assertions here, because I did so in the discussion of Azara's opinions on this issue.

14. The modesty of the home Pernety describes stands in contrast to the luxury of some of the houses in Buenos Aires at that time. For testimony on that subject that includes pictures of furniture, see Furlong (1969: 320–41).

15. Pernety's ability not only to appreciate the landscape's beauty, but also to see its potential for exploitation, confirms what Núñez calls the "*consideraciones prácticas*" ("practical considerations ") of the European travelers (1989: xi). This discursive shift from the classical topic of the *locus amoenus* (where only esthetic elements are at play) to the topic of the abundant place (whose foundation is more pragmatic and economic than esthetic) was discussed earlier, in the chapter dedicated to the conflict over Colonia do Sacramento.

16. Bougainville, the leader of the expedition, portrays the inhabitants of Montevideo in a similar way (1980: 38). Another foreigner, Tadeo Haenke (who traveled to the River Plate in 1789 to join the Malaspina expedition), dedicates a long paragraph to commenting on Montevideans' scant inclination to work. In that passage, he blames the abundance of natural resources and the lack of moral values for the lack of social progress he observed in the region (1943 [1795]: 101–2).

17. This eighteen-year-old observer left his impressions (a little *hâtif*, according to Duviols) on the itinerary of the circumnavigation voyage and on Montevideo in a few pages, from which I quote.

18. Vivez also alludes to the women's penchant for lascivious dances (Taillemite 1977: 193).

19. It is interesting to compare Pernety's account with that of Concolorcorvo, another European subject who was outraged by the wanton African dances: "The blacks' amusements are the most barbaric and vulgar imaginable. . . . Their dances consist of moving their bellies and hips with immodesty, accompanied by ridiculous gestures which bring to mind the celebrations made by witches on Saturday [the sabbath]" (1985: 175–76). On the disgust that these dances engendered among Europeans and colonial authorities and prohibitions against them, see Furlong (1969: 163–65).

20. Furlong presents a picture of colonial society in the seventeenth and eighteenth centuries that has some points of contact with the barbaric sensibility studied by Barrán: "Thanks to the memories left by many French and English travelers who visited the River Plate at the end of the seventeenth and during the eighteenth century,

we know today, for sure, that the society of that era was not sad, narrow, or stifling at all. On the contrary, the joy and happiness of the people, due to the abundance with which nature presented them, was universal" (Furlong 1969: 107).

21. A slightly divergent view that does not emphasize sloth as the main cause of the chaos in the rural areas of the Banda Oriental blames instead the irrational exploitation and lack of responsibility of both the authorities and the owners. See Brito Stífano (1953: 345, 353, 355, and *passim*).

22. Almost all of Azara's suggestions can also be found in the anonymous memoir dated 1794. For a comparative analysis of these documents and two others, see Pivel Devoto (1957 [1952]: 59–69).

23. On the issues of authorship, biography, and circumstances of the production of this work, see Antonio Lorente Medina's introduction (Carrió de la Vandera 1985: xi).

24. Espinosa y Tello's impressions of Montevideo are far more complete than those left by Francisco Xavier de Viana, the only Uruguayan member of the expedition, who also wrote a diary (Viana 1958). His descriptions of the lands and peoples of the Banda Oriental have the peculiarity of commenting on those recorded by Concolorcorvo.

25. Karen Stolley discusses the genre to which *El lazarillo* should be assigned (1992: 25–47). She argues that, because of some of the strategies it employs, the text cannot be analyzed as a typical eighteenth-century travel book. One of those strategies involves the narrator's presenting himself as an enlightened author in order to question the veracity of travel books (ibid.: 46). I believe that Stolley's argument deserves careful attention. However, I include *El lazarillo* in this chapter dedicated to travelers because, in my opinion, its gaze is as tentative as that of the other travelers. Further, *El lazarillo* presents itself as interested in producing knowledge about the region being explored and, at the same time, shows a scientific attitude toward description—two traits that Stolley acknowledges are present in the book (ibid.: 34–37). Therefore, although I acknowledge that *El lazarillo* is not a typical eighteenth-century travel book, I believe that it can certainly be seen as related to that family of texts. The very fact that Stolley needed to produce an extensive and careful generic analysis in order to distinguish the text from travel literature suggests that it contains many similarities to that genre.

26. A similar view can be found in Espinosa y Tello (1938).

27. Again, for a discussion of clothing in Concolorcorvo's text, see Meléndez (1995).

28. Melo provides a less derogatory description: "These are the peons, the gauchos, *poor men whom necessity forces to take what they think has no owner,* to the advantage of those who pay miserable salaries" (1865: 279; emphasis added). Compare this passage with that by the anonymous author of the 1794 memoir: "Because they are used to a licentious life and a lucrative practice, *nothing is more difficult than to reduce them to Civility* (in Brito Stífano 1953: 360; emphasis added}. Haenke also portrays the gauchos as the opposite of civilization when he laments the fate of a (fictitious) laborious Galician immigrant whose son, in the absence of urban centers, turns his back on European work habits and "degenerates into a guaderio [*sic*]" (1943 [1795]: 101–2). The gaucho is represented this way even by twentieth-century *Criollo* critics who continue to view the nation with borrowed, Europeanized eyes. See the works by Azarola Gil in which he deals with the gauchos; Coni (1945); and many others.

29. Like so many others, Espinosa y Tello records the overpopulation of cattle in the region (1938: 281).

30. Recall that, in a passage quoted earlier, Azara referred to a similar smelly situation.

31. Although the gaucho appeared as a referent in Chapter 4, when we examined the letter/poem about the siege of the fortress ("Relación exacta" 1920), Concolorcorvo's text predates it. *El lazarillo* was written between the years 1773 and 1776, according to specialists on that text, whereas the *décimas* were written in 1778, at the earliest. According to Richard W. Slatta, an even earlier reference to the gaucho can be found in Jorge Juan and Antonio de Ulloa's *Noticias secretas de América* (1918) (Slatta 1983: 8). However, as Slatta acknowledges, the term "gaucho" in that work appears to refer to rural people in general in the area of Concepción, Chile (ibid.). What Slatta does not mention is that Juan and Ulloa use the term "*guasos*," not "gauchos" or "*gauderios*" (see Juan and Ulloa 1991: 572). The reason for this omission may lie in the fact that Slatta was using the 1918 Editorial América edition (instead of the 1991 edition from which I quote), in which the word "gauchos" is used instead of the original "*guasos*" (see Juan and Ulloa 1918: 2:247). A more extensive portrayal of the *guasos* by Ulloa, which includes a detailed description of their clothing, their skill in handling weapons (the *lanza* and the lasso), and their abilities as horsemen, can be found in *Viaje a la América meridional, vol. B* (Ulloa 1990: 268–70). For a discussion of authorship issues surrounding this book—that is, whether it was a solo effort by Ulloa or a joint effort with Juan—see Andrés Saumell's preface in ibid. (1:13).

32. A few decades later, in 1797, the locals tell the British traveler Sir John Constanse Davie that contraband is still a serious problem for the government (Davie 1805: 36–37).

33. I use this term in the sense that Walter Ong gives it: "Writing makes 'words' appear similar to things because we think of words as the visible marks signaling words to decoders: we can see and touch such inscribed 'words' in texts and books. Written words are residue. Oral tradition has no such residue or deposit" (1987 [1982]: 11). *Gauchesca* literature can also be considered an example of oral culture's "residue."

34. Interestingly, his love interest (whose name is the all-too-obvious Blanca, which means "white" in Spanish), is also a Spanish woman.

Conclusion

1. I take the image of the blank page from de Certeau (1988: xxv). I have argued elsewhere that a research agenda is needed that concentrates on studying the documentary evidence of European origin and the available archaeological data to help produce a more complex view of the territory in colonial times (Verdesio 1997a). In that paper, I also study the image of the territory and its inhabitants that is created by maps of the region.

2. For more information about these cultures, see, among others, Taddei (in Barrios Pintos 1989: 25–45).

3. Good examples of this are the articles by Carlos Ferrés and Juan H. Figueira (as quoted in Vidart 1996b: 20).

4. Renzo Pi Hugarte disagrees with this new model (1993: 46), although he does not say why. Another author who disagrees is Daniel Vidart, who attempts to support his position via infantile reasoning and logical fallacies. His repertoire of inaccuracies includes the attribution of ridiculous assertions—that the mound builders held slaves, for example, and that the population can be estimated at 300,000—to the most recent investigators, who never uttered such nonsense (1996b: 48, 51, 52, 54). Another of Vidart's outrageous assertions is that the only contribution the new investigations have made consists of a pumpkin seed, because the other objects found are not novel in the history of excavating the mounds (ibid.: 21, 36). To highlight the absurdity of this statement, suffice it to say that the mere exhumation of objects is useless without a reasonable archaeological chronology and context. That is something that the current investigators' predecessors—most of them mere aficionados—were never able to produce.

5. In an earlier article, the investigators advanced the opposite hypothesis—that is, of an egalitarian society—based on the objects (polished lithics, bones, fangs, shell beads, etc.) associated with the dead in the interments that they analyzed (Femenías et al. 1990: 352).

6. See Ferrés and Figueira (as quoted in Vidart 1996b).

7. For a survey of the elevations identified as "*bichaderos*" and for a summary description of them, see Femenías (1983).

8. For a synthesis of the hypotheses and findings from the most recent excavations, see Verdesio (1999).

9. In the contemporary Uruguayan social imaginary, Guaraní is almost synonymous with Paraguayan. However, there is some awareness of the Guaraní's presence in extensive parts of the territory of today's Brazil.

10. See Lopes de Souza (1926: 266–67). See also Barlow (1932: 156), in which the name is spelled "biguais."

11. On the diffusionist theories that postulate a panorama of civilizational evolution achieved by the succession of migratory waves, see López Mazz and Bracco (1989).

12. The *roza* involves burning parts of the soil in order to facilitate cultivation.

13. Fregeiro's speculation is based on agricultural vestiges from 860 B.P., which predates the period in which the Guaraní are believed to have arrived in the territory.

14. An exception to this practice of summer occupation might be found in the attack Cabot suffered in San Salvador at the hands of an unidentified ethnic group on August 14—winter in the Southern Hemisphere—according to Harrisse (1882: 213), who bases his date on Ramírez's text: "The night before the day of Our Lady of August" ("*Víspera de Na. Sa. de Agosto*" ["Carta de Luiz Ramírez,"] in Madero 1892: 1:333).

15. In the versions of this episode by Peter Martyr (1892: 459–60, Decade III, Liber X, Caput II), Herrera (1945 [1601–15]: 308), and others, the banquet takes place immediately after the killing.

16. We cannot, of course, rule out the possibility that official documents referring to the mound builders will come to the surface in the future.

17. Further confirmation of the temporal coincidence of the European and mound-building cultures can be found at sites excavated in what today is the Department of Treinta y Tres (Prieto et al. 1970: 35).

18. Although it is not advisable to identify archaeological evidence with historical-time ethnic groups, I will point out that abundant evidence of Guaraní utensils has been found in the mounds, especially in their most recent layers. One could, however, argue that the proportion of Guaraní utensils compared with the total number of exhumed objects is low (Cabrera 1992: 113). This presents yet another mystery: What happened to the Guaraní who settled in the lowlands or on the territory's eastern coasts? Did they return to the territory of modern-day Brazil? Did they undergo transculturation?

19. According to Mignolo, territoriality has different meanings for different subjects. For the members of a specific cultural tradition, it implies the appropriation of the territory in order to construct a past for it (a cultural abode), whereas for scholars, it means a field of knowledge (1986: 152). As should be obvious by now, I understand territoriality in the latter sense.

20. The Inter-American Bank for Development, the International Monetary Fund, and the General Agreement on Tariffs and Trade.

Bibliography

Abreu, Capistrano de. 1900. "Prologue." Pp. i–xxxvi in Simão Pereira de Sá. *Historia topográphica e bellica da Nova Colonia do Sacramento do Rio da Prata.* Rio de Janeiro: Typographia Leuzinger.

Acosta y Lara, Eduardo. 1961. *La guerra de los charrúas en la Banda Oriental.* Montevideo: Monteverde.

Adorno, Rolena. 1986. *Guaman Poma: Writing and Resistance in Colonial Peru.* Austin: University of Texas Press.

———. 1988a. "El sujeto colonial y la construcción cultural de la alteridad." *Revista de Crítica Literaria Latinoamericana* 14, no. 28: 55–68.

———. 1988b. "Nuevas perspectivas en los estudios coloniales hispanoamericanos." *Revista de Crítica Literaria Latinoamericana* 14, no. 28: 11–28.

———. 1989. "Arms, Letters and the Native Historian in Early Colonial Mexico." Pp. 201–24 in *Re/Discovering Colonial Writing.* Hispanic Issues 4. Ed. René Jara and N. Spadaccini. Minneapolis: Prisma Institute.

Aguirre, Juan Francisco. 1905. "Diario de Aguirre." Pp. 4:1–151 in *Anales de la Biblioteca.* Ed. Paul Groussac.

Aínsa, Fernando. 1977. *Los buscadores de la Utopía.* Caracas: Monte Avila.

Albo, Francisco. 1888. "Diario o derrotero del viage de Magallanes desde el cabo de San Agustin en el Brasil, hasta el regreso a España de la nao Victoria, Escrito por Francisco Albo." Pp. 213–56 in José Toribio Medina. *Colección de documentos inéditos para la historia de Chile.* Vol. 1. Santiago de Chile: Imprenta Ercilla.

Anderson, Benedict. 1983. *Imagined Communities.* London: Verso.

Anderson Imbert, Enrique. 1954. *Historia de la literatura hispanoamericana.* 2 vols. México: Fondo de Cultura Económica.

Angelis, Pedro de. 1910a. "Discurso preliminar a la *Argentina* de Barco Centenera." Pp. i–viii in *Colección de Obras y Documentos relativos a la Historia Antigua y Moderna de las Provincias del Río de la Plata.* 2nd ed. Vol. 2. Buenos Aires: Librería Nacional de J. Lajouane & Cia.

———. 1910b. "Discurso preliminar a la Historia del P. Guevara." Pp. i–vii in *Colección de Obras y Documentos relativos a la Historia Antigua y Moderna de las Provincias del Río de la Plata.* 2nd ed. Vol. 2. Buenos Aires: Librería Nacional de J. Lajouane & Cia.

"Año de 1762. Relación exacta del sitio de la Colonia del Sacramento, Plaza Portuguesa en la costa del N. del Rio de la Plata. Formada por uno que se halló en el mismo sitio, con todas las reflexiones conducentes á la mas cabal intelijencia de sus circunstancias." 1982 [1849]. Pp. 13–14 in *Biblioteca del Comercio del Plata. T. VII. Biblioteca de Impresos Raros Americanos. T. XI.* Montevideo: Universidad de la República.

Aranguren, Carlos M. 1963. *Hernandarias. Primer gran estanciero criollo del Río de la Plata.* Paraná, Argentina: Nueva Impresora de Brest y Viñas París.

Ayestarán, Lauro. 1950. *La primitiva poesía gauchesca en el Uruguay. Vol. 1 1812–1838.* Montevideo: El Siglo Ilustrado.

Azara, Félix de. 1847. *Descripción e historia del Paraguay y Río de la Plata.* 2 vols. Madrid: Sanchiz.

———. 1904. *Geografía física y esférica de las provincias del Paraguay y Misiones guaraníes.* Ed. Rodolfo Schuller. Montevideo: Anales del Museo Nacional de Montevideo.

———. 1943. *Memoria sobre el estado rural del Río de la Plata y otros informes.* Buenos Aires: Bajel.

———. 1969 [1923]. *Viajes por la América Meridional.* Madrid: Espasa Calpe.

Azarola Gil, Luis Enrique. 1927. *Crónicas y linajes de la gobernación del Plata.* Buenos Aires: J. Lajouane & Cía.

———. 1931. *La epopeya de Manuel Lobo.* Madrid: Compañía Ibero-Americana de Publicaciones S.A.

———. 1933. *Los orígenes de Montevideo 1607–1749.* Buenos Aires: "La Facultad."

Bakhtin, M. M. 1981. *The Dialogic Imagination.* Trans. Caryl Emerson and Michael Holquist. Austin: University of Texas Press.

Barco Centenera, Martín del. 1602. *La Argentina y conquista del Río de la Plata, con otros acaecimientos de los Reynos del Perú, Tucumán, y estado del Brasil.* Lisbon: Pedro Crasbeck.

Barlow, Roger. 1932. *A Brief Summe of Geographie.* Second Series, no. 69. London: Hakluyt Society.

Barrán, José Pedro. 1991 [1989]. *Historia de la sensibilidad en el Uruguay. La cultura "bárbara" (1800–1860).* Vol. 1. Montevideo: Ediciones de la Banda Oriental.

———. 1991 [1990]. *Historia de la sensibilidad en el Uruguay. El Disciplinamiento (1860–1920).* Vol. 2. Montevideo: Ediciones de la Banda Oriental.

Barrios Pintos, Anibal. 1989. "Los indígenas del tiempo histórico." Pp. 25–45 in *Artigas: de los aborígenes cazadores al tiempo presente.* Ed. A. Barrios Pintos. Vol. 1. Montevideo: Ministry of Education and Culture.

———. 1991. *Los aborígenes del Uruguay.* Montevideo: Linardi y Risso.

Bauzá, Francisco. 1965 [1880, 1895–98]. *Historia de la dominación española en el Uruguay.* Vol. 2. In *Colección de clásicos uruguayos.* Ed. Juan E. Pivel Devoto. Montevideo: Biblioteca Artigas.

Becco, Horacio J., Félix Weinberg et al. 1977. *Trayectoria de la poesía gauchesca.* Buenos Aires: Plus Ultra.

Bennett, Tony. 1985. "Texts in History: The Determinations of Readings and Their Texts." *Journal of the Midwest MLA* 18, no. 1: 1–16.

Bermejo de la Rica, Antonio. 1920. *La Colonia del Sacramento.* Toledo, Spain: Imp. de la Editorial Católica Toledana.

Beverley, John. 1993. *Against Literature.* Minneapolis: University of Minnesota Press.

Bhabha, Homi K. 1983. "The Other Question. . . ." *Screen* 24, no. 6: 18–36.

Bolaños, Alvaro Félix. 1994. *Barbarie y canibalismo en la retórica colonial. Los indios Pijaos de Fray Pedro Simón.* Bogotá: CEREC.

Borrero, Fernando. 1911. "Descripción del territorio oriental por uno de los demarcadores de 1783–1801." *Revista Histórica* 4, no. 10: 795–813.

Bosch, Felipe. 1971. *Historia del antiguo Buenos Aires.* Buenos Aires: Alborada.

Bougainville, L. A. de. 1954. *Viaje alrededor del mundo por la fragata del rey la "Boudeuse" y la fusta la "Estrella" en 1767, 1768 y 1769.* Buenos Aires: Espasa Calpe.

———. 1980. *Voyage de la frégate la Boudese et de la flute L'Etoile autour du monde.* Paris: Maspero.

Bourdieu, Pierre. 1998. "Neo-Liberalism, the Utopia (Becoming a Reality) of Unlimited Exploitation." Pp. 94–105 in Pierre Bourdieu. *Acts of Resistance: Against the New Myths of Our Time.* Trans. Richard Nice. Cambridge: Polity Press.

Bracco, Diego. 1998. *Guenoas.* Montevideo: Ministry of Education and Culture.

Bracco, Roberto. 1990. "Dataciones 14C en sitios con elevación." *Revista Antropología* 1, no. 1: 11–17.

———. 1992. "Desarrollo cultural y evolución ambiental en la región Este del Uruguay." Pp. 1:48–73 in *Ediciones del Quinto Centenario.* Ed. Pi Hugarte et al.

Brenkman, John. 1987. *Culture and Domination.* Ithaca, N.Y., and London: Cornell University Press.

Brennan, Timothy. 1990. "The National Longing for Form." Pp. 44–70 in *Nation and Narration.* Ed. Homi Bhabha. London and New York: Routledge.

Brito Stífano, Rogelio. 1953. "Dos noticias sobre el estado de los campos de la Banda Oriental al finalizar el siglo XVIII. Noticias sobre los campos de la Banda Oriental [Madrid 1794]." *Revista Histórica* 18, no. 52–54: 301–527.

———. 1955. "El relato del viaje de William Toller al Río de la Plata en 1715." *Revista Histórica* 23, no. 67–69: 193–263.

Buschiazzo, Mario J., ed. 1941. *Buenos Aires y Córdoba en 1729. Según cartas de los padres C. Cattaneo y C. Gervasoni S. J.* Buenos Aires: C.E.P.A.

Cabrer, José María. 1882. "Diario de Cabrer." Pp. 108–84 in Melitón González. *El límite oriental del territorio de misiones.* Vol. 1. Montevideo: El Siglo.

Cabrera Pérez, Leonel. 1989a. "El pasado que negamos. . . ." *Anales del VI° encuentro nacional y IV° regional de historia* 1, no. 1: 115–17.

———. 1989b. "Los 'indios infieles' de la Banda Oriental y su participación en la guerra guaranítica." *Estudios Ibero-americanos* 15, no. 1: 215–27.

———. 1992. "El indígena y la conquista en la cuenca de la Laguna Merín." Pp. 1:97–122 in *Ediciones del Quinto Centenario.* Ed. Pi Hugarte et al.

Cabrera Pérez, Leonel, and María del Carmen Curbelo. 1987. "Aspectos socio-demográficos de la influencia guaraní en el sur de la antigua Banda Oriental." Pp. 117–41 in *Annais do VII Simposio Nacional de estudos missioneiros. As Missoes Jesuítico-Guaranis: cultura e sociedade.*

Cabrera Pérez, Leonel, and Jorge Femenías. 1990. "Etnohistoria y arqueología en la cuenca de la Laguna Merin: hacia la revisión de los modelos generales del área." Pp. 1–22 in *Avances de Investigación. Material de Intercambio.* Montevideo: Universidad de la República.

Calvo, Carlos. 1865. *Memoria de los tratados, convenciones, capitulaciones, armisticios, cuestiones de límites y otros asuntos diplomáticos y políticos de todos los estados comprendidos entre el golfo de Méjico y el Cabo de Hornos, desde el año de 1493 hasta nuestros días.* 7 vols. Paris: Durand, Garnier, Denné-Schmidt.

Campal, Esteban F. 1967. *Hombres, tierras y ganados.* Montevideo: Arca.

Canal Feijóo, Bernardo. 1984. "La época colonial. Del Renacimiento al Barroco." In *Historia de la Literatura Argentina. Desde la Colonia hasta el Romanticismo.* Vol. 1. Buenos Aires: Centro Editor de América Latina.

Carrió de la Vandera, Alonso (Concolorcorvo). 1985. *El lazarillo de ciegos caminantes.* Introduced and annotated by Antonio Lorente Medina. Caracas: Biblioteca Ayacucho.

Carroll, David. 1987. "Narrative, Heterogeneity, and the Question of the Political: Bakhtin and Lyotard." Pp. 69–106 in *The Aims of Representation.* Ed. Murray Krieger. New York: Columbia University Press.

Casas, Fray Bartolomé de las. 1957 [1875–76]. *Obras escogidas de Fray Bartolomé de las Casas.* Ed. Juan Pérez de Tudela Bueso. Vol. 2. Madrid: Biblioteca de autores españoles.

Cattaneo, Gaetano. 1752a. "Lettera Prima." Pp. 220–75 in Ludovico Antonio Muratori. *Il Cristianesimo felice nelle missioni dei padri della Compagnia di Gesú del Paraguai.* Venice: Giambattista Pasquali.

———. 1752b. "Lettera Seconda." Pp. 275–91 in Muratori. *Il Cristianesimo felice nelle missioni dei padri della Compagnia di Gesú del Paraguai.* Venice: Giambattista Pasquali.

———. 1752c. "Lettera Terza." Pp. 220–75; 290–323 in Muratori. *Il Cristianesimo felice nelle missioni dei padri della Compagnia di Gesú del Paraguai.* Venice: Giambattista Pasquali.

Caviglia, Buenaventura. 1925. *La etimología del nombre Montevideo. Pistas y sugestiones para rastrearla en un primitivo Mòt. ví. dì.* Montevideo: El Siglo Ilustrado.

Certeau, Michel de. 1984. *The Practice of Everyday Life.* Trans. Steven Rendall. Berkeley: University of California Press.

———. 1988. *The Writing of History.* Trans. Tom Conley. New York: Columbia University Press.

———. 1989 [1986]. *Heterologies. Discourse on the Other.* Trans. Brian Massumi. Minneapolis: University of Minnesota Press.

Cevallos, Francisco J. 1986. "La retórica historiográfica y la aculturación en tres cronistas peruanos." *Revista de estudios hispánicos* 20, no. 3 (October): 55–66.

Charlevoix, Pedro Francisco Javier de. 1910 [1756]. *Historia del Paraguay.* Trans. Pablo Hernández. Vol. 1. Madrid: Victoriano Suárez.

Chiappelli, Fredi, ed. 1976. *The First Images of America: The Impact of the New World on the Old.* Vol I. Berkeley and Los Angeles: University of California Press.

Clendinnen, Inga. 1993. "'Fierce and Unnatural Cruelty': Cortés and the Conquest of Mexico." Pp. 12–47 in *New World Encounters.* Ed. Stephen Greenblatt. Berkeley: University of California Press.

Coester, Alfred. 1938 [1916]. *The Literary History of Spanish America.* New York: Macmillan.

Colón, Cristóbal. 1982. *Los cuatro viajes del Almirante y su testamento.* Madrid: Espasa Calpe.

Coni, E. 1945. *El gaucho. Argentina–Brasil–Uruguay.* Buenos Aires: Sudamericana.

Coni, Emilio A. 1929. "La introducción del ganado vacuno en el Uruguay por San Gabriel, Santo Domingo Soriano y las Misiones del Alto Uruguay." *La Mañana* (July 7): 1–2.

———. 1930. *Historia de las vaquerías de Río de la Plata (1555–1750).* Madrid: Tipográfica de Archivos.

Constant, Louis. 1980. "Introduction." Pp. i–xxviii in *Voyage de la frégate la Boudese et de la flute L'Etoile autour du monde.* Paris: Maspero.

Cornejo Polar, Antonio. 1980. *Literatura y sociedad en el Perú: La novela indigenista.* Lima: Lasontay.

———. 1989a. *La formación de la tradición literaria en el Perú.* Lima: CEP B.

———. 1989b. "Los sistemas literarios como categorías históricas." *Revista de Crítica Literaria Latinoamericana* 15, no. 29: 19–25.

Crosby, Alfred W. 1996 [1986]. *Ecological Imperialism: The Biological Expansion of Europe, 900–1900.* New York: Cambridge University Press.

Curtius, Ernst Robert. 1975 [1948]. *Literatura europea y edad media latina.* Vol. 1. México: Siglo XXI.

Davie, Sir John Constanse, Esq. 1805. *Letters from Paraguay: Describing the Settlements of Montevideo and Buenos Ayres; the Presidencies of Rioja Minor, Nombre de Dios, St. Mary and St. John, &. &. With the Manners, Customs, Religious Ceremonies, &. of the Inhabitants. Written during a Residence of Seventeen Months in that Country.* London: G. Robinson, Paternoster-Row.

Derrida, Jacques. 1976. *Of Grammatology.* Trans. Gayatri Spivak. Baltimore and London: Johns Hopkins University Press.

———. 1981 [1972]. *Positions.* Trans. Alan Bass. Chicago: University of Chicago Press.

———. 1988. "Signature Event Context." Pp. 1–23 in *Limited Inc.* Trans. Samuel Weber and Jeffrey Mehlman. Evanston, Ill.: Northwestern University Press.

Díaz de Guzmán, Ruy. 1882. *La Argentina.* Buenos Aires: C. Casavalle.

Díaz del Castillo, Bernal. 1984. *Historia verdadera de la conquista de la Nueva España.* Ed. Miguel León-Portilla. Madrid: Historia 16.

Duviols, Jean-Paul. 1975. "Montevideo et sa région en 1767 (Extraits inédits du journal de Ch. F. P. Fesche)." *Caravelle* 24: 10–15.

———. 1985. *L'Amérique espagnole vue et rêvée. Les livres de voyages de Christophe Colomb à Bougainville.* Paris: Promodis.

Eagleton, Terry. 1976a. *Criticism and Ideology.* London: New Left Books.

———. 1976b. *Marxism and Literary Criticism.* London: Methuen.

———. 1983. *Literary Theory: An Introduction.* Minneapolis: University of Minnesota Press.

Elliott, J. H. 1974. "The Discovery of America and the Discovery of Man." Pp. 101–25 in *Proceedings of the British Academy.* Vol. 63 (1972). London: British Academy.

Ercilla, Alonso de. 1979. *La Araucana.* Ed. Marcos Morínigo and Isaías Lerner. 2 vols. Madrid: Castalia.

Espinosa y Tello, José de. 1938. "Estudio sobre las costumbres y descripciones interesantes de la América del Sur." Pp. 276—342 in *Viaje al Río de la Plata en el siglo XVIII. Reedición de los documentos relativos al viaje de las corbetas "Descubierta" y "Atrevida" e informes de sus oficiales sobre el virreinato, extraídos de la obra de Novo y Colson.* Ed. Héctor Ratto, Capitán de Fragata (R.). Buenos Aires: La Facultad.

Fabian, Johannes. 1983. *Time and the Other: How Anthropology Makes Its Object.* New York: Columbia University Press.

Femenías, Jorge. 1983. "Amontonamientos artificiales de piedras en cerros y elevaciones de nuestro territorio," *Revista Antropológica* 1, no. 1: 13–16.

Femenías, Jorge, José M. López, Roberto Bracco, Leonel Cabrera, Carmen Curbelo, Nelsys Fusco, and Elianne Martínez. 1990. "Tipos de enterramiento en estructuras monticulares ('cerritos') en la región de la cuenca de la Laguna Merín (R. O. U.)." *Revista do CEPA* 17, no. 20: 345–56.

Fernández de Navarrete, Martín. 1955 [1825–37]. *Colección de viajes y descubrimientos que hicieron por mar los españoles desde fines del siglo XV.* Ed. Carlos Seco Serrano. Vol. 2. Madrid: Biblioteca de autores españoles.

Fernández de Oviedo, Gonzalo. 1959 [1535–47]. *Historia General y Natural de las Indias.* Madrid: Biblioteca de autores españoles.

Ferreira da Sylva, Silvestre. 1748. *Relaçaô do sitio, que o governador de Buenos Aires D. Miguel de Salcedo poz no anno de 1735 à Praça da Nova Colonia do Sacramento.* Lisbon: Impres. da Congregaçaô Camer. da S. Igreja de Lisboa.

Fish, Stanley. 1980. *Is There a Text in This Class?* Cambridge, Mass., and London: Harvard University Press.

Foucault, Michel. 1970 [1966]. *The Order of Things. An Archaeology of the Human Sciences.* New York: Pantheon Books.

———. 1971. *L'ordre du discours.* Paris: Gallimard.

———. 1982 [1969]. *La arqueología del saber.* Trans. Aurelio Garzón del Camino. México: Siglo XXI.

Frege, Gottlob. 1973. "Sobre el sentido y la denotación." Pp. 3–27 in *Semántica filosófica: problemas y discusiones.* Ed. Thomas Moro Simpson. Trans. Eduardo Rabossi and Eugenio Bulygin. Buenos Aires: Siglo XXI.

Fregeiro, Ana Inés. 1996. "Trabajo final de licenciatura. Antropología, opción Arqueología." Montevideo: Facultad de Humanidades, Universidad de la República.

Funes, D. Gregorio. 1816. *Ensayo de la historia civil del Paraguay, Buenos-Ayres y Tucumán.* Vol. 1. Buenos Aires: M. J. Gandarillas.

Furlong, Guillermo, S. J. 1969. *Historia social y cultural del Río de la Plata 1536–1810. El trasplante social.* Buenos Aires: Tipográfica Editora Argentina.

Galeano, Eduardo. 1997 [1971]. *Las venas abiertas de América Latina.* México: Siglo XXI.

Gandía, Enrique de. 1942. *Aventuras de Jaime Rasquín.* Buenos Aires: EMECE.

———. 1945. "Prologue." In Ruy Díaz de Guzmán. *La Argentina.* Buenos Aires and México: Espasa Calpe Argentina.

———. 1946. "Introduction." In Ruy Díaz de Guzmán. *La Argentina.* 2nd ed. Buenos Aires: Estrada.

García Méndez, Javier. 1992. "Tabaré o la Leyenda Blanca." *Brecha* 7, no. 322 (January 31): 15–17

Gates, Jr., Henry Louis. 1985. "Editor's Introduction: Writing Race and the Difference It Makes." *Critical Inquiry* 12, no. 1: 2–20.

Gerbi, Antonello. 1960 [1955]. *La disputa del Nuevo Mundo. Historia de una polémica 1750–1900.* México and Buenos Aires: Fondo de Cultura Económica.

Godzich, Wlad. 1989 [1986]. "Foreword: The Further Possibility of Knowledge." Pp. vii–xxi in de Certeau. *Heterologies.*

González, Luis Rodolfo, and Susana Rodríguez Varese. 1990. *Guaraníes y paisanos. Nuestras raíces 3*. Montevideo: Nuestra Tierra.

González, Melitón. 1882. *El límite oriental del territorio de misiones*. Vol. 1. Montevideo: El Siglo.

Gossman, Lionel. 1978. "History and Literature. Reproduction or Signification". Pp. 3–39 in *The Writing of History*. Ed. Robert H. Canary and Henry Kozicki. Madison: University of Wisconsin Press.

———. 1986. "History and Decipherment: Romantic Historiography and the Discovery of the Other." *New Literary History* 18: 23–57.

Graham, Joseph, ed. 1985. *Difference in Translation*. Ithaca, N.Y., and London: Cornell University Press.

Greenblatt, Stephen. 1991. "Marvelous Possessions." Pp. 52–85 in *In Marvelous Possessions. The Wonder of the New World*. Ed. Stephen Greenblatt. Chicago: University of Chicago Press.

Grimaldi, Marqués de. 1982 [1849]. "Respuesta del Marqués Grimaldi sobre la cuestión de límites en la Banda Oriental del Río de la Plata." In *Biblioteca del Comercio del Plata. T. VII. Biblioteca de Impresos Raros Americanos. T. XI*. Montevideo: Universidad de la República.

Groussac, Paul, ed. 1905. "Diario de Aguirre." *Anales de la Biblioteca* 4: 1–151.

Guastavino, Juan Estevan. 1928. *Hernandarias. Fundador de Corrientes*. Buenos Aires: Talleres Gráficos G. Pesce.

Guevara, José. 1910 [1832]. *Historia del Paraguay, Río de la Plata y Tucumán*. Ed. Pedro de Angelis. *Colección de Obras y Documentos relativos a la Historia Antigua y Moderna de las Provincias del Río de la Plata*. Vol. 2. Buenos Aires: Librería Nacional de J. Lajouane & Cia.

Haenke, Tadeo. 1943 [1795]. *Viaje por el virreinato del Río de la Plata*. Buenos Aires: Emecé.

Harley, J. B. 1988. "Silences and Secrecy: The Hidden Agenda of Cartography in Early Modern Europe." *Imago Mundi* 40: 57–76.

———. 1990. *Maps and the Columbian Encounter*. Milwaukee: Golda Meir Library.

Harrisse, Henry. 1882. *Jean et Sebastien Cabot. Leur origine et leur voyages*. Paris: Ernest Leroux.

Herder, Johann Gottfried von. 1968. *Reflections on the Philosophy of the History of Mankind*. Trans. T. O. Churchill. Chicago and London: University of Chicago Press.

Hernandarias. 1937. "Cartas y memoriales de Hernandarias." *Revista de la Biblioteca Nacional* 1, no. 1 (January–March): 130–57.

Hernández Sánchez-Barba, Mario. 1978. *Historia y literatura en Hispanoamérica (1492–1820)*. Madrid: Castalia/Fundación Juan March.

Herrera, Antonio de. 1945 [1601–15]. *Historia general de los hechos de los castellanos, en las islas, y Tierra-firme de el Mar Océano*. Vol. 2. Asunción: Guaranía.

Hidalgo, Bartolomé. 1979. *Obra completa*. Ed. Walter Rela. Montevideo: Editorial Ciencias.

Hulme, Peter. 1986. *Colonial Encounters. Europe and the Native Caribbean, 1492–1797*. London and New York: Methuen.

"Informe del procurador José González de Melo al cabildo de Montevideo." 1921. *Revista del Archivo General Administrativo* 2: 73.

Invernizzi Santa Cruz, Lucía. 1986. "*Naufragios* e *Infortunios:* Discurso que transforma fracasos en triunfos." *Dispositio* 11: 99–111.

Iser, Wolfgang. 1974. *The Implied Reader: Patterns of Communication in Prose Fiction from Bunyan to Beckett.* Baltimore: Johns Hopkins University Press.

Jameson, Fredric. 1981. *The Political Unconscious.* Ithaca, N.Y.: Cornell University Press.

Jan Mohamed, Abdul R. 1985. "The Economy of Manichean Allegory: The Function of Racial Difference in Colonial Literature." *Critical Inquiry* 12, no. 1: 59–87.

Jauss, Hans Robert. 1982. *Toward an Aesthetic of Reception.* Trans. Timothy Bahti. Minneapolis: University of Minnesota Press.

Jitrik, Noé. 1983. *Los dos ejes de la cruz.* Puebla, Mexico: Universidad Autónoma de Puebla.

Juan, Jorge, and Antonio de Ulloa. 1918. *Noticias secretas de América.* 2 vols. Madrid: Editorial América.

———. 1991 (repr. ed.). *Noticias secretas de América.* Ed. Luis J. Ramos Gómez. Madrid: Historia 16.

Klor de Alva, J. Jorge. 1995. "The Postcolonization of the (Latin) American Experience: A Reconsideration of 'Colonialism,' 'Postcolonialism,' and 'Mestizaje.'" Pp. 241–75 in *After Colonialism. Imperial Histories and Postcolonial Displacements.* Ed. Gyan Prakash. Princeton, N.J.: Princeton University Press.

Kristeva, Julia. 1986. *The Kristeva Reader.* Ed. Toril Moi. New York: Columbia University Press.

Laguarda Trías, Rolando A. 1982. *El hallazgo del Río de la Plata por Amerigo Vespucci en 1502.* Montevideo: Academia Nacional de Letras.

Lamas, Andrés. 1873. "Introduction." Pp. i–cxlvi in Pedro Lozano. *Historia de la conquista del Paraguay, Río de la Plata y Tucumán.* Ed. Andrés Lamas. Buenos Aires: Imprenta Popular.

Levillier, Roberto, ed. 1915. *Correspondencia de los Oficiales Reales de Hacienda del Río de la Plata con los Reyes de España.* Vol. 1. Madrid: Sucesores de Rivadeneyra.

Lewis, Thomas E. 1979. "Notes Toward a Theory of the Referent." *PMLA* 94, no. 3 (May): 459–75.

———. 1987. "The Referential Act." Pp. 158–74 in *On Referring in Literature.* Ed. Anna Whiteside and Michael Issacharoff. Bloomington and Indianapolis: Indiana University Press.

Lockhart, James. 1992. *The Nahuas after the Conquest. A Social and Cultural History of the Indians of Central Mexico, Sixteenth Through Eighteenth Centuries.* Stanford, Calif.: Stanford University Press.

Lopes de Souza, Pero. 1926. *Diario da navegaçâo. 1530–1532.* Rio de Janeiro: Typographia Leuzinger.

López de Gómara, Francisco. 1877 [1552]. *Historia general de las Indias. Historiadores primitivos de Indias.* Madrid: Biblioteca de autores españoles.

López Mazz, José María. 1992. "Aproximación a la génesis y desarrollo de los cerritos de la zona de San Miguel (Departamento de Rocha)." Pp. 1:76–96 in *Ediciones del Quinto Centenario.* Ed. Pi Hugarte et al.

———. 1995a. "Aproximación al territorio de los 'constructores de cerritos.'" Pp. 65–78 in *Arqueología en el Uruguay. VIII Congreso Nacional de Arqueología*

Uruguaya. Ed. Mario Consens, José María López Mazz, and María del Carmen Curbelo. Montevideo.

———. 1995b. "El fósil que no guía y la formación de los sitios costeros." Pp. 92–105 in *Arqueología en el Uruguay.* Ed. Consens, López Mazz, and Curbelo.

———. 1996. "Trabajos en tierra y complejidad cultural en el Rincón de los Indios." Photocopy, 1–14.

López Mazz, José María, and Roberto Bracco. 1989. "Las sociedades prehistóricas: viejas y nuevas aproximaciones." Pp. 107–14 in *Anales del Vi° encuentro nacional y IV° regional de historia* I, no. 1.

———. 1992. "Relación hombre-medio ambiente en las poblaciones prehistóricas de la zona Este del Uruguay." Pp. 259–82 in *Archaeology and Environment in Latin America.* Ed. Omar Ortiz-Troncoso and Thomas van der Hammen. Amsterdam: Universitat van Amsterdam.

Lopreto, Gladys. 1996. *"... que vivo en esta conquista." Textos del Río de la Plata, Siglo XVI.* La Plata, Argentina: Editorial de la Universidad de la Plata.

Lozano, Pedro. 1873. *Historia de la conquista del Paraguay, Río de la Plata y Tucumán.* Ed. Andrés Lamas. 3 vols. Buenos Aires: Imprenta Popular.

Ludmer, Josefina. 1988. *El género gauchesco. Un tratado sobre la patria.* Buenos Aires: Sudamericana.

Lyotard, Jean F. 1977. *Instructions païennes.* Paris: Galilée.

———. 1981. *The Postmodern Condition.* Minneapolis: University of Minnesota Press.

MacCormack, Sabine. 1989. "Atahualpa and the Book." *Dispositio* 36–38: 169–85.

Macherey, Pierre. 1978 [1966]. *A Theory of Literary Production.* Trans. Geoffrey Wall. London, Henley, and Boston: Routledge and Kegan Paul.

Madero, Eduardo. 1892. *Historia del Puerto de Buenos Aires.* Vol. 1. Buenos Aires: Imprenta de la Nación.

Mártir de Anglería, Pedro (Peter Martyr). 1892. *De Orbe Novo. Decades Octo.* Ed. Joachim Torres Asensio. Vol. 1. Madrid: Viuda e Hijas de Gómez Fuentenebro.

———. 1990. *Cartas sobre el Nuevo Mundo.* Madrid: Ediciones Polifemo.

Maturana, Humberto, and Francisco Varela. 1980. *Autopoiesis and Cognition: The Organization of the Living.* Dordrecht, Boston, and London: D. Reidel Publishing.

Mattos, Tomás de. 1989. *Bernabé, Bernabé.* Montevideo: Ediciones de la Banda Oriental.

Medina, José Toribio. 1888. *Colección de documentos inéditos para la historia de Chile.* 3 vols. Santiago de Chile: Imprenta Ercilla.

———. *Juan Díaz de Solís.* 1897. *Estudio histórico.* Vols. 1–2. Santiago de Chile: Edición del autor.

———. 1908a. *El veneciano Sebastián Caboto al servicio de España.* Vols. 1–2. Santiago de Chile: Imprenta y Encuadernación Universitaria.

———. 1908b. *Los viajes de Diego García de Moguer. Estudio histórico.* Santiago de Chile: Imprenta Elzeviriana.

Meléndez, Mariselle. 1995. "La vestimenta como retórica del poder y símbolo de producción cultural en la América colonial: de Colón a *El Lazarillo de ciegos caminantes.*" *Revista de estudios hispánicos* 29, no. 3: 411–39.

Melo, Cipriano. 1865. "Informe de D. Manuel Cipriano Melo sobre la otra Banda, límites, fuertes y guardias. Buenos Aires, 16 de julio de 1790." In Calvo. *Memoria de los tratados, convenciones, capitulaciones, armisticios, cuestiones de límites y otros asuntos diplomáticos y políticos de todos los estados comprendidos entre el golfo de Méjico y el Cabo de Hornos, desde el año de 1493 hasta nuestros días.* Vol. 1. Paris: Durand, Garnier, Denné-Schmidt.

Meltzer, Françoise. 1987. "Renaming in Literature: Faces of the Moon." Pp. 70–83 in *On Referring in Literature.* Ed. Whiteside and Issacharoff.

Menéndez, Elisa A. 1953. *Antes de 1810.* Montevideo: Mosca Bros.

Menéndez Pidal, Ramón. 1968. *La lengua de Cristóbal Colón.* 5th ed. Madrid: Espasa Calpe.

Meyer, Jean. 1982. "Le context des grandes voyages d'exploration au XVIIIe siécle." Pp. 17–39 in *L'importance de l'Exploration Maritime au Siécle del Lumières (Apropos du voyage de Bougainville). Table Ronde. Paris, 8 et 9 décembre 1978.* Ed. E. Taillemite and M. Mollat. Paris: Éditions du Centre National de la Recherche Scientifique.

Mignolo, Walter. 1980. "What Is Wrong with the Theory of Literature?" Pp. 305–27 in *The Sign: Semiotics Around the World.* Michigan Slavic Contributions no. 9. Ed. L. Matejka, R. W. Bailey, P. Steiner. Ann Arbor: Michigan Slavic Publications.

———. 1981. "El metatexto historiográfico y la historiografía indiana." *MLN* 96: 358–402.

———. 1982. "Cartas, crónicas y relaciones del descubrimiento y la conquista." Pp. 57–117 in *Historia de la literatura hispanoamericana. Tomo I. Epoca colonial.* Ed. Luis Iñigo Madrigal. Madrid: Cátedra.

———. 1983a. "Comprensión hermenéutica y comprensión teórica." *Revista de literatura* 14, no. 90: 1–35.

———. 1983b. "Semiosis y universos de sentido." *Lexis* 7, no. 2: 219–35.

———. 1986a. "La historia de la escritura y la escritura de la historia." In *De la crónica a la nueva narrativa mexicana: coloquio sobre literatura mexicana.* Merlín H. Forster and Julio Ortega, eds. Oaxaca, México: Editorial Oasis, 13-28.

———. 1986b. "La letra, la lengua, el territorio (o la crisis de los estudios literarios coloniales)." *Dispositio* 11, no. 28–29: 135–60.

———. 1989a. "Literacy and Colonization: The New World Experience." Pp. 51–96 in *Re/Discovering Colonial Writing.* Ed. Jara and Spadaccini.

———. 1989b. "¿Teorías literarias o teorías de la literatura? ¿Qué son y para qué sirven?" Pp. 4–42 in *La teoría literaria en la actualidad.* Ed. Graciela Reyes. Madrid: El Arquero.

———. 1990. "Tradiciones orales, alfabetización y literatura (o de las diferencias entre el corpus y el canon)." *IX Congreso internacional da associaçao de lingüística e filologia da América Latina.* Campinas, São Paulo, photocopy, 1–13.

———. 1991. "Teorizar a través de fronteras culturales." *Revista de Crítica Literaria Latinoamericana* 17, no. 33: 103–12.

———. 1992. "Putting the Americas on the Map (Geography and the Colonization of Space)." *Colonial Latin American Review* 1, no. 1–2: 25–63.

———. 1993. "Misunderstanding and Colonization: The Reconfiguration of Memory and Space." *South Atlantic Quarterly* 92, no. 2: 209–60.

Millau, Francisco. 1947. *Descripción de la provincia del Río de la Plata (1772).* Ed. Richard Konetzke. Buenos Aires: Espasa Calpe.

Molina, Raúl A. 1948. *Hernandarias. El hijo de la tierra.* Buenos Aires: Lancestremere.

Montaigne, Michel de. 1979. *Essais.* Paris: Garnier-Flammarion.

Montalvo, Hernando de. 1915. "Carta del tesorero del Río de la Plata, Hernando de Montalvo, al Rey, sobre la expedición de Juan Ortiz de Zárate y otros asuntos de la provincia. Puerto de San Salvador, Marzo 29 de 1576." Pp. 286–312 in *Correspondencia de los Oficiales Reales de Hacienda del Río de la Plata con los Reyes de España.* Ed. Roberto Levillier. Vol. 1. Madrid: Sucesores de Rivadeneyra.

Montrose, Louis. 1993. "The Work of Gender in the Discourse of Discovery." Pp. 177–217 in *New World Encounters.* Ed. Greenblatt. Berkeley: University of California Press.

Mouffe, Chantal. 1979. *Gramsci and Marxist Theory.* London: Routledge and Kegan Paul.

Muratori, Ludovico Antonio. 1752. *Il Cristianesimo felice nelle missioni dei padri della Compagnia di Gesú del Paraguai.* Venice: Giambattista Pasquali.

Murena, H. A. 1969. *El pecado original de América Latina.* Buenos Aires: Sudamericana.

Núñez, Estuardo, ed. 1989. *Viajeros hispanoamericanos (Temas continentales).* Caracas: Biblioteca Ayacucho.

O'Gorman, Edmundo. 1958. *La invención de América.* México: Fondo de Cultura.

Ong, Walter. 1987 [1982]. *Orality and Literacy: The Technologizing of the Word.* London and New York: Methuen.

Ortega, Julio. 1988. "Para una teoría del texto latinoamericano: Colón, Garcilaso y el discurso de la abundancia." *Revista de Crítica Literaria Latinoamericana* 14, no. 28: 101–15.

Ottsen, Henrich. 1617 [1603]. *Iornael oft daghelijcx register van de voyagie no Rio de Plata.* Amsterdam: M. Colijn.

———. 1945 [1603]. *Corto y verídico relato de la desgraciada navegación de un buque de Amsterdam.* Ed. Armando Tonelli. Buenos Aires: Editorial Huarpes.

Oyárvide, Andrés de. 1865. "Memoria de Oyárvide." Pp. 1–352 in Carlos Calvo. *Memoria de los tratados, convenciones, capitulaciones, armisticios, cuestiones de límites y otros asuntos diplomáticos y políticos de todos los estados comprendidos entre el golfo de Méjico y el Cabo de Hornos, desde el año de 1493 hasta nuestros días.* Vol. 7. Paris: Durand, Garnier, Denné-Schmidt.

Pagden, Anthony. 1982. *The Fall of Natural Man: The American Indian and the Origins of Comparative Ethnology.* Cambridge: Cambridge University Press.

Parras, Pedro José de. 1992. "Navegamos desde la altura del Janeiro hasta Montevideo. Entramos en Montevideo: descríbese esta ciudad y navegamos a Buenos Aires (1749)." In *Viajeros, marinos y naturalistas en la Banda Oriental del siglo XVIII.* Ed. Walter Rela. Montevideo: Ediciones de la Plaza.

Pastor, Beatriz. 1988 [1983]. *Discursos narrativos de la Conquista: mitificación y emergencia.* Hanover, N.H.: Ediciones del Norte.

Peña, Enrique. 1916. *Don Francisco de Céspedes. Noticias sobre su gobierno en el Río de la Plata (1624–1632).* Buenos Aires: Coni Bros.

Pereira de Sá, Simão. 1900. *Historia topográphica e bellica da Nova Colonia do Sacramento do Rio da Prata.* Rio de Janeiro: Typographia Leuzinger.

Perelli, Carina, and Juan Rial. 1986. *De mitos y memorias políticas. La represión, el miedo y después . . .* Montevideo: EBO.

Pernety, Antoine Joseph. 1770. *Histoire d'un voyage aux îles Malouines, fait en 1763 et 1764; avec des observations sur le détroit de Magellan et sur les Patagons.* Vol. 1. Paris: Chez Saillant et Nyom.

Pierce, Frank. 1968. *La poesía épica del Siglo de Oro.* 2nd ed. Madrid: Gredos.

Pigafetta, Antonio. 1888. *Viaje alrededor del mundo por el caballero Pigafetta. Colección de documentos inéditos para la historia de Chile.* Vol. 2. Ed. José Toribio Medina. Santiago de Chile: Imprenta Ercilla.

Pi Hugarte, Renzo. 1993. *Los indios del Uruguay.* Madrid: Mapfre.

Pivel Devoto, Juan E., ed. 1957 [1952]. *Raíces coloniales de la revolución oriental de 1811.* Montevideo: Medina.

Pizarro, Ana, ed. 1985. *La literatura latinoamericana como proceso.* Buenos Aires: Centro Editor de América Latina.

Pratt, Mary Louise. 1992. *Imperial Eyes. Travel Writing and Transculturation.* London and New York: Routledge.

Prieto, O., et al. 1970. "Información preliminar sobre investigaciones arqueológicas en el Departamento de Treinta y Tres, R.O.U." *Publicaçoes Avulsas.* Vol. 1. S. Leopoldo, Brazil: Instituto Anchietano de Pesquisas.

Pupo-Walker, Enrique. 1982. *La vocación literaria del pensamiento histórico en América. Desarrollo de la prosa de ficción: siglos XVI, XVII, XVIII y XIX.* Madrid: Gredos.

Rabasa, José. 1993. *Inventing A-m-e-r-i-c-a: Spanish Historiography and the Formation of Eurocentrism.* Norman, Okla., and London: Oklahoma University Press.

Rama, Angel. 1982 [1976]. *Los gauchipolíticos rioplatenses. Capítulo. Serie complementaria: Sociedad y cultura/4.* Buenos Aires: CEDAL.

———. 1984. *La ciudad letrada.* Hanover, N.H.: Ediciones del Norte.

Ramírez, Luiz. 1892. "Carta de Luiz Ramírez." Pp. 330–52 in Eduardo Madero. *Historia del Puerto de Buenos Aires.* Vol. 1. Buenos Aires: Imprenta de la Nación.

Ratto, Héctor, Capitán de Fragata (R.), ed. 1938. *Viaje al Río de la Plata en el siglo XVIII. Reedición de los documentos relativos al viaje de las corbetas "Descubierta" y "Atrevida" e informes de sus oficiales sobre el virreinato, extraídos de la obra de Novo y Colson.* Buenos Aires: La Facultad.

Rela, Walter, ed. 1992. *Viajeros, marinos y naturalistas en la Banda Oriental del siglo XVIII.* Montevideo: Ediciones de la Plaza.

"Relación exacta de lo que ha sucedido en la expedición a Buenos-Ayres que escrive un Sargento de la Comitiua en este Año de 1778 en las siguientes décimas." 1920. Pp. 276–94 in Antonio Bermejo de la Rica. *La Colonia del Sacramento.* Toledo: Imp. de la Editorial Católica Toledana.

Restuccia, Alberto. 1985. *Salsipuedes (El exterminio de los charrúas). Libro de documentos.* Montevideo: Teatro Uno.

Reyes, Alfonso. 1942. *Ultima Tule.* México: Imprenta Universitaria.

Rodríguez Prampolini, Ida. 1948. *Amadises de América. La hazaña de Indias como empresa caballeresca.* México: n.p.

Rojas, Ricardo. 1924. *Obras. vol. X. La literatura argentina. Los coloniales I.* Buenos Aires: "La Facultad."

Rosenblat, Angel. 1977. *Los conquistadores y su lengua.* Caracas: Universidad Central de Venezuela.

Russell, Bertrand. 1973. "Sobre el denotar." Pp. 29–48 in *Semántica filosófica: problemas y discusiones.* Ed. Thomas Moro Simpson. Trans. Thomas M. Simpson and Néstor Míguez. Buenos Aires: Siglo XXI.

Said, Edward. 1989. "Representing the Colonized: Anthropology's Interlocutors." *Critical Inquiry* 15, no. 2: 205–25.

Sallaberry, Juan F., S. J. 1926. *Los charrúas y Santa Fe.* Montevideo: Gómez y Cía.

Sambarino, Mario. 1969. *La cultura nacional como problema. Nuestra Tierra No. 46.* Montevideo: Nuestra Tierra.

Sans, Mónica. 1992. "Genética e historia: hacia una revisión de nuestra identidad como 'país de inmigrantes.'" Pp. 1:21–42 in *Ediciones del Quinto Centenario.* Ed. Renzo Pi Hugarte et al. Montevideo: Universidad de la República.

Schiaffino, Rafael. 1928. "La 'Relación del Sitio, toma y desalojo de la Colonia nombrada del Sacramento, en que se hallavan los Portugueses desde el año 1680, en el Río de la Plata a vista de las Islas de S. Gabriel.'" *Revista del Instituto Histórico y Geográfico del Uruguay* 6, no. 1: 204–10.

Schmidel, Ulrico. 1947. *Derrotero y viaje a España y las Indias.* Trans. Edmundo Wernicke. Buenos Aires: Espasa-Calpe Argentina.

Schuller, Rodolfo. 1904. "Prologue." Pp. vi–cxxxii in Azara. *Geografía física.*

———. 1906. *Sobre el orijen de los Charrúa.* Santiago de Chile: Imprenta Cervantes.

Searle, John R. 1973. "Las objeciones de Russell a la teoría de Frege sobre el sentido y la denotación." Pp. 49–55 in *Semántica filosófica.* Ed. Simpson.

———. 1975. "The Logical Status of Fictional Discourse." *New Literary History* 6: 619–32.

Seed, Patricia. 1995. *Ceremonies of Possession in Europe's Conquest of the New World.* Cambridge: Cambridge University Press.

Slatta, Richard W. 1983. *Gauchos and the Vanishing Frontier.* Lincoln, Neb., and London: University of Nebraska Press.

Sommer, Doris. 1986. "Not Just Any Narrative: How Romance Can Love Us to Death." Pp. 47–73 in *The Historical Novel in Latin America.* Ed. Daniel Balderston. Gaithersburg: Hispamérica.

———. 1990. "Irresistible Romance: The Foundational Fictions of Latin America." Pp. 71–98 in Homi K. Bhabha. *Nation and Narration.* London and New York: Routledge.

Spalding, Karen. 1984. *Huarochirí. An Andean Society under Inca and Spanish Rule.* Stanford, Calif.: Stanford University Press.

Spivak, Gayatri C., ed. 1988a. "Explanation and Culture: Marginalia." Pp. 103–17 in *In Other Worlds.* New York and London: Routledge.

———. 1988b. "Subaltern Studies: Deconstructing Historiography." Pp. 197–221 in *In Other Worlds.* New York and London: Routledge.

Stern, Steve. 1982. *Peru's Indian Peoples and the Challenge of Spanish Conquest: Huamanga to 1640.* Madison: University of Wisconsin Press.

Stolley, Karen. 1992. *El lazarillo de ciegos caminantes: Un itinerario crítico.* Hanover, N.H.: Ediciones del Norte.

Strawson, Peter F. 1973. "Sobre el referir." Pp. 57–86 in *Semántica filosófica.* Ed. Simpson.

Taillemite, Étienne, ed. 1977. *Bougainville et ses compagnons aoutour du monde. 1766–1769.* Vol. 1–2. Paris: Imprimerie Nationale.

Tainter, Joseph. 1978. "Mortuary Practices and the Study of Prehistoric Social Systems." In *Advances in Archaeological Method and Theory.* Vol. 1. New York: Academic Press.

Tani, Rubén. 1982. "Fundamentos para una semiótica filosófica: Las oscuridades de *On Denoting* (1905)." Pp. 253–63 in *Actas de las Jornadas de Lingüística del Uruguay.* Montevideo: Departamento de Publicaciones, Facultad de Humanidades y Ciencias.

Techo, Nicolás del. 1897 [1673]. *Historia de la Provincia del Paraguay de la Compañía de Jesús.* Trans. Manuel Serrano y Sanz. Vol. 1. Madrid: Uribe y Cia.

Tiscornia, Ruth. 1973. *Hernandarias estadista. La política rioplatense a principios del siglo XVII.* Buenos Aires: Eudeba.

Todorov, Tzvetan. 1992 [1982]. *The Conquest of America: The Question of the Other.* New York: Harper Collins.

Toller, William. 1955. "Reproducción facsimilar de la 'Historia de un Viaje al Río de la Plata y Buenos Aires desde inglaterra. Año MDCCXV' por William Toller." *Revista Histórica* 23, no. 67–69: 201–63.

Transilvano, Maximiliano. 1888. "Relación escrita por Maximiliano Transilvano de cómo y por quién y en qué tiempo fueron descubiertas y halladas las islas Molucas, donde es el propio nacimiento de la Especería, las cuales caen en la conquista y marcación de la Corona Real de España. E divídese esta relación en veinte párrafos principales. 5 de octubre de 1522." Pp. 1:256–97 in Medina. *Colección de documentos inéditos.*

Ulloa, Antonio de. 1990. *Viaje a la América meridional.* Ed. Andrés Saumell. 2 vols. Madrid: Historia 16.

Viana, Francisco Xavier de. 1958. *Diario de Viaje.* 2 vols. *Colección clásicos uruguayos.* Montevideo: Biblioteca Artigas.

Verdesio, Gustavo. 1993a. "*La Argentina:* tipología textual y construcción de los referentes." *Revista de crítica literaria latinoamericana* 38: 345–60.

———. 1993b. "Escritura e identidad cultural en el Uruguay colonial." *Letterature d'America: Rivista Trimestrale* 13, no. 49: 23–43.

———. 1995. "Una ausencia en el canon: los discursos coloniales del Uruguay en el marco de la historiografía literaria uruguaya y los estudios coloniales latinoamericanos." *Revista Iberoamericana* 169–70: 249–68.

———. 1997a. "Las representaciones territoriales del Uruguay colonial: Hacia una hermenéutica pluritópica." *Revista de Crítica Literaria Latinoamericana* 23, no. 46: 135–61.

———. 1997b. Review of *Conquista y contraconquista. La escritura del nuevo mundo.* Ed. Julio Ortega and José Amor and Vázquez. México: Brown University, El Colegio de México. *Hispanic Review* 65, no. 1: 123–25.

———. 1999. "Hacia la descolonización de la mirada geográfica: las prácticas territoriales indígenas en la 'prehistoria' de la ribera norte del Río de la Plata." *Revista Iberoamericana* 186: 59–80.

———. Forthcoming. "The Original Sin Behind the Creation of a New Europe: Economic and Ecologial Imperialism in the River Plate." In *Mapping Colonial Latin America.* Ed. Santa Arias and Mariselle Meléndez. Lewisburg, Pa.: Bucknell University Press.

Vidal, Hernán. 1976. *Literatura hispanoamericana e ideología liberal: surgimiento y crisis.* Buenos Aires: Hispamérica.

———. 1985. *Socio-Historia de la Literatura Colonial Hispanoamericana: Tres lecturas orgánicas.* Minneapolis: Institute for the Study of Ideologies and Literature.

Vidart, Daniel. 1996a. *El mundo de los charrúas.* Montevideo: Ediciones de Banda Oriental.

———. 1996b. *"Los cerritos de los indios" del Este uruguayo.* Montevideo: Ediciones de Banda Oriental.

Washburn, Wilcomb E. 1976. "The Clash of Morality in the American Forest." Pp. 335–50 in *The First Images of America: The Impact of the New World on the Old.* Vol. 1. Ed. Fredi Chiappelli. Berkeley and Los Angeles: University of California Press.

White, Hayden. 1978. "Interpretation in History." Pp. 51–80 in *Tropics of Discourse.* Baltimore and London: Johns Hopkins University Press.

Whiteside, Anna. 1987. "Theories of Reference." Pp. 175–208 in *On Referring in Literature.* Ed. Whiteside and Issacharoff.

Williams, Raymond. 1977. *Marxism and Literature.* Oxford: Oxford University Press.

———. 1980. *Problems in Materialism and Culture.* London: New Left Books.

Zabala, D. Bruno Mauricio de. 1982 [1849]. "Diario del gobernador de Buenos Aires." *Biblioteca del Comercio del Plata. T. I. Biblioteca de impresos raros americanos. T. VII.* Montevideo: Universidad de la República.

Zamora, Margarita. 1993. *Reading Columbus.* Berkeley: University of California Press.

Zavala, Iris M. 1989. "Representing the Colonial Subject." Pp. 323–48 in *Re/Discovering Colonial Writing.* Hispanic Issues 4. Ed. R. Jara and N. Spadaccini. Minneapolis: Prisma Institute.

Zorrilla de San Martín, Juan. 1956. *Tabaré.* Montevideo: Ministerio de Instrucción Pública y Previsión Social.

Zum Felde, Alberto. 1967 [1920]. *Proceso histórico del Uruguay.* Montevideo: Arca.

Index

Abayubá, 50, 54–55, 68
Abreu, Capistrano de, 76, 78
Acosta y Lara, Eduardo, 153
Acuña, Rodrigo de, 32
Adorno, Rolena, 11, 108, 164, 166, 170, 172–73, 176–78
Aguirre, Francisco, 7, 134, 136
Aínsa, Fernando, 170, 179
Albo, Francisco, 29
altepetl, 2
Anderson, Benedict, 105
Andes, 1–2, 56, 101, 160, 163, 173
Angelis, Pedro de, 94, 170
Arachans, 154
Aranguren, Carlos M., 65, 173–74
La Araucana, 43, 50–51, 56, 60
Areizaga, Juan de, 32
La Argentina, 4, 43, 47, 50–51, 53, 55–57, 60, 170
La Argentina manuscrita, 56–57
Asunción, 5, 67, 100, 170
Atahualpa, 36
Ayestarán, Lauro, 91–92, 138, 175
ayllu, 2
Azara, Félix de, 7, 15, 23–24, 26, 56, 99–107, 122, 131–32, 135–36, 153, 167, 173, 176–77, 179–81
Azarola Gil, Luis Enrique, 5, 59–60, 62, 67–70, 73–74, 80, 83–85, 153, 162, 174–75, 180
Aztecs (also Mexica), ix, xi

Bakhtin, Mikhail M., 165, 176
Bandeirantes, 73, 156, 174
Barco Centenera, Martín del, 4, 20–21, 28, 43, 45–55, 57, 59, 68, 78, 94, 96–99, 102–3, 108, 120–21, 131, 155, 167, 170–72
Barlow, Roger, 153, 182
Barrán, José Pedro, 88, 129–30, 136, 139, 179
Barrios Pintos, Aníbal, 40–41, 150, 152, 181
Bauzá, Francisco, 15, 162, 173
Becco, Horacio J., 175
Bennett, Tony, 12
Betanzos, Juan de, 101
Beverley, John, 11
Bhabha, Homi K., 164
Bohanes, 121
Bolaños, Alvaro F., xi, 166, 173, 177
Borrero, Fernando 7, 133
Bosch, Felipe, 169
Bougainville, L. A. de, 124, 131, 142, 179
Bourdieu, Pierre, 163
Bracco, Diego, 105, 153, 169, 175–77
Bracco, Roberto, 147–48, 154, 182
Brenkman, John, 165
Brennan, Timothy, 177
Brito Stífano, Rogelio, 112, 134, 139, 142, 178, 180
Buenos Aires, 3, 6, 39, 61–63, 66–70, 73–74, 77, 81, 83–84, 86, 100, 112, 117, 119–20, 128, 131, 136, 155–56, 170, 173, 177–79
Buffon, George Louis Leclerc, 101, 176
Buschiazzo, Mario, 178

Cabeza de Vaca, Alvar Núñez, 27, 60, 168, 170
Cabot, Sebastian, 3, 4, 22, 30–31, 33–36, 38, 64, 68, 78, 114, 155, 167–69, 178, 182
Cabrer, José María, 7, 81, 133–34, 136
Cabrera Pérez, Leonel, 24, 154, 169, 183
Calenda, 129–30
Canal Feijóo, Bernardo, 170
Caribs, 16, 18, 20, 25, 47, 49, 57, 166, 171, 176

Carrió de la Vandera (Concolorcorvo), 7, 110, 136–38, 141–43, 157, 168, 175, 179–81
Carroll, David, 165
Castillos, 83, 114, 116, 156
catalanense, 147
Cattaneo, Gaetano, 7, 116–25, 157, 179
Caviglia, Buenaventura, 168, 178
Certeau, Michel de, 37, 108–9, 164, 169, 172, 177, 181
Céspedes, Francisco de, 5, 66–70, 72, 75, 174
Cevallos, Francisco, 164
Cevallos, Viceroy, 6, 88, 90–91
Chaná, 66–67, 70, 79, 105, 154, 158
Chaná-Beguas, 41, 149–50, 153, 182
Chaná-Timbús, 42, 150
Charlevoix, Pedro Francisco Javier de, 16, 22–23
Charrúas, 3, 4, 23–25, 35, 40–42, 50–57, 59–61, 64, 66–70, 75, 79, 84, 97–99, 102–5, 120–23, 132, 144, 149, 151–56, 158, 160, 167, 169–70, 172–74, 176
City of the Caesars, 64
Clendinnen, Inga, 170
Coester, Alfred, 170
Colonia, Department of, 24, 40, 152
Colonia do Sacramento, 6, 10, 68–69, 75–77, 81, 83–84, 87–88, 90–91, 116–18, 150, 155–57, 179
Columbus, Christopher, 5, 16, 26–27, 34, 37, 45–47, 49, 63–64, 78, 82, 159, 166–68, 171–72, 176
Commerson, Philibert, 128, 131
Coni, Emilio, 60, 68, 162, 173–74, 180
Constant, Louis, 124
Cornejo Polar, Antonio, 165, 175
Cortés, Hernán, 26–27, 155, 159, 167–68, 176
Crosby, Alfred, 163
cuareimense, 147
Curtius, Ernst Robert, 174

Davie, Sir John Constanse, 111, 181
Dávila, Francisco, 32
deconstruction, 9
Derrida, Jacques, 8, 164
Díaz de Guzmán, Ruy, 15, 56–58, 94, 97, 103, 167
Díaz del Castillo, Bernal, 44, 159, 167
Duviols, Jean-Paul, 28, 127–28, 168, 174, 177–79

Eagleton, Terry, 8
Elliott, J. H., 176
Elysian Fields, 81–82, 89, 126, 128, 174
Entre Ríos, 39, 173
Ercilla, Alonso de, 43, 46, 51, 56
Espinosa y Tello, José de, 136, 138–42, 158, 180–81

Fabian, Johannes, 164
Femenías, Jorge, 24, 148, 169, 182
Fernández de Navarrete, Martín, 16, 23–24
Fernández de Oviedo, Gonzalo, 15, 17–18, 21–22, 24–25, 27–28, 50, 93, 166
Ferreira da Sylva, Silvestre, 6, 78, 81, 132
Ferrés, Carlos, 149, 181–82
Fesche, Ch. F. P., 127–28, 134
Figueira, Juan H., 181–82
Fish, Stanley, 48
Foucault, Michel, 166
Frege, Gottlob, 52
Fregeiro, Ana Inés, 150, 182
Funes, Gregorio, 15
Furlong, Guillermo, S. J., 127, 178–80

Galeano, Eduardo, 166
Gandía, Enrique de, 56–57, 59
Garay, Juan de, 53, 60, 174
García Méndez, Javier, 144
García, Diego, 3, 4, 25, 30–33, 38, 63, 132, 168–69
Garcilaso de la Vega, Inca, 159
Garro, Governor, 74–75
Gates, Jr., Henry Louis, 176
gauchesca poetry, 90, 140–41, 144, 175, 181
gauchos, 89–92, 137–44, 156–57, 161–62, 174–75, 180–81
Gerbi, Antonello, 176
Godzich, Vlad, 164
González Garaño, Alejo, 112
González, Luis Rodolfo, 25, 152
González, Melitón, 81
Gossman, Lionel, 51, 177
Graham, Joseph, 87
Greenblatt, Stephen, 170
Grimaldi, Marquis of, 77–78
Groussac, Paul, 134–36
Guaman Poma de Ayala, 159, 178
Guaraní, 23, 25, 35, 39–40, 47, 51, 73, 95, 97, 105, 117–19, 122, 149–50, 152–54, 157–58, 170–71, 182–83
Guastavino, Juan Esteban, 65, 173
Guenoa, 3, 105, 122–23, 153, 167, 175–77
Guevara, José, 56, 94, 97, 99, 103, 106, 173

Habermas, Jurgen, 165
Haencke, Tadeo, 91, 179–80
Harley, J. B., 146, 171
Harrisse, Henry, 182
Herder, Johann Gottfried von, 164

Hernandarias (Hernando Arias de Saavedra), 5, 6, 10, 17, 59–68, 70–72, 82, 89, 114, 153, 155–56, 158, 173–74
Hernández Sánchez-Barba, Mario, 168, 171
Herrera, Antonio de, ix, 3, 15, 19–23, 30–31, 35, 101, 182
Hidalgo, Bartolomé, 175
Hulme, Peter, 172, 176

Invernizzi Santa Cruz, Lucía, 168
Iser, Wolfgang, 164

Jameson, Fredric, 10, 164, 168
Jaques, Cristobal, 35, 38, 169
Jauss, Hans Robert, 12
Jitrik, Noe, 37, 46, 78, 111, 170–71
Jordan River, 146
Juan, Jorge, 181

Klor de Alva, J. Jorge, 57
Kristeva, Julia, x, 3–4

Laguarda Trías, Rolando, 164
Lamas, Andrés, 94–96
Las Casas, Bartolomé de, ix, 16, 18–19
Léry, Jean de, 153
Les Luthiers, 14
Levillier, Roberto, 54
Lévi-Strauss, Claude, 20
Lewis, Thomas E., 53, 172
Lobo, Manuel, 73–75, 80, 155
Lockhart, James, 2, 163
locus amœnus, 81–82, 88, 133, 174, 179
Lopes de Souza, 4, 15, 39–42, 77, 153–54, 182
López de Gómara, Francisco, 3, 15, 18, 23
López Mazz, 147–48, 182
Lopreto, Gladys, 177
Lorente Medina, Antonio, 180
Los Tontos, 59
Loaysa (or Loaisa), García Jofre de, 4, 30–32, 169–70
Lozano, Pedro, 7, 16, 23, 26, 56, 65, 83, 87, 94–100, 102–3, 106, 131, 166, 173–74
Ludmer, Josefina, 138, 175
Lyotard, Jean F., 165

MacCormack, Sabine, 170
Macherey, Pierre, 8–9
Madero, Eduardo, 15–16, 21, 24, 166–67, 169, 173–74, 182
Magellan, Ferdinand, 4, 20, 27, 29–31, 35, 37–38
Magellan, Straight of, 28, 33, 124, 170
Maldonado, 21, 23, 41, 59, 73, 83, 131, 142–43
Manchados, 121
Martidanes, 121
Martín García, 21–23
Mártir de Anglería, Pedro (Peter Martyr), ix, 3, 16–18, 22, 27, 166, 172, 182
Mattos, Tomás de, 144
Mayas, ix, xi
Medina, José Toribio, 15–16, 21–22, 24–25, 29, 32–33, 35, 114, 152, 166–67, 169, 178
Meléndez, Mariselle, 168, 180
Melo, Cipriano, 133, 180
Meltzer, Françoise, 52–53, 172
Mendoza, Pedro de, 4, 15, 42, 155
Menéndez, Elisa, 174
Menéndez Pidal, Ramón, 172
Mesoamerica, 1–2, 56, 101, 160, 163, 173
Meyer, Jean, 177
Mignolo, Walter, 5, 11–12, 44, 46, 146, 159, 165, 171, 173, 176, 183
Millau, Francisco, 82
Minuans, 79, 81, 84–87, 92, 105, 131–32, 153, 156, 158, 161, 175–77
Molina, Raúl A., 61, 65, 173–74
Montaigne, Michel de, 53, 97, 176
Montalvo, Hernando de, 43, 53–55, 68, 153–54
Monte Seredo, 114, 116, 146, 178
Montes, Enrique, 32, 35–36
Montevideo, 6, 21, 23, 29, 61–62, 68–69, 72–73, 82–86, 88–89, 114–19, 124–31, 136–37, 139, 141, 143, 150, 156–57, 168, 174–75, 179–80
Montoya (accountant), 33–34, 169
Montrose, Louis, 177
mounds *(cerritos de indios)*, 147–49, 154, 158, 182–83
Muratori, Ludovico, 116, 179
Murena, H. A., 15, 166

Nassau-Siegen, Charles Othon de, 131–32
Nietzche, Friedrich, 3
Núñez, Estuardo, 114, 178–79

O'Gorman, Edmundo, x, 171
Ong, Walter, 181
Ortega, Julio, 45, 47, 82
Ortiz de Zárate, Juan, 4, 15, 43, 51, 53–54, 56, 59–60, 68, 99, 155, 170
Ottsen, Henrich, 111–16, 125, 143, 157, 178
Oyárvide, Andrés de, 7, 133–36

Pagden, Anthony, 166, 171, 176
Paraná River, 58, 60, 97, 121, 168
Parras, Francisco José de, 134
Pastor, Beatriz, 26, 28, 33, 45–46, 167, 171

Pauw, Cornelius de, 101, 176
Pereira de Sá, Simao, 6, 76–82, 88–89, 126
Pernety, Antoine Joseph, 7, 124–32, 139, 143, 157, 179
Pierce, Frank, 170
Pigafetta, Antonio, 28–29, 38
Pi Hugarte, Renzo, 149–50, 182
Pijaos, xi
Pivel Devoto, Juan, 180
place of abundance *(lugar de la abundancia)*, 82, 158, 174, 179
Pratt, Mary Louise, 93, 124
Prieto, O., 182
Puerto, Francisco del, 33–36, 167, 169
Pupo-Walker, Enrique, 171

Rabasa, José, 93, 146, 177
Rama, Angel, 100, 175–76
Ramírez, Luiz, 169, 182
Ramírez, Melchor, 32, 36
Rasquín, Jaime, 59
Real de San Carlos, 90
Restuccia, Alberto, 144
Reyes, Alfonso, 28, 171
Rivera, Fructuoso, 151
Rocha, Department of, 147, 154
Rodríguez Prampolini, Ida, 168
Rodríguez Varese, Susana, 25, 152
Rojas, Ricardo, 56–57, 94, 170
Rosenblat, Angel, 171
Russell, Bertrand, 52, 172

Sahagún, Bernardino de, 101
Said, Edward, 165
Sallaberry, Juan F., S. J., 173
Salto, Department of, 147
Sambarino, Mario, 164
San Cristóbal, 29–30
San Gabriel, 42, 53, 60, 68, 72–73, 75, 77, 83, 116–17, 155, 169, 174
San José, Department of, 39
San Salvador, 33, 59, 169, 182
Sans, Mónica, 150
Santa Catarina, 6, 32, 35–36, 61, 88, 168–69
Santa Cruz, Alonso de, 21–22, 28, 33, 167
Santa Fe, 39, 62, 100, 173, 177
Santa Lucía, 61–62, 114–15
Santa María, Cape of, 29–30, 33–35, 40–41, 146
Santo Domingo Soriano, 5, 120
Sapateo, 129
Saumell, Andrés, 167, 181
Schiaffino, Rafael, 175
Schmidel, Ulrich, 4, 42–43, 170
Schuller, Rodolfo, 35, 41–42, 170
Searle, John R., 172
Seed, Patricia, 170
Slatta, Richard W., 181
Solís, Juan Díaz de, 3–4, 15–27, 29–33, 37–38, 40, 68, 78, 102, 146, 151–52, 166–69
Sommer, Doris, 166
Southern Cone, x
Spalding, Karen, 2, 163
Spivak, Gayatri Chakravory, 164, 177
Staden, Hans, 153
Stern, Steve, 2, 163
Stolley, Karen, 138, 180
Strawson, Peter, 52–53

Tabaré, 144
Taillemite, Etienne, 128, 131, 179
Tainter, Joseph, 148
Tani, Ruben, 172
Tapes, 73, 79, 84, 174
Techo, Nicolás del, 94
Timbú, 20
Tiscornia, Ruth, 173
Todorov, Tzvetan, 36, 65, 103, 170, 173
Toller, William, 7, 111, 114–16, 125, 178
Tordesillas treaty, 73, 77, 155
trace(s), concept of, 8–9
Transilvano, Maximiliano, 29
Treinta y Tres, Department of, 182

Ulloa, Antonio de, 16, 167, 181
Uruguay River, 61–62, 74, 121, 146, 174

Verdesio, Gustavo, 163–64, 170, 179, 181–82
Vespucci, Amerigo, 78, 164, 177
Viana, Francisco Xavier de, 180
Vidart, Daniel, 149–51, 181–82
Vivez, François, 127, 179

Washburn, Wilcomb E., 104
Weinberg, Félix, 175
White, Hayden, 51, 172
Whiteside, Anna, 52–53, 172
Williams, Raymond, 10

Yamandú, 5
Yaros, 121–23

Zabala, Bruno Mauricio de, 81, 83–85, 156–57, 175
Zamora, Margarita, x, 163
Zapican, 50–51, 55, 68
Zavala, Iris, 106, 172, 177
Zorrilla de San Martín, Juan, 144